PREACHER'S HOMILETIC LIBRARY

PROCLAIMING THE NEW TESTAMENT

The Gospel of Matthew

PROCLAIMING THE NEW TESTAMENT

Edited by Ralph G. Turnbull

The Gospel of Matthew

by
Herschel H. Hobbs

BAKER BOOK HOUSE
Grand Rapids, Michigan

Copyright © 1961 by
Baker Book House Company

Reprinted, January, 1972

Library of Congress Catalog Card
Number: 61-10006

ISBN: 0-8010-6912-2

Preacher's Homiletic Library
ISBN: 0-8010-6916-5

Photolithoprinted by Cushing-Malloy, Inc.
Ann Arbor, Michigan, United States of America

DEDICATED

to

JERRY AND LYNNE

with the prayer that their lives together
may be used in the service of the King.

Editor's Foreword

In the series, Proclaiming the New Testament, an attempt is made to provide homiletical comments and ideas. The busy pastor needs to spend time in meditation if he is to offer the bread of life to his people. One of the best known methods of Bible study is to work through one book of the Bible at a time. This gives depth as well as breadth. It provides for the preaching of the whole counsel of God and not just a part of that revelation. As truth must reach people in various stages of growth and at different levels of reception, so there must be variety of communication.

The intention of this series is to stimulate men in the ministry to more definite study. Believing that the first rule of homiletics is to read and study the actual text of Scripture, this method brings ideas and suggestion. Here illustrations are limited as the individual should find his own as he reads or mingles with people, and as he is open to all the winds of God. No pastor can lead his people to a level of thought and spiritual experience higher than the one he occupies. God will not honor lazy men or men who imagine the Holy Spirit should prompt alone. God has given us a mind to use, a heart to love, a spirit to pray, and a will to study.

These results are possible from this approach. *One,* the pastor and student will find suggestive ideas. As Charles H. Spurgeon said of William Gurnall (1616-79), a Puritan, "I have found his work the best thought-breeder in all our library. I should think more discourses have been suggested by it than by any other. I have often resorted to it when my own fire has been burning low...." *Two,* the user will see how to study an entire book of the Bible for preaching values. *Three,* the man of God will be encouraged to begin the study of the Bible book for himself and find by this method other treasures of homiletical insight.

While using the King James or Authorized Version, the student should compare with all other versions and translations as well as the original text when available.

Many and varied are the commentaries available for the profit of the preacher. These include the following:

I. *Critical.* This deals with the text in the light of biblical criticism, seeking to apply historical principles and a rational approach to the text, e.g., *The International Critical Commentary, The Moffatt New Testament Commentary, The Expositor's Greek Testament,* and the commentaries of H. A. W. Meyer, and Keil and Delitsch.

II. *Exegetical.* This seeks to lead out the exact meaning of the text in terms of the words and idioms in the light of their background and use originally, e.g., *The Westminster Commentaries, The New International Commentary on the New Testament, The Evangelical Commentary on the New Testament,* and the commentaries of R. C. H. Lenski, J. P. Lange, and W. Hendriksen.

III. *Expository.* This expounds and applies the dominant theme of each section or unit in the light of history and with relevance to the present, e.g., *The Expositor's Bible, The Interpreter's Bible, Calvin's Commentaries, The Pulpit Commentary,* and *An American Commentary on the New Testament.*

IV. *Devotional.* This brings out the inner sense or the spiritual essence as applied to the soul in meditation. Here is the stimulus to the spiritual life of the believer, e.g., *A Devotional Commentary,* and Matthew Henry's *Commentary on the Whole Bible.*

The present type of book is neither a Bible study book nor a book of outlines. It is not a commentary as the above. We seek to encourage the preacher to engage in the reading and studying of the book to find the homiletical units. As "the servant of the Word" let him work toward this ideal:

the Historical setting,
the Expository meaning,
the Doctrinal value,
the Practical aim,
the Homiletical form

The First Presbyterian Church
of Seattle, Washington

Ralph G. Turnbull
General Editor

Introduction

The Gospel of Matthew is the Gospel of the King. It was possibly written to convince the Jews that Jesus was their Messiah, the long-awaited King. As such it makes much use of Old Testament prophecy.

This volume is written on the assumption that this Gospel was written by Matthew or Levi, the publican. According to Papias, as quoted by Eusebius, Matthew wrote the *Logia,* a record of Jesus, in Hebrew or Aramaic. Some see this Gospel as a Greek translation of the *Logia.* However, there is no reason why Matthew could not have written both. As a publican Matthew was accustomed to keeping records. One can almost see him taking notes as Jesus taught. Thus we are not surprised to see the great detail with which Matthew reports the teachings of Jesus: the Sermon on the Mount (Chapters 5-7) ; the parables (Chapter 13) ; the denunciation of the Pharisees (Chapter 23) ; and the eschatalogical discourse (Chapters 24-25) .

The date of this Gospel calls for attention. Because of the detailed description of the destruction of Jerusalem (Chapter 24) , some would date it after A.D. 70. But if one accepts the deity of Jesus Christ, there is no reason why it could not have been written prior to that time. Thus it becomes prophecy of the event rather than a history of it. Matthew, like Luke, makes much use of the material found in Mark. Therefore it must have been written after Mark. It could have been written either before or after Luke. However, Matthew shows no reliance upon Luke's account. This may or may not show the priority of Matthew over Luke. The order of the two is not certain, nor is it of great importance. Mark's Gospel probably was written as early as A.D. 50. If so, then sometime between A.D. 55-60 would serve as a probable date for Matthew.

The purpose of this volume is quite plain. It is neither a commentary nor an exposition. It is not a book of sermons. Rather it is intended as an aid in sermon or devotional preparation. With it goes the prayer that it may save busy servants of the King many precious hours of research, and that through them its ministry may be enhanced beyond measure.

Herschel H. Hobbs

Pastor's Study
First Baptist Church
Oklahoma City, Oklahoma
February 1961

Contents

Matthew 1

THE SAVIOURHOOD OF JESUS CHRIST

1:21 "And she shall bring forth a son, and thou shalt call his name JESUS: for he shall save his people from their sins."

I. HISTORICAL SETTING. This is the climax of the genealogical introduction to The Gospel of Matthew. The Jews placed great importance upon their genealogical line, which was traced through the line of the father. Since Matthew is writing primarily for the Jews to prove the Messianic lineage of Jesus, he traces it through the Davidic line of Joseph. But since both Joseph and Mary were of the line of David, the genealogy is a true one with the exception of Jesus' immediate parentage. Matthew is careful to point out that Joseph is not the actual, but legal, father of Jesus (1:16-25). Luke writing for Gentile readers, gives the actual genealogy of Jesus through Mary.

II. EXPOSITORY MEANING. The words "bring forth" (cf. 1:23) render a Greek verb meaning "to give birth." Its noun form is "child." Literally, "she shall child a son." The verbs "bring forth," "call," and "save" are all prophetic future tenses. "JESUS" is the Greek equivalent of the Hebrew word *Joshua* or *Jehoshuah* (cf. English, John; and Spanish, Juan), meaning "Jehovah is helper," "Help of Jehovah," or "Jehovah is salvation." "He" in Greek is emphatic, "He Himself." "Save" means to preserve or deliver. It sometimes refers to physical danger (8:25), disease (9:21-22), or death (24:22). More often it is related to spiritual salvation. "People" could refer to Israel, or to all people (Luke 2:10). Probably it refers to the spiritual Israel (Rom. 9:25-26, 30). He will save all who trust in Him. "Sins" renders a Greek word meaning "to miss the mark" or target, the target being the will and righteousness of God. Literally, "He Himself, and no other, shall save

His people from their sins." "From" translates the Greek preposition *apo,* away from. Jesus will save away from sins. They
will be cast away from and out of sight (cf. Ps. 103:12; Isa.
38:17). Although Matthew wrote primarily for Jewish readers,
the scope of Jesus' saving ministry includes the whole world
(John 3:16).

III. DOCTRINAL VALUE. The major doctrine involved is
the person and work of Jesus Christ. This doctrine also includes the virgin birth, the nature of sin, the crucifixion, resurrection, ascension, and the continued intercession of the
Son of God. Study Luke's account of the birth of Jesus and the
prophetic utterances in Isaiah 7:10-16; 9:1-7. Note also Acts
4:10-12 and Philippians 2:5-11.

IV. PRACTICAL AIM. To show that God has moved in
history to redeem a lost world. This salvation is not military,
political, or social. It is spiritual. Of his own accord man is
unable to save himself. It required a mighty act from God.
But man is saved as an individual. What is God's part? What
is man's role in his salvation?

V. HOMILETICAL FORM
    Theme: "The Saviourhood of Jesus Christ."
    Introduction: Joseph was betrothed to Mary, which in Jew-
ish life was little short of marriage. Before they came together
in marriage Joseph discovered that Mary was with child. As
a *just* man, living according to the law, Joseph felt that he
was unable to enter into marriage with Mary. But because of
his love for her he was not *willing* to embarrass her publicly.
Therefore he *wished* to divorce her privately, which was his
right under the law. While Joseph was in this state of mind,
an angel of the Lord revealed in a dream the true nature of
Mary's condition. The climax of this revelation is the key
verse of the chapter in which is expressed the redemptive
purpose of God. Herein we find the Saviour identified; the
Saviour specified; the salvation classified.

    A. *The Saviour Identified* — "Thou shalt call his name
JESUS." This is the focal point of prophecy. God had made
promises concerning the "seed" of the woman (Gen. 3:15)

and the "seed" of Abraham (Gen. 22:18; Gal. 3:16). Through Isaiah He had promised a child born of a virgin (7:15; 9:6-7). The hopes of Israel, even of the entire world, centered upon these promises.

To Joseph, therefore, the evangel was given that God was moving in history for His eternal redemptive purpose. The child of promise shall be called "Jesus," meaning *Jehovah is salvation*.

Conceived of the Holy Spirit, He is God. Born of the virgin Mary, He is man. He is the God-man. Only thus could the person of God find interplay with the person of man. Christ, the anointed one, is His eternal name. Jesus, help of Jehovah, is His human name. He is Emmanuel, God with us, to help and to save.

Jesus is the Greek equivalent of the Hebrew Joshua. Like Joshua, the prophet, He prophesies, "The Lord will do great wonders among you" (Josh. 3:5). Like Joshua, the priest, He will deliver the captives from their bondage (Ezra 2:2). Like Joshua, the ruler, He will lead into the salvation promised of the Lord (Josh. 1:6). He is Prophet, Priest, and King!

B. *The Saviour Specified* — "He [himself] shall save." Matthew's quotation (1:22-23) refers back to Isaiah 7-9. Ahaz sought deliverance by military alliances, soothsayers, and wizards. He refused to trust in the promises of Jehovah. In the time preceding and following the first century, the Jews trusted in many false military "messiahs" to their own hurt and loss. Monuments and inscriptions abound in the title "Saviour" applied to the Caesars and others. Even the Gentiles looked for a saviour of their own making and choosing. God says that Jesus himself shall save. He is set apart and above all others.

After two thousand years man still looks for salvation from his own ranks. The frustration seen on every hand is the direct result of such futile hopes. Amid the desolate cries of every failure of man may be heard the still small voice of God, "JESUS . . . he [himself] shall save" (cf. Acts 4:10-12).

C. *The Salvation Classified* — "He shall save his people from their sins." This salvation is a deliverance. The Jews thought in terms of military and political deliverance. The apochryphal writing of the Jews just before and during the lifetime of Jesus pictured the Messiah as a military conqueror. Under him Israel would drive out the Romans, and from Jerusalem would rule the world (cf. Luke 24:21; Acts 1:6). Such a deliverance included only the Jews.

From the New Testament it is clear that "his people" involves all men. "God so loved the world [inhabited earth] ... whosoever believeth..." (John 3:16; cf. John 10:16). The Jews regarded themselves alone as God's people. But Paul is careful to point out that not all citizens of political Israel were God's people (Rom. 9:6-13; Rom. 11:1-4; cf. Matt. 3:7-9). Furthermore those who were formerly not a people shall be called the people of God (I Peter 2:9-10; cf. of Rom. 11:17-32). This new relationship is not genetical or political, but spiritual.

This is the scope of the New Testament. It is involved in Matthew 1:21.

Matthew 2

THE RECEPTION OF THE KING

2:1. "Now when Jesus was born in Bethlehem of Judaea in the days of Herod the king, behold, there came wise men from the east to Jerusalem,"

2:2. "Saying, Where is he that is born King of the Jews? for we have seen his star in the east, and are come to worship him."

2:3. "When Herod the king had heard these things, he was troubled, and all Jerusalem with him."

I. HISTORICAL SETTING. The time is 6 or 5 B.C. Matthew dates Jesus' birth in the closing years of the reign of Herod the Great who died in 4 B.C. A. T. Robertson gives eight reasons for the above date of Jesus' birth (*A Harmony of the Gospels,* Broadman, Nashville) : death of Herod, slaughter of the infants, the star, language of Luke 2:14 about "peace on earth," beginning of the ministry of John the Baptist, beginning of the ministry of Jesus, building of the temple, Roman census of Luke 2:1 f.

The place is Bethlehem of Judaea, near Jerusalem, not the Bethlehem near Nazareth mentioned by Josephus (*Antiquities* XIX. 15). Bethlehem was the home of David. Being of his lineage Joseph and Mary went there to enroll for taxation (Luke 2:1-4).

The wise men may have come from Babylon, Persia, Parthia, Arabia, or elsewhere, probably from somewhere east of Palestine. The number "three" is legendary, inferred from the number of gifts brought. Legend also names them Caspar, Balthasar, and Melchoir; and suggests that they represent Shem, Ham, and Japheth. They were probably astrologers.

II. EXPOSITORY MEANING

Matt. 1:1. "When" is not in the Greek. The form is a genitive absolute construction. Literally it reads, "Now about the birth of Jesus." "Was born" is a passive participle of the verb *to beget*. "In the days of Herod" is an indefinite time referring to the evil time in which Jesus was born. *Herod* was the son of Antipater, an Edomite, and an Arabian mother, so not a Jew. He had been appointed "king" by the Roman senate (cf. "sceptre . . . from Judah," Gen. 49:10). The "wise men" were "Magi," astrologers. Herodotus speaks of a tribe of Magi among the Medians. "East" translates a word meaning "from the risings" of the sun, so probably east of Palestine.

Matt. 2:2. "Born King" suggests a contrast. Jesus was "born King." Herod was appointed king. "Have seen" is from a verb to see with the eyes, so not an imaginary vision. "Star" is the word for one star (*astēr*), not a group of stars (*astron*) as some suggest. It was "his star," not "a star." Actually they saw it not *in* the eastern sky, but *while they were in the east.* "Worship" literally means to kneel or prostrate in homage or obeisance.

Matt. 2:3. "Troubled" renders a verb meaning *to agitate* as water; to trouble the mind; or, as here, to terrify.

III. DOCTRINAL VALUE.
This passage bears witness to the Kingship of Jesus Christ. It speaks of the response made to the Kingship both by inanimate nature and by human personality. *The Gospel of Matthew* emphasizes that Jesus is the King of the Jews and of the whole world.

IV. PRACTICAL AIM.
To set forth the varying responses given to the Kingship of Jesus and the resultant consequences. Regardless of a man's position he must answer the question, "What shall I do then with Jesus which is called Christ?" (Matt. 27:22).

V. HOMILETICAL FORM

Theme: "The Reception of the King."

Introduction: Even in His birth hour Jesus confronted men and nature with His claims upon them. God is sovereign in that He does that which He wills and which is in accord with His nature. But man is a person endowed with a free will. As such he is responsible for his choices. To accept God's sovereign will is to rise to the heights of greatness. To reject that will is to go down to the depths of ruin both in time and in eternity. This twofold truth is clearly demonsrated in Matthew 2.

A. *The Response of Inanimate Nature* — "His star in the east...." Various efforts have been exerted to explain this phenomenon. Kepler suggested that it was a conjunction of Jupiter and Saturn in 747 A.U.C (Roman Timetable) to which was added Mars in 748. Chinese records refer to a comet in the spring of 749. Reverend C. Pritchard, as confirmed at Greenwich, suggests that the above constellation could not have appeared as one star. They were never nearer one another than double the diameter of the moon. The suggestion that the Magi had weak eyes is preposterous. The word used means *a star,* not a group of stars. A normal star would have been as far from the Magi in Bethlehem as "in the east." This star "came, and stood over where the young child was." It was a miracle. God said, "Let His star come into being," and it was so. Inanimate nature responded to God's sovereign will.

It was always true. Water, wind, vegetation, rocks, and physical disease responded to his word. "The heavens declare the glory of God; and the firmament showeth his handywork" (Ps. 19:1). The universe came into being at His word. Seasons, seed-time and harvest all respond to His will. In the realm of nature Christ is King. His law is absolute.

B. *The Response of Science* — "There came wise men...." While they were astrologers they suggest the advanced wisdom of their day. They could have been Jewish proselytes who held to the Messianic hope. Even Virgil, the Roman poet, had caught such a vision.

Whatever the source of their knowledge, in faith, they followed the vision to worship and to lay their treasures at the feet of the Christ child. They followed God's guidance, refusing to make their knowledge the instrument of a tyrant bent upon defeating the purpose of God. Thus they became a symbol of science and knowledge which recognizes the source of all wisdom and dedicates it to the salvation, not the destruction, of men.

Unhappily this is not always true. Greek philosophy achieved unprecedented heights of greatness in mental power. It formed the basis of modern scientific investigation and achievement. Yet it set itself up against "the wisdom of God" (cf. I Cor. 1:20-28). Refusing to recognize God, God gave it over to a reprobate mind, one that is void of judgment (Rom. 1:28). The very wisdom of modern man has produced products which largely either corrupt man or threaten to destroy him altogether. The greatest need today is a worship of and thorough dedication to God in Christ within the realm of modern man's intellect and its fruits.

C. *The Response of Government* — "When Herod the king had heard these things, he was troubled, and all Jerusalem with him." As a non-Jew Herod had no right to the throne of Judaea. This knowledge, plus his jealous nature, led him to destroy every seeming threat to his position: his two favorite sons, Aristobulus and Alexander; his favorite wife, their mother, Mariamne; Antipater, another son; the brother and mother of Mariamne; and her uncle, his faithful adviser. Augustus Caesar said that it was better to be Herod's sow (*hus*) than his son (*huios*), for the former had a better chance to live.

Thus this suspicious and jealous king was troubled or terrified when he heard of one "that is born King of the Jews." Herod was merely *appointed* king of the Jews. He occupied the place which rightly belonged to Jesus. Wherever governments usurp the place of God they have a right to be terrified. "And all Jerusalem with him." When those in power defy God, those over whom they rule may well be terrified as well.

But Jesus had no kingly aspirations in the political sense. Had Herod joined the Magi in worship and in placing his crown at Jesus' feet, he would have received it back enhanced and glorified. For government is ordained of God for his purpose. But Herod sought to intervene between men and God's redemptive ministry. No government has that right. Soul liberty is man's right, not something bestowed or withheld by rulers.

Herod's attitude may be described in two ways. First, he feigned a desire to worship Jesus (2:7-8). Second, he desired only to destroy Jesus (2:16). His slaughter of the infants, probably about twenty, was so insignificant an event in comparison with his other murders that extra-biblical history ignores it. But God's word records it. Though secular history ignores the hypocritical lip-service paid to God and tends to minimize the destructive work of ungodly rulers, the records of God in time and eternity indelibly record them. Such nations are judged of God in the context of history. Herod died a horrible, loathsome death less than two years later. All of the Herods die, but Jesus Christ lives on in triumph over them.

D. *The Response of the Soul* — "We . . . are come to worship him . . . bring me word again, that I may come and worship him also" (2:2, 8). The outward attitude is the same; the inward purpose is different. The difference rested within their separate wills. The one was humble, sincere, and benevolent. The other was hypocritical, cynical, and destructive. "But the hour cometh, and now is, when the true worshippers shall worship the Father in spirit and in truth: for the Father seeketh such to worship him" (John 4:23).

True spiritual worship must be a willing response within the souls of men. Note the contrast — a babe in a manger versus the wisdom and the political power of men. But in the babe was the wisdom of God and the power of God (I Cor. 1:24). As a babe He had no power to compel either the Magi or the king. As a man He did not compel obeisance by force. It must be willingly and personally given. When this is done, men rejoice (2:10). When it is not done, men are troubled in heart, and the whole world with them (2:3).

Men withhold themselves from Him now to their own hurt and loss. But the day will come when He will be "King of Kings and Lord of Lords" (Rev. 17:14; Rev. 19:16).

Matthew 3

THE SHADOW OF COMING EVENTS

3:16. "And Jesus, when he was baptized, went up straight-way out of the water: and, lo, the heavens were opened unto him, and he saw the Spirit of God descending like a dove, and lighting upon him:"

3:17. "And lo a voice from heaven, saying, This is my be-loved Son, in whom I am well pleased."

I. HISTORICAL SETTING. The time is probably A.D. 26. The place is the Jordan River near Bethany. Thirty years have elapsed since Jesus' birth (Luke 3:23). This event breaks eighteen years of silence concerning Jesus (Luke 2:42). Six months earlier John the Baptist had begun his ministry as the forerunner of the Messiah. Multitudes came to hear his preaching, and many received his baptism of repentance. Word of his ministry reached Galilee. So Jesus came to pre-sent Himself for baptism. The time had arrived when the King should present himself. The Kingdom of Heaven is at hand.

II. EXPOSITORY MEANING

Matt. 3:16. "When he was baptized" translates a participle, "being baptized." "Baptize" transliterates a Greek word meaning to dip, plunge, or submerge. Metaphorically it means to be overwhelmed as by calamities. John's *baptism* (*baptisma*, not the act but its significance) was symbolically with reference to repentance, or a willingness to participate in Messiah's kingdom.

Matt. 3:16. "Spirit of God." The third person of the Trin-ity. This is not the Spirit's entrance into the world. He was active both in the Old Testament and in the birth of Jesus. It is an anointing of the King.

23

Matt. 3:16. "dove." It is symbolic of gentleness and sweetness. Matthew says, "As a dove." Luke says, "In a bodily shape like a dove."

Matt. 3:16. "Voice." This is the Father, the first person of the Trinity. Note the presence of the Trinity — Son, Spirit, Father.

Matt. 3:17. Literally, "This is my Son, the beloved." "Well pleased" is an aorist tense of point action covering eternity and time. It is God's approval of Jesus' life up to this point. Note also Matthew 17:5 and II Peter 1:17.

III. DOCTRINAL VALUE. In His baptism Jesus symbolized His death and resurrection, that which He did for man's redemption. This involves the triune God. Secondarily He authenticated the ministry of John; He identified Himself with man; He identified Himself with the Suffering Servant of Isaiah (cf. Isa. 40:3-5; 42:6-21; 53).

IV. PRACTICAL AIM. To reveal the King as the Suffering Servant of Jehovah in whom the triune God wrought salvation for lost men. Though a King He became one with sinful man, becoming obedient to death in the eternal Spirit. In His resurrection God declared Him to be the Son of God with power in whom the Father is well pleased. This is the heart of the Kingdom which He established.

V. HOMILETICAL FORM
Theme: "The Shadow of Coming Events."

Introduction: The author of Hebrews refers to the Levitical rituals as "a shadow of good things to come" (Heb. 10:1). In a very real sense the same may be said of Jesus' baptism. It was a shadow of coming events which would climax the redemptive purpose which God activated in the incarnation of His Son. That this purpose involved the entire Godhead is seen in this event which marked the beginning of Jesus' public ministry. Here is symbolized the truth that "God was in Christ, reconciling the world unto himself..." (II Cor. 5:19). This is seen in first, the baptism of the Son; second, the anointing by the Spirit; third, the approval of the Father.

A. *The Baptism of the Son* — "And Jesus, when he was

baptized ...." Why was Jesus baptized? Not for repentance, because He had no sin from which to repent. The sinlessness of Jesus is at the heart of the gospel. To set an example? Perhaps. To authenticate John's ministry? In a sense. As dedication for His own ministry? Possibly so. But these are fringe ideas read into the event after the fact.

What did this baptism mean to Jesus? "To be baptized" (3:13) is an infinitive of purpose. "By him" (3:13) links His ministry to that of the herald of the Kingdom, a Kingdom which is rooted in God's redemptive love whose greatest expression is seen in the crucifixion and resurrection (cf. Isa. 40:3-5; Isa. 42:21; 53). After this event Jesus spoke of His baptism only twice (Matt. 20:22; Luke 12:50) both of which referred to His death. In His initial baptism He fulfilled that which was right as He joined others who were being baptized. Sinless, yet He identified Himself with sinners as later He did on the cross. His baptism was a prophecy of His death and resurrection. Ours is a symbol of these events in which we as sinners saved by grace symbolically identify ourselves with Him who knew no sin, yet for our sake became sin, that we might become the righteousness of God through Him (Rom. 6:3-4; II Cor. 5:21).

B. *The Anointing by the Spirit* — "The Spirit of God ... lighting upon him...."

The Cerinthian Gnostics, insisting that God was neither born nor did He die, said that Deity came upon Jesus at His baptism and left Him on the cross (Matt. 27:46). But the whole of the New Testament contradicts this.

What is the significance of this anointing? It is the anointing of the King. The dove is symbolic of gentleness, innocence, and meekness (Matt. 10:16). The Levitical law prescribed one dove, along with a lamb, or two doves only for the poor, as a sacrificial offering (Lev. 12:6; Lev. 14:22; cf. Luke 2:24). This would be the primary thought suggested to Matthew's Hebrew readers.

This was not Jesus' first contact with the Holy Spirit. By Him He had been born and had developed into manhood. He will continue to be with Him. Thus this anointing was not one of power for His ministry of mighty works and teaching. He is not to be a King in the popular Hebrew sense. It was His anointing for sacrifice. As one who was gentle, innocent, and meek He would be the sacrifice for sin. It corresponds to the lamb and dove for those who could afford it, or to two doves for the poor. Thus Jesus is to be the comprehensive sacrifice for sin for all who will receive Him. He will be offered "through the eternal Spirit" (Heb. 9:14). As the dove He is weak in His sacrifice. As the Spirit He is powerful in His salvation.

C. *The Approval of the Father* — "This is my beloved Son . . . well pleased."

This harks back to Psalm 2. Here the Father speaks of the only begotten Son to whom He will give the heathen for an inheritance. He shall be His "king upon my holy hill of Zion." Though the heathen shall rage and kings shall plot, the Son is promised victory. His victory shall not be military but spiritual. The Jews looked for the former. God gives the latter. He will go through the cross to the throne. Once again the thought of sacrifice appears.

Note Heb. 10:5-9; Matt. 17:5; Luke 9:31; Rom. 1:4-5. The one approved will be raised and crowned. Thus He is our Sacrifice, Hope, and King.

Matthew 4

THE VICTORIOUS KING

4:1. "Then was Jesus led up of the Spirit into the wilderness to be tempted of the devil."

4:3. "If thou be the Son of God, command that these stones be made bread."

4:6. "If thou be the Son of God, cast thyself down . . . ."

4:9. "All these things will I give thee, if thou wilt fall down and worship me."

I. HISTORICAL SETTING. Immediately (straightway, Mark 1:12) after His baptism the Holy Spirit led (driveth, Mark 1:12) Jesus into the wilderness of Judea. The time is A.D. 26. The traditional Mount of Temptation is a wild, barren mountain just west and north of Jericho. From the time of the crusades it was called Quarantania. After forty days of fasting Jesus was tempted of the devil. The fasting was not mere ritual. It was a fasting of preoccupation with the will of God, wherein Jesus felt no hunger. "He was afterward ahungered" (Matt. 4:2). The order of the temptations varies in Matthew and Luke, with the sequence of the second and third being reversed. Luke follows the geographical order. Matthew gives the natural and climactic. At the outset of His public ministry the King faces the Adversary who challenges His right to reign.

II. EXPOSITORY MEANING

Matt. 4: "led" means to lead from a lower to a higher place, from the valley to the mountain. "Of the spirit" or by the agency of the Spirit. The choice was of God not of Satan. "To be tempted" is an infinitive of purpose meaning to test, to prove, either in the good or evil sense. God would

27

prove the good; Satan would prove the evil. Note "of the **spirit**" and "of the devil." "Devil" means slanderer. It is the proper name of a person (masculine). The Devil slanders God to man (Gen. 3:4) and man to God (Job 1:9-11).

Matt. 4:3. "If thou be [the] Son of God . . . ." A condition of the first class (Greek) assumed as true. "Command" is the imperative form of "say," a *command* of the devil for Jesus to *command*.

Matt. 4:6. "If thou be . . . ." Again a condition assumed as being true.

Matt. 4:9. "All these things" refers to the "kingdoms of the cosmos" (4:8), including the rule of the world, not merely Palestine. "Fall down and worship me" or prostrate before Satan, the usual form of oriental worship.

III. DOCTRINAL VALUE. The temptations of Jesus involve primarily both His humanity and deity. Involved also are the doctrines of Satan and of evil. The place and power of the Word of God in temptation are seen. The Messianic mission and method are evident. This entire event is cast against the background of the will of God and the way of the cross. Both the King and the nature of His Kingdom are brought into clear focus.

IV. PRACTICAL AIM. To show that in Jesus Christ we have a King or High Priest who "was in all points tempted like as we are, yet without sin" (Heb. 4:15). He is therefore able to help us when we are tempted. Here Christ truly becomes one with us; He is the Pioneer of our faith who shows the way to triumphant, Godly living.

V. HOMILETICAL FORM
    Theme: "The Victorious King."

Introduction: This initial temptation of Jesus in His public ministry is the first of which there were many. Jesus, as a man, had the capacity to yield to these temptations or else they were not real. The glorious truth is that He was "tempted . . . yet without sin" (Heb. 4:15). In so doing He justified the demands of God's law. He proved Himself to be "just" or righteous in order that He might become the "justifier of him which believeth in Jesus" (Rom. 3:26). He "was in all points tempted like as we are" (Heb. 4:15). Luke says that He endured "every kind of temptation" (4:13, author's translation). Satan tempted Eve in the realms of the physical, aesthetic, and of ambition (Gen. 3:6). He tempted Jesus in the realms of physical need, spiritual trust, and divine mission. Sin is the illegitimate expression of a legitimate desire.

A. *The Realm of Physical Need* — "If thou be the Son of God, command that these stones be made bread."

Satan assumes the truth of the words of the Father at Jesus' baptism. As the Son of God Jesus should possess divine power, a power which He had not used as yet. Satan suggests that Jesus use this power for selfish ends, something that He never did. In this temptation is the subtle suggestion that God is not benevolent (cf. Gen. 3:1). Likewise he implies failure of Jesus' divine mission at the outset. Suppose that He should die of starvation. What then? Furthermore Satan suggests that Jesus assert His deity to the abandonment of His humanity or His identity with the weakness of man. Involved also is the thought that God cannot be trusted. "Take things into your own hands."

This temptation is common to every man. Man must have bread. If he cannot get it one way, then get it in another. But Jesus says, "Take no thought [be not overly anxious] for your life, what ye shall eat . . . is not the life more than meat . . .?" (cf. Matt. 6:25 ff.).

In essence this was Jesus' answer to Satan (Matt. 4:4). Note His use of Scripture, the sword of the Spirit, as He quoted from Deuteronomy 8:3. There is more to man than the physical body. He is a soul which feeds upon God's every word. At the very beginning the King renounces self-will for the will of God. Those who aspire to places of authority should do likewise.

B. *The Realm of Spiritual Trust* — "Cast thyself down. . . ."

Once again Satan assumes the deity of Jesus. He also assumes His humanity as he appeals to the human weakness of dizziness from the heights. Basic, however, is the temptation to doubt God's promises. To put God to such a test is to doubt. Satan said, "Do not trust, but dare. Instead of throwing yourself upon God's promise, throw yourself from the pinnacle of the temple. Create a crisis, and call God's hand."

Note that in reply to Jesus' use of Scripture, the Devil replies in kind (cf. Ps. 91:11-12). He can use Scripture to his own nefarious ends. Note again that he misquotes by omitting a vital part. Lifting it out of its context he seeks to create doubt rather than faith.

The all-inclusive element of this temptation is to use the spectacular rather than prosaic faith in God to obtain a desired end. By such a deed Jesus would immediately receive acclamation as the Messiah. According to God's promise it would involve no real danger, only seem to do so. In truth it involved hypocrisy on Jesus' part. Such acclamation would be but surface in nature. The Kingdom could not be founded upon such. God's purpose must be achieved in such a way that those who received Jesus must do so in true faith. His Kingdom must be founded upon truth, a truth which was forged in the fires of suffering and tempered in the waters of the resurrection. Jesus chose to be identified with a cause which failed, according to man's standards, but which triumphed in the will and purpose of God. Man should never employ the risque to achieve personal or divine ends.

Thus His second reply from Scripture (Matt. 4:7; cf. Deut. 6:16). "Tempt" here is the same word as used in Matthew 4:1 with the prefixed preposition. This adds force to the word, and clearly gives it the evil sense. He will not try God to see if He will fail. Instead He will trust in God, knowing that His will must succeed.

C. *The Realm of Divine Mission* — "All these things will I give thee . . . if. . . ."

Note the rising sequence of the temptations: self-preservation; public acclamation; world domination. From "an exceeding high mountain" Jesus saw the adjoining kingdoms. "In a moment of time" (Luke 4:5) in a vision He beheld the "kingdoms of the cosmos," or orderly world, and their glory. This was destined of God to be Jesus' realm. Satan implies that such shall come to be. But note that he quotes no Scripture. Not the Father's will but only that of Jesus is to be involved. God's promise to the Son is in the background (cf. Ps. 2:8-12). The issue is not the fact but the method to be employed.

Note the false claim involved: "I will give thee . . . ." Were they his to give? Note the false method suggested: "If thou wilt fall down and worship me." Would-be conquerors have always fallen into Satan's trap and ultimately have failed. Satan promises and does not, yea, cannot deliver (cf. John 8:44-45). God promises and does deliver (cf. Matt. 5:5).

Note the two methods involved (cf. John 6:15; Matt. 27:40-43; Matt. 16:25; Luke 9:5). Note Jesus' final answer to Satan. "Begone Satan" (author's translation). cf. Deut. 6:13.

Matthew 5

THE CHARACTER OF THE CHRISTIAN

5:3. "Blessed are the poor in spirit: for theirs is the kingdom of heaven."

5:4. "Blessed are they that mourn: for they shall be comforted."

5:5. "Blessed are the meek: for they shall inherit the earth."

5:6. "Blessed are they which do hunger and thirst after righteousness: for they shall be filled."

5:7. "Blessed are the merciful: for they shall obtain mercy."

5:8. "Blessed are the pure in heart: for they shall see God."

5:9. "Blessed are the peacemakers: for they shall be called the children of God."

5:10. "Blessed are they which are persecuted for righteousness' sake: for theirs is the kingdom of heaven."

5:11. "Blessed are ye, when men shall revile you, and persecute you, and shall say all manner of evil against you falsely, for my sake."

5:12. "Rejoice, and be exceedingly glad: for great is your reward in heaven: for so persecuted they the prophets which were before you."

I. HISTORICAL SETTING. The sermon on the Mount was delivered probably near the middle of Jesus' public ministry or about A.D. 28. The place is uncertain, but it was at a level place (Luke 6:17) on a mountain (Matt. 5:1) in Galilee. It may have been the Horns of Hattin between Capernaum and Nazareth. Some scholars insist that this is not a sermon, but a collection of Jesus' sayings delivered on various occasions. Others distinguish the account of Luke from that of Matthew as being distinct sermons delivered on different occasions. But they probably are different accounts of the same sermon. After a night of prayer Jesus chose the twelve apostles (Mark 3:13-19; Luke 6:12-16). The sermon was delivered to the Twelve although the "multitude" heard it also. In it Jesus set forth the character and conditions of life pertaining to citizens of His Kingdom. It has been called the Constitution of the Kingdom of God. Doctor Oswald Dykes called it "The Manifesto of the King."

II. EXPOSITORY MEANING

Matt. 5:3. "Blessed" means "happy," not a gift from without but a condition of character realized within one's life, and resulting in happiness or blessedness. "Poor" means deep poverty (cf. Luke 16:20, 22). "In spirit" is a recognition of spiritual poverty as the publican (Luke 18:13).

Matt. 5:4. "mourn." This means to be sad, to lament, not only over one's own sins, but over the sins of others. The "poor in spirit" will "mourn." "Comforted" is the verb from which comes "Comforter' (John 14:16), the one called alongside for comfort or encouragement.

Matt. 5:5. "meek." This is not effeminacy but the inner calm of strength. The meek man recognizes the source of this strength and seeks to use it for God's glory and man's blessedness.

Matt. 5:6. "hunger" and "thirst." These are the primary drives, food and drink. "Righteousness" is personal righteousness, but which is desired for all men. Jesus gives to these natural drives a spiritual content. "Filled" is used of feeding and fattening cattle.

Matt. 5:7. "merciful." This quality means full of mercy, pity, or compassion as opposed to censorious criticism (cf. Matt. 7:1-2). This is the law of sowing and reaping.

Matt. 5:8. "pure in heart." This purity is not outer but inner cleanliness. The Jews practiced the opposite.

Matt. 5:9. "peacemakers." Over against warmongers Jesus acclaims the makers of peace. The primary reference is with respect to peace between God and man. The Son of God is the perfect peacemaker (cf. Eph. 2:14 f.). Such shall be like Him.

Matt. 5:10. "persecuted." This word sometimes means to pursue in a good sense. Here it means to pursue with malignity.

Matt. 5:11. "revile." This means to "reproach" (ASV) or to insult with evil language. "Falsely" is a participle meaning "lying."

Matt. 5:12. "Rejoice . . . exceeding glad." The first word is the common word for joy. The latter words denote exhultation in joy (cf. Luke 6:23, "leap" for joy).

III. DOCTRINAL VALUE. The Beatitudes set forth the character of the Kingdom man. This character involves the nature of the Kingdom as an inner condition resulting in outward attitudes and aptitudes. Involved is the contrast between the Messianic kingdom envisioned by the Jews and the Kingdom as seen through the eyes of Jesus.

IV. PRACTICAL AIM. To see the Christian character not as something to possess but as a *being* and *doing* for Christ's sake. The Christian life is a gift of grace. But it is more than a gift. It is a stewardship of character to be developed and used in bringing the rule of God into the hearts of all men.

V. HOMILETICAL FORM

Theme: "The Character of the Christian"

Introduction: When the King would set forth the nature of His Kingdom, He turned His back upon a popular movement and selected a small group of men. The nature of the Kingdom which He declared to them was in direct contrast to that sought by the masses. During the four hundred years between Malachi and Matthew Jewish literature created the popular image of a conquering military Messiah whose reign would be characterized by power, pomp, and plenty. In sharp contrast Jesus pictures His reign as one of submission, service, and suffering. As such the King's followers are not to be soldiers but "salt" (5:13), not legions but "light" (5:14). It is not a matter of conquest but of character. This character is presented as essence, expression, and experience.

A. *The Essence of Christian Character* — "Blessed . . . poor in spirit . . . mourn . . . meek . . . hunger and thirst . . . ."

Happiness (blessedness) is the desired goal of every man. False roads lead to frustration. Those who first heard these words of Jesus, including the Twelve, followed the path of performance and possessing. Jesus emphasized the importance of being and sharing. After two thousand years man follows the former and ignores the latter. The enigma of man is the paradox of Jesus. Natural man says, "Happy . . . the rich . . . joyful . . . proud . . . satisfied." Jesus says, "Happy . . . the poor . . . mournful . . . meek . . . hungry." Note the progression in Matthew 5:3-6.

The "poor in spirit" is conscious of his spiritual need, and thus surrenders to the will of the King (5:3). Aware of his own inability, he is willing to be governed. Such receives the Kingdom as he submits to the King. Recognizing his weakness he *mourns* for his own sins and those of others (5:4). But he is comforted by Him who stands alongside him in forgiveness and strength. Thus he realizes the inner strength of *meekness* (5:5). He achieves happiness not in new circumstances, but his happiness alters his circumstances. Thus he inherits the earth. Therefore he *hungers and thirsts* more and more for a richer experience with the King, not for himself alone but for all men (5:6). In his submission he receives a continuous infilling of the Spirit, who enables him to experience *happiness* and to share it with others who through his zeal are brought to submit to the King.

B. *The Expression of Christian Character* — "Blessed . . . the merciful . . . pure in heart . . . peacemakers . . . ."

Note again the progression in Matthew 5:7-9. The passive essence of Christian character evolves into the active expression of that character in evangelistic zeal. Such a person does not give way to captious criticism of those who lack the Christian character. Rather he is "merciful" (5:7) as he declares God's love and grace to them. In so doing he receives not their judgment (Matt. 7-12), but their mercy in return. It is "a self-acting law of the moral world" (Bruce). In such an attitude the Christian becomes "pure in heart" (5:8). His heart is undivided as he presses his one aim in life — to share Christian happiness with others. With absolute loyalty to the King, he sees God in the fulness of His love and grace, for himself and for all men. So wherever he goes he exemplifies the atmosphere of peace (5:9). Not only is he at peace within himself and with God, but he is a *peacemaker* between man and man and between God and man. As such he becomes like the King (Eph. 2:14-16), and in truth is a child of God.

C. *The Experience of Christian Character* — "Persecuted ...revile...."

Verses 10-12 retrogress to verses 3-9. Jesus never promised the Christian "flow'ry beds of ease" (cf. Matt. 16:24; John 16:33). But He does promise happiness in tribulation. The Christian is not to seek suffering for suffering's sake. It is to be found only in his zeal after righteousness (5:10) as He does the will of the King (5:11). The Christian character should never *deserve* persecution and reproach. Neither should he seek to avoid it in the line of duty. In his suffering he is in a glorious succession (the prophets) and a royal one (the King Himself); cf. Heb. 2:10.

Matthew 6

THE PRIMACY OF KINGDOM VALUES

6:1. "Take heed that ye do not your alms before men, to be seen of them...."

6:2. "Therefore when thou doest thine alms, do not sound a trumpet before thee, as the hypocrites do in the synagogues and in the streets, that they may have glory of men. Verily I say unto you, They have their reward."

6:5. "And when thou prayest...."

6:16. "Moreover when ye fast...."

6:19. "Lay not up for yourselves treasures upon earth...."

6:33. "But seek ye first the kingdom of God, and his righteousness; and all these things shall be added unto you."

I. HISTORICAL SETTING. This is a continuance of the Sermon on the Mount. The King turns from essential character and social relationship to the personal righteousness of the Kingdom man as it relates him to God and His rule. It is a contrast of current practices in religion with the pure motives which should activate the Kingdom man with respect to the kingdom of this world and to the Kingdom of God.

II. EXPOSITORY MEANING

Matt. 6:1. "Take heed." This is an imperative form meaning to set the mind. Followed by the negative particle *(mē)*, as here, it means to beware. G. Campbell Morgan calls it the "flaming sword" guarding holy ground. "Alms" translates the word for "righteousness." It includes alms (6:2), prayer (6:5), and fasting (6:16). "To be seen" is an infinitive of purpose. From it comes our word *theatrical.*

Matt. 6:2. "alms." The word means any eleemosynary deed. It does not refer to church finances. "Trumpet." Preceded by the negative particle it means "stop sounding a trumpet." Jewish writings do not list such a practice. But it probably refers to the custom of some to sound a small trumpet to call beggars to them and to advertise their generosity. "Hypocrites." This is a theatrical word (cf. 6:1) for *play actor,* one who plays a part. Only Jesus applied this word to men (cf. Matt. 23). "They have their reward." "They have" renders an intensive form of *have.* The papyri lists it as a commercial term meaning "payment in full."

Matt. 6:16. "fast." This is self-denial in communion with God. It could be good (Matt. 4:2) or evil, as here. The motive flavors the act.

Matt. 6:19. "Lay not up." This is an imperative preceded by the negative. Literally, "stop laying up." "Treasures." The word means *caskets* (Matt. 2:11) or *storehouses* (Matt. 13.52). Here it means that which is stored up. In this instance it could include "reward" as contrasted in Matthew 6:1-2, 5, 16, as well as material goods. "Yourselves." Literally this means "to you" rather than to God.

Matt. 6:33. "seek." This is an imperative form meaning to desire, to strive to obtain that which is desired. "First the kingdom and the righteousness of him." "God" is not in the best manuscripts. "First" is in the emphatic position. The definite article before *kingdom* and *righteousness* emphasizes both. "And all these things shall be added unto you." "These things" refer primarily to physical benefits, but include "reward" also. "Added." This means here "to super-add," abundance.

III. DOCTRINAL VALUE. This chapter bears witness to true Kingdom values as over against worldly aims and desires. The former is inner and spiritual rather than outer and material. Such values are indestructible. The Kingdom man seeks a proper relationship with God rather than the plaudits of men. Involved is the true righteousness versus the ostentatious hypocrisy of those outside the Kingdom. This includes a proper concept of charity, prayer, and fasting. The true treasures are those of the heart. Singlehearted devotion

to God supersedes every other possession. The whole passage
teaches the primacy of God's rule and righteousness.

IV. PRACTICAL AIM. To enable the Christian to seek to be
well pleasing to God as he places the values of life in their
relative importance. By way of suggestion it is to challenge
lost men to seek first God's will and way in the renunciation
of that which perishes and fades away.

V. HOMILETICAL FORM
   Theme: "The Primacy of Kingdom Values."
   Introduction: The Christian is a citizen of two worlds, the
earthly and the heavenly, with each striving for the mastery
(cf. Rom. 7:14-25). As such the Kingdom man becomes a
battleground between God and man, and God and mammon.
In this conflict the good becomes the enemy of the best. In
Chapter 5 Jesus warns His followers against the evils which
assail them in their relationships to other men. Now He
warns against the subtler temptations in their relationship to
God. If Satan cannot defile them through personal or social
sins, he will attack them in the realm of personal righteousness, that which would rightly relate their lives to the will
of God. The Christian can do *right* things in the *wrong* way.
The result is sin. Jesus warns against such as He pictures the
lure of man, the love of mammon, and the loyalty to God.
   A. *The Lure of Man* — "To be seen of them . . . ."
   Because of his new nature the Kingdom man is inclined
toward deeds of righteousness. Satan, knowing that he can
not stifle this desire, seeks to pervert it to evil ends. He directs
it toward men rather than toward God. "To be seen" is an
infinitive of purpose. Thusly perverted man's purpose is to
receive the praise of men rather than to receive divine commendation and benefits. This truth Jesus illustrates with
three righteous deeds: alms, prayer, and fasting.
   The logical order reverses that which Jesus used. True
"fasting" is self-denial resulting from a pre-occupation with
the will of God. "Prayer" is communion between God and
man. "Alms" is but the outward expression of the God-like-
ness of the Kingdom man whose giving stems from the grace
of God. Fasting evolves into prayer which results in the spirit

of giving. When directed toward God alone, they become true righteousness. But "before men" they are perverted into selfish, hypocritical deeds for self-glory.

Note the outcome of such righteousness. It is not that they may appear unto God to fast, but "unto men" (6:16). It is to be "seen of men," not heard of God, that they pray (6:5). The end of their charity is "that they may have glory of men" (6:2). This is in contrast with the Kingdom ideal (5:16).

Men receive that for which they seek. "They have their reward." They seek to be seen of and glorified by men. They receive it. *Paid in full!* To such God has no obligation.

B. *The Love of Mammon.* "For yourselves treasures upon earth . . . ."

The Bible does not discourage the making of money. It exhorts to diligence in business, thrift, and the stewardship of wealth. But Satan perverts these virtues into miserliness. Against such the Kingdom man is warned.

The rich fool is not accused of dishonesty. His sin lay in the wrong purpose in the hoarding of wealth. Of him Jesus said, "These things are requiring thy soul [life] of thee" (Luke 12:20, author's translation). Note Jesus' words about inordinate anxiety (Matt. 6:25 ff.).

"For where your treasure is, there will your heart be also" (6:21). Likewise, "where your heart is, there will your treasure be also."

The Kingdom man must make money honestly, invest money wisely, and dedicate money religiously. He cannot serve two masters (6:24).

C. *The Loyalty to God.* "Seek ye first . . . ."

Note the order of "first" things: "the kingdom of him;" "the righteousness of him." His Kingdom, the rule of God, is primary over the rule of man. A man must first submit to the rule of God in his own life. Then the coming of the Kingdom in other men's lives must be the Kingdom man's first desire. The first real petition of the Model Prayer (6:10) is "Thy kingdom come . . . ." Before daily bread (6:11) comes the Kingdom. God must supersede mammon in his loyalty.

"The righteousness of him" must displace self-righteousness

in the Kingdom man. Money, fasting, prayer, and alms to him
are not the means to an end — self-glory, self-righteousness —
but the outgrowth of God's righteousness which indwells him.
Only thus may they fulfil their purpose in the will of God.

When a man is rightly related to God "all these things"
shall be "super-added" to him.

Matthew 7

THE GOLDEN RULE

7:12 "Therefore all things whatsoever ye would that men should do unto you, do ye even so to them: for this is the law and the prophets."

I. HISTORICAL SETTING. The Golden Rule comes near the close of the Sermon on the Mount. Luke (6:31) places it just after Matthew 5:42. This verse complements Matthew 5:17. These two verses may well be regarded as parentheses which encompass all that comes between. In its immediate setting the Golden Rule is a climax to Matthew 7:1-12. The Kingdom man is warned against condemnatory judgment (7:1-5), but is called upon to exercise discrimination (7:6). To exercise properly these elements he is to ask, seek, and knock in order to be empowered of God. It is in such power that he is able to exercise the Golden Rule.

II. EXPOSITORY MEANING

Matt. 7:12. "Therefore." This word harks back not only to Matthew 5:17 ff. It calls for reexamination of Matthew 7:1-11 in particular. It calls for soul-searching.

Matt. 7:12. "All things." This is one word in Greek, and precedes "therefore." It is thus in the emphatic position. "Therefore" is followed by "whatsoever." "All things . . . whatsoever" emphasize the scope of that which Jesus has in mind.

Matt. 7:12. "would." This translates a verb "to will." It is more than a mere wish, but delves into man's will.

Matt. 7:12. "should do." This is a subjunctive form, "all things . . . whatsoever . . . men should do . . . ." The scope of possibilities is infinite.

Matt. 7:12. Literally, "so also you do [imperative] to them." "You" is emphatic.

45

III. DOCTRINAL VALUE. In this verse Jesus laid down the comprehensive rule for Christian conduct with regard to all men. It does not, except by implication, touch upon one's responsibility to God. This is not a justification for a purely social gospel. It furnishes a guide for the Kingdom man in all of his social relationships. The Christian religion is both Godward and manward (cf. Matt. 22:37-40). Only as one is rightly related in the former may he achieve the latter.

IV. PRACTICAL AIM. To show that the Kingdom man is not to be burdened with a multiplicity of rules of conduct. There is but one rule: love for God and man. The latter will never exceed the former; and without the former the latter is impossible.

V. HOMILETICAL FORM
Theme: "The Golden Rule."

Introduction: God simplifies; man complicates. This is true whether one considers the plan of salvation or the personal living of the saved man. The question is constantly being asked, "Is it right to do this or that?" Volumes have been written in an effort to answer this question in the realms of diplomacy, ethics, philosophy, psychology, sociology, and religion. Jesus answers it with one simple statement — the Golden Rule. It is unique, inclusive, and conclusive.

A. *It is Unique* — "Whatsoever ye would that men should do to you, do ye ... to them ...."

Some insist that this is not a new teaching, but an old one in new dress. As proof, various teachers are cited. Confucius: "Do not unto others that which you would not they should do unto you." Socrates: "What stirs your anger when done to you by others, that do not to others." Philo: "One must not himself do what he hates to have done to him." Hillel: "What is hateful to thee, do not do to another. This is the whole law; the rest is explanation of it."

But there is a decided difference. These rules are negative; that of Jesus is positive. These are passive; that is active. Theirs is the "Silver Rule;" Jesus' is the "Golden Rule." The "silver" is prohibitory; the "golden is exhortatory. The Silver

Rule prohibits murder, theft, falsehood, and adultery. The Golden Rule commands love, giving, truth, and purity. The former forbids the criminal act; the latter exhorts to Christian living. One can abide by the Silver Rule even though he passively watches another starve, so long as he does not kill him. The Golden Rule demands that one feed another to preserve his life. The one is the basis of human ethics; the other is the basis of Christian morality.

Lesser teachers taught but gave no power with which to obey. Jesus taught and empowered His followers for obedience (Matt. 7:7 ff.). Out of self respect the worldly man may do the former. But only by divine power may the Kingdom man continuously do the latter.

B. *It is Inclusive* — "Therefore all things whatsoever . . . men . . . to them . . . ."

Certain situations have been cited thus far in the Sermon. But Jesus does not stop there. The Christian cannot cite chapter and verse for every situation. Jesus did not teach rote rules for specific situations. He laid down a principle to cover all experiences. "Therefore" recaps the specifics of Matthew 5:17–7:11. "All things whatsoever" includes the general, covering the whole of life. "Man . . . to them" is not limited to blood kin, friends, neighbors, or Christians. It involves strangers, enemies, foreigners, all racial and national groups, unbelievers, — not all men *en masse,* but every man as an individual.

In short Jesus said, "Put yourself in another's place. Then act accordingly." If this simple rule were followed what wars, crimes, and injustices would be prevented! What peace, social benefits, and righteousness would result! Living by the Silver Rule has turned the world into a sea of misery, suspicion, and conflict. Redeemed men living by the Golden Rule would bring the Kingdom of God into the hearts of men.

C. *It is Conclusive* — "For this is the law and the prophets."

This is the King's answer to those who said that He would disannul the law and the prophets. Instead He endues each Kingdom man with a power which brings the law and the prophets to their intended end. The Law said, "Thou shalt have no other gods before me" (Exod. 20:3). It said, "Thou shalt love the Lord thy God with all thy heart . . . soul . . . mind" (Deut. 6:5). Only the Kingdom man can do this. The Law said, "Thou shalt not kill . . . commit adultery . . . steal . . . bear false witness against thy neighbor" (Exod. 20:13-16). It said, ". . . thou shalt love thy neighbor as thyself" (Lev. 19:18). Only the Kingdom man can do this.

Since the Golden Rule stems from the law and the prophets, it follows that only the Kingdom man possesses the qualities intended by Jesus. Wrong motives produce the wrong results. In the hands of a criminal, this rule would produce crime. Only when it is followed by a Kingdom man may its fruits be the God-kind-of-righteousness.

In Jesus, not only the law but the prophets as well, find their fulfilment. He not only taught the Golden Rule, but He followed it. His life certifies this. Its supreme example is in His death. On the cross every vestige of Isaiah found its complete fulfilment (cf. also Ps. 22). Jesus put Himself in man's place.

". . . Christ also suffered for us, leaving us an example, that ye should follow his steps: who did no sin, neither was guile found in his mouth: who, when he was reviled, reviled not again; when he suffered, he threatened not: but committed himself to him that judgeth righteously: Who his own self bare our sins in his own body on the tree, that we, being dead to sins, should live unto righteousness: by whose stripes ye were healed" (I Peter 2:21-24).

Matthew 8

A STUDY IN CONTRASTS

8:24. "And, behold, there arose a great tempest in the sea ... but he was asleep."

8:25. And his disciples came to him, and awoke him, saying, Lord, save us: we perish."

8:26. "And he saith unto them, Why are ye fearful, O ye of little faith? Then he arose, and rebuked the winds and the sea; and there was a great calm."

8:27. "But the men marveled, saying, What manner of man is this, that even the winds and the sea obey him!"

I. HISTORICAL SETTING. This event followed shortly the Sermon on the Mount. According to A. T. Robertson's *A Harmony of the Gospels* it marks the end of Jesus' "Busy Day." Fitting Matthew's Gospel into the framework of Mark's Gospel, Doctor Robertson places it in the early evening of a day marked by many striking events (Mark 3:19 — 4:34; Matt. 12:22 — 13:53; Luke 8:4-21). This may be confusing to some. But Synoptic Criticism has proved the probable priority of Mark. It shows that Matthew and Luke, for the most part, followed the framework of Mark, while using other sources as well. The event occurred while Jesus and the Twelve were crossing the Sea of Galilee from west to east. Sudden windstorms rushing down the canyons focussing on this sea are common even today.

II. EXPOSITORY MEANING
Matt. 8:24. "tempest." The Greek word is *seismos*, like seismograph, or earthquake. The sea was turbulent as an earthquake. Mark and Luke call it a whirlwind. "asleep." The Greek tense (imperfect) means "He kept on sleeping."

49

Matt. 8:25. "Lord." This word may mean "sir" or "lord," as one over others. Here it means deity, probably in the sense of "Lord" in the Old Testament, the usual translation in the KJV for Jehovah.

"Save ... perish." "Save" (aorist) means rescue from danger, heal from disease, or spiritual salvation. The first meaning applies here. "Save at once" "Perish" means to destroy utterly. The present passive voice as here means "we are being utterly destroyed."

Matt. 8:26. "O ye of little faith." In Greek this is one word meaning one whose faith is small and weak. "Was a great calm." "Was" is an aorist tense. "Immediately there was a great calm," a miracle. Note the contrast: "a great tempest" (8:24) ; "a great calm" (8:26).

Matt. 8:27. "marveled." This is an ingressive aorist of the verb to wonder with admiration and/or astonishment. They "began to marvel."

Matt. 8:27. "What manner of man ... !" This is one word in Greek. Basically, "of what country!" Here it may mean "what kind " or "how great!"

Matt. 8:27. "obey." It translates a compound verb meaning "to hear under" with the idea of submission or obedience. The present tense suggests continuous action.

III. DOCTRINAL VALUE. This passage teaches the King's miraculous power. Indeed this is the thought throughout Chapter 8. The physical (disease), natural (wind and sea), and spiritual (demons) elements obeyed His will. The will of man refused Him. This chapter sets forth the sovereignty of God and the free will of man (8:34).

IV. PRACTICAL AIM. To contrast the faith of man and the faith of the King; the power of God's will and of man's will. The physical and natural realms are submissive to God's will. The will of man rebels to its own loss.

V. HOMILETICAL FORM
  Theme: "A Study in Contrasts."
  Introduction: This is a chapter marked by great contrasts: the plight of the leper and the power of Jesus (8:2-4) ; the

faith of a pagan and the doubt of Israel (8:5-13) ; the fever
of a woman and the fortitude of the Son of Man (8:14-15) ;
the great tempest and the great calm (8:23-27) ; the grace of
God toward a demoniac and the greed of men toward their
swine (8:28-34). It is a contrast between the power of evil
and the power of God. Note the varied expressions of evil:
disease, storm, demons, and greed; and the varied methods of
divine power: touch of the hand and the spoken word. The
focal point of contrast is seen in verses 24-27. Here we see
fear versus faith, futility versus fortitude, and astonishment
versus achievement.

A. *Fear versus Faith* — "Why are ye fearful?" (8:26). "But
he was asleep" (8:24).

The sea rocked and rolled as if in the teeth of an earthquake. The frail boat was enveloped in the waves. The
turmoil in nature was transferred to the spirits of the Twelve.
They feared for their boat and for their lives. But a deeper
fear seized them, fear for the safety of Jesus. What if He
should perish? What would happen to His mission and Kingdom? In all this natural and spiritual turmoil Jesus "was
asleep." No fear raged within Him.

To their cry Jesus replied, "Why are ye fearful, O ye of
little faith?" Their fear was the product of their lack of
faith: faith in Jesus' ability to care for them; faith in the
providence and purpose of God. So long as they were with
Jesus they were safe. So long as the King was in the boat
it could not sink. Any cause centered in Jesus will succeed.

Fear is always due to the absence of faith. So long as we
are in the will of God there is no place for fear. Though
the forces of evil may seem to be on the verge of triumph,
God is still in control. The sleep of Jesus was not one of
unconcern but one of confidence. So long as He is in such
a sleep, we have nothing to fear. The ship of God's purpose
is plowing through the waves of adversity toward the haven
of God's will and peace.

B. *Futility versus Fortitude* — "Lord, save us: we perish."

This boat was manned by skilful seamen. Jesus was a land-
lubber. The Twelve, through their own skill, had weathered

many storms. Now they had done their best. But still the ship threatened to sink. They had come to their wits end. Futility characterized their every effort. It was then that they turned to the Lord.

This is the essence of true prayer. Men do not really pray until they come to the end of their own abilities. Prayer is too often an escape hatch from the seat of responsibility. So long as man can do, he should. When he has reached the end of his own powers, he should *awaken* the Lord (8:25). "Man's extremity is God's opportunity."

What these men of the sea could not do, the God of the sea did. Their power was finite; His infinite. His strength is made perfect in our weakness.

C. *Astonishment versus Achievement* — "What manner of man is this, that even the wind and the sea obey him."

Apparently the previous miracles recorded in this chapter did not overly impress the Twelve. But the spectacular nature of the miracle at sea aroused astonishment and admiration. Literally, "The men began to marvel ... the sea kept on obeying him." While man wonders, God keeps on working. Men marvel at the healing *miracles* of medical science, but the healing power is of God. Men are astonished at the space miracles of science, but the laws are the laws of God.

But the greatest miracle was yet to come. cf. Mark 5:15; Luke 15:7.

Matthew 9

THE PHYSICIAN OF SOULS

9:11. "And when the Pharisees saw it, they said unto his disciples, Why eateth your master with publicans and sinners?"

9:12. "But when Jesus heard that, he said unto them, They that be whole need not a physician, but they that are sick."

9:13. "...for I am not come to call the righteous, but sinners to repentance."

I. HISTORICAL SETTING. According to A. T. Robertson's *A Harmony of the Gospels* this event is placed in the great Galilean ministry prior to the Sermon on the Mount. Jesus had just called Matthew from his business as a tax-gatherer to follow Him as His disciple, later to become an apostle. In recognition of the occasion Matthew gave a dinner in Jesus' honor. To it were invited Jesus' disciples, and other publicans, perhaps friends and fellow tax-gatherers with Matthew. Others, called "sinners," also were guests. In keeping with the custom of the time others, including the Pharisees and some of John the Baptist's disciples, stood about and watched as the guests ate. Eating with publicans and sinners Jesus violated the customs of the Pharisees. In answer to their criticism Jesus taught a great spiritual truth.

II. EXPOSITORY MEANING
Matt. 9:11. "Pharisees." They were the conservative religious party of Jesus' day. They accepted all of the Old Testament as Scripture, believing in angels, miracles, and the resurrection from the dead. In contrast with the Sadducees, rationalists and more political than religious, who accepted only the Mosaic writings and denied angels, miracles, and the resurrection, the Pharisees were more numerous but

less politically powerful. In interpreting their Scriptures the Pharisees had devised a multitude of customs and rules which were burdensome to obey.

Matt. 9:11. "master." This means "teacher," in contrast with their teachers who refrained from social contacts with publicans and sinners. While in some versions "Master" is capitalized, they did not so use the word.

Matt. 9:11. "publicans and sinners. " "Publican" renders a word meaning one who collects public revenue. The English word is from the Latin *publicanus,* one who did public duty. Roman taxes were farmed out to the highest bidder, who, in turn, employed others to collect the taxes. They were noted for graft and extortion, and were considered as traitors to their nation. As such they were commonly regarded as the companions of sinners, hence "publicans and sinners," social outcasts.

Matt. 9:12. "whole." This means in good health. "Physician" is one who heals. The sense here is physical healing, but it implies the spiritual element also. "Sick." This renders an adverb, "ill, badly." Its root carries the basic thought of evil. Both the physical and spiritual aspects are involved here. This was probably a common proverb.

Matt. 9:13. "righteous, but sinners." This transfers the thought from a social to a spiritual connotation. "To repentance," while implied, is not in the best manuscripts.

III. DOCTRINAL VALUE. This passage presents the King as a social being whose compassion reaches out to all men, regardless of their social strata. It involves a recognition of the true nature of sin. Here the Saviour is seen as the friend of sinners, the Physician of souls.

IV. PRACTICAL AIM. To point out that all men, regardless of social position or culture, are sinners in need of a Saviour. Men judge by outward appearances and conduct. Jesus looks to inner attitudes and needs. The greater sin involves the latter not the former.

V. HOMILETICAL FORM
   Theme: "The Physician of Souls"

THE GOSPEL OF MATTHEW

Introduction: Jesus was a social being. But His social activities were purposeful. As a physician must come into contact with the diseased bodies of men, so the Great Physician was bound to experience intimate contact with social outcasts. He dealt with their sin, but Himself was free from it. Herein is the example for those who would follow Him. Many lessons are taught by this passage, but three are outstanding: the wrong diagnosis; the logical deduction; the proper treatment.

A. *The Wrong Diagnosis* — "publicans and sinners."

The Pharisees, then and now, assume that sin is only outward. To be sure "out of the abundance of the heart the mouth speaketh" (Matt. 12:34). But the outward expression is but the revelation of an inward condition. The mortal disease is not always evident to the natural, untrained eye. The Pharisees were quack practitioners posing as specialists.

The Great Physician rightly diagnoses all diseases. He recognized the illness in the souls of the publicans and sinners. But He also saw the more vicious disease in the hearts of the Pharisees (cf. Heb. 4:12-13). Note Jesus' reference to Micah 6:6-8 (Matt. 9:13). Outwardly the Pharisees were healthy. Inwardly their souls were sick unto death as seen in their unmerciful, critical attitude, with regard both to God and to man.

Jesus never condoned outward sin. But His most serious condemnation was directed toward wrong spiritual attitudes, especially hypocrisy (Matt. 23). Man is careful about the outward and careless about the inward disease, physical and spiritual. God is concerned about both.

B. *The Logical Deduction* — "whole need not a physician, but they that are sick."

This is a logical conclusion. Since the Pharisees regard the publicans and sinners as ill, where else would they expect the Physician to be? But there is also irony in Jesus' words. Who are the real victims of disease? With one reference to the Scriptures which the Pharisees claimed to know so well, Jesus wipes the cosmetics of self-righteousness from their pallid faces, and flashes before them the "X-ray" of their own souls. Therefore, they also need to see the Physician. The ministry of the gospel is necessary both in the slums and in the choice residential districts, in palaces as well as in hovels, to the up-and-outs as well as to the down-and-outs. "Rescue missions" are just as necessary on Park Avenue as in the Bowery. "For all have sinned, and come short of the glory of God" (Rom. 3:23).

C. *The Proper Treatment* — "... I am not come to call the righteous, but sinners to repentance."

In the original Greek "not" is emphatic. It emphasizes in a negative way the positive purpose of Jesus. He does not call the Pharisees "righteous," but ironically takes them at their word. In His sight they are the greater sinners, but more hopelessly so, because they are unaware of their condition.

Hardly will a man seek a physician unless he believes himself to be ill. The greater his recognition of his illness, the more anxious he is to see the physician. Hence the "publicans and sinners." However great the disease or its inroads, no man should consider himself incurable. By his own skill he may be, but the skill of the physician is another matter (cf. Ps. 103:3).

So Jesus calls all sinners, excluding none. He calls you. But the Physician cannot heal you unless you submit yourself to Him.

Matthew 10
THE DEMANDS OF DISCIPLESHIP

10:32. "Whosoever therefore shall confess me before men, him will I confess also before my Father which is in heaven."

10:33. "But whosoever shall deny me before men, him will I also deny before my Father which is in heaven."

10:34. "Think not that I am come to send peace on earth: I came not to send peace, but a sword."

10:39. "He that findeth his life shall lose it: and he that loseth his life for my sake shall find it."

I. HISTORICAL SETTING. Following A. T. Robertson's *A Harmony of the Gospels,* this chapter comes sometime after the Sermon on the Mount. Since then Jesus has taught and trained the twelve apostles. Now he sends them forth on their first independent evangelistic mission through Galilee. He told them where to go, reminded them of their message, what equipment to carry, the dangers awaiting them, and how they were to meet them. But they will receive no worse treatment than their Master already has endured. But they are not to be afraid. The heavenly Father who watches over the sparrows most assuredly will care for them. He closed this first *commission* by stating the conditions of discipleship. He will not judge the Twelve by statistical results but by their faithfulness to duty.

II. EXPOSITORY MEANING
Matt. 10:32. "whosoever." Actually this translates two words, literally, "all whosoever." It emphasizes the inclusion of all without exception. "Confess." Twice it is a future tense involving all future time. This is a changeless condition. "Confess" in Matthew 10:32 is literally "confess in me"

and "confess in him." In both cases "in" means "in the sphere of." Note the intimate relationship between Christ and the one confessing. "Before" here and in verse 33 means in front of, or before the face of.

Matt. 10:33. "Deny." In Matthew 10:33a it is an aorist tense suggesting complete and final denial of Christ. "Before men" suggests a public denial. This will result in Jesus' denial of such before God. Jesus impresses the Twelve with the gravity of their mission.

Matt. 10:34. "Think not." It is an aorist subjunctive preceded by a negative particle. Possibly the Twelve were thinking only of peace. Jesus said, "Stop thinking" thusly. "Send." This word, meaning to cast or throw, twice appears as an aorist infinitive of instant action. Just as the Twelve expected Jesus to send immediate peace, He hurled a sword into their midst.

Matt. 10:39. "Findeth...loseth" are aorist participles of definite, point action. They refer to definite, final decisions as to one's attitude. Note the paradox: "findeth...shall lose ...loseth...shall find." The word "life" in both instances is the same, meaning either physical or spiritual life. Here it means first one and then the other. The paradox turns upon these meanings.

III. DOCTRINAL VALUE. In these verses Jesus sets forth the conditions inherent in being a Christian. Herein are found the basis of Kingdom citizenship, the absolute Lordship of the King, and the path to triumphant Kingdom living. The King makes strong demands, but He gives great rewards.

IV. PRACTICAL AIM. To show that Jesus never tried to make His way attractive. He sought only those who were willing to pay the price. To both Jesus and man Satan offers the easy path. Jesus rejected it, and so must those who would follow Him. The road to the throne leads through the cross.

V. HOMILETICAL FORM
    Theme: "The Demands of Discipleship."
    Introduction: One of the greatest problems in present-day churches is the inactive member. Once enthusiastic, they have

grown cold and indifferent. Trials and the desire for easy living take their toll. Certainly one explanation of this is the manner in which members are received. Lenient standards may pad the church rolls, but they do not produce genuine, faithful followers of Christ. Jesus never sought numbers for numbers' sake. He emphasized not quantity but quality. This is seen in His instructions given to the Twelve as they launched forth on their first evangelistic effort as a group. The demands of discipleship are listed as confession, conflict, and consecration.

A. *The Demand for Confession* — "... confess me before, men, him will I also confess...."

To confess is to declare a thing to be true and to commit one's self to it. A Christian confession is an open declaration of the truth of the gospel in Christ, and a commitment to Him. Note the confession "before men." It is more than a verbal statement. It is to choose a way of life and to walk in it. To confess "in Christ" is to place one's self in the whole sphere of Christ. Paul's phrase "in Christ" in another way of saying it.

Note that of such a person Jesus says that before the Father He will "confess in him." The man in Christ and Christ in the man presents him blameless before God (cf. John 15:1-8). Before man the Christian says of Christ, "He is mine." Before God Christ says of the Christian, "He is mine." In like fashion the man who ultimately, publicly, and finally says of Christ, "I know Him not," of him before the Father Christ says, "I know him not." Note that in both confession and denial, God holds man responsible. Christ's work for man's redemption is finished. God now calls upon man to act.

B. *The Demand for Conflict* — "... not to send peace, but a sword."

Too often the evangelist and the evangelized look beyond confession to immediate peace. It is not so with Jesus. He demands absolute loyalty which often produces conflict. The gospel unites to Christ, but it may divide from men. Even the intimate family circle may be broken. In early Christian persecution, the informants often were members of one's own household (10:36).

The true Christian must be prepared to pay a price for his faith. The word "loveth" in Matthew 10:37 has to do with choice, not with mere emotion (cf. Rom. 9:13). He must be ready even to die, if necessary for his faith in Christ (10:38). To take up one's cross meant to bear it to the place of crucifixion. In Paul's day to confess "Jesus is Lord" (Rom. 10:9, author's translation) rather than "Caesar is Lord," could mean death. "Faithful unto death" means "faithful unto the point of dying" (Rev. 2:10). Jesus does not ask His disciples to do more than He did, but He asks no less.

C. *The Demand of Consecration* — "... findeth his life ... loseth his life for my sake shall find it."

The Christian life is a paradox. Jesus lives by dying. So do His disciples. Satan offered Jesus life (cf. Matt. 4), but Jesus saw the fallacy. The selfish life is the dying life. But he who dies to self lives unto God. Finding by losing, keeping by giving, living by dying — in so doing the Christian mounts the stairs to the throne. If man confesses in Christ and Christ is to confess in him, there can be no other way.

Matthew 11

THE GREAT INVITATION

11:28. "Come unto me, all ye that labor and are heavy laden, and I will give you rest."

11:29. "Take my yoke upon you, and learn of me; for I am meek and lowly in heart: and ye shall find rest unto your souls."

11:30. "For my yoke is easy, and my burden is light."

I. HISTORICAL SETTING. The events of this chapter form a sequence: the perplexity of John; the unreasonableness of the age; the impenitent cities; the simpleminded, trusting "babes." These are the different attitudes confronting the King. He encountered them in Galilee on a given day. The chapter concludes with one of Jesus' great invitations, issued to all of these attitudes.

II. EXPOSITORY MEANING
Matt. 11:28. "Come." This is an exclamation like "come hither," and is used as an imperative, a command. "Labor" is a participle, the ones fainting from weariness. "Heavy laden." This perfect participle indicates a permanent state of weariness. "And I" is emphatic as opposed to other teachers such as the rabbis. "Give you rest" is one verb. "I will refresh or rejuvenate you."

Matt. 11:29. "Take" is an aorist imperative of point action. "Yoke." This does not relate to oxen pulling a load. "To take the yoke" was a rabbinical phrase meaning to enroll under a teacher. "Learn" is an imperative, "be taught of me." "Meek and lowly." The ancients did not regard these as virtues. "Ye shall find rest." This was sought but not found through other teachers.

61

Matt. 11:30. "easy." Moffatt translates this "kindly." "Burden" here is contrasted with "heavy laden" in verse 28. They are kindred words.

III. DOCTRINAL VALUE. This passage involves the experience of the Christian life from regeneration through sanctification. Man seeks a full knowledge of God only to be frustrated in his search. Jesus is the Teacher who fully understands and reveals God. His revelation is offered to all men, but is received only as they forsake worldly wisdom to become as babes in Christ.

IV. PRACTICAL AIM. To set forth the Christian experience as submission to the Teacher and application under His guidance. God is not comprehended through knowledge but through faith. That which is impossible to the "wise and prudent" becomes easy to "babes."

V. HOMILETICAL FORM
Theme: "The Great Invitation."
Introduction: This invitation is found only in Matthew, although it reflects the sensitivity of John. The Christ of the one is the Christ of the other. Jesus saw men as sheep having no shepherd (cf. Matt. 9:36). Everywhere men were searching for the better life. Underneath their doubts (Matt. 11:2 ff.), indifference (11:16 ff.), and sin (11:20 ff.) was a thirst and hunger after God. In their midst Jesus stood and called. He is doing so today. In His call is a challenge, a condition, and a promise.

A. *The Challenge* — "Come unto me...."
This challenge is issued to those who "labor and are heavy laden." The former suggests active toil. The latter depicts endurance. This is a metaphor. Men seek a knowledge of God. They are burdened with a lack of this knowledge. The Greeks sought the *summum bonum* through wisdom. The Jews were burdened with ritual and works of the law. There is no labor so wearisome, no burden so heavy, as that which ends in frustration.

Jesus says, "You have sought elsewhere in vain. Come unto me... and I will refresh, rejuvenate you." He offers rest

from the letter in the spirit, from form by reality, from con-
jecture by certainty, from past traditions by the present voice
of God (cf. A. B. Bruce, *The Expositor's Greek Testament*,
in loco).

B. *The Condition* — "Take my yoke... learn of me...."

Jesus used many figures to illustrate the Christian experience (cf. new birth, John 3, and marriage, Matt. 9:15). Here
He sees it as enrolling in school (cf. disciple, pupil). The
second one is born he is a child. At marriage he becomes a
husband. The split second he enrolls in school, he becomes
a pupil. He may be a disobedient child, a thoughtless husband, or an indolent pupil. But he is what he has become. The
Christian may prove to be disappointing to God, but he is
nevertheless a Christian.

Beyond the initial coming into being is a continuous becoming. In the above examples it involves growth, develop-
ment, reproduction, learning, and service. No Christian can
be content simply to be. He must become. He must fulfil
his purpose of being. This involves justification, sanctification, and glorification. The first is a fixed condition. The
degrees of the others are determined by one's application to
the learning, and resultant serving, process.

C. *The Promise* — "my yoke is easy... burden light."

This does not mean that the process involves no toil. But
it is a toil of love and joy. The yoke is kindly to wear. In
one sense it is the heaviest of yokes. Jesus makes strong demands. But for that reason it is light. High ideals and their
accomplishment remove the sense of wearisome toil and rug-
ged endurance. Though Jesus asks much, He provides the
power to respond. Both teacher and pupil rejoice in the resultant achievements. The toil of the road will seem as nothing when one reaches the end, or goal, of the way.

Matthew 12

THE UNPARDONABLE SIN

12:24. "But when the Pharisees heard it, they said, This fellow doth not cast out devils, but by Beelzebub ...."

12:28. "But if I cast out devils by the Spirit of God, then the kingdom of God is come unto you."

12:31. "Wherefore I say unto you, All manner of sin and blasphemy shall be forgiven unto men: but the blasphemy against the Holy Ghost shall not be forgiven unto men."

12:32. "And whosoever speaketh a word against the Son of man, it shall be forgiven him; but whosoever speaketh against the Holy Ghost, it shall not be forgiven him, neither in this world, neither in the world to come."

I. HISTORICAL SETTING. This marks the beginning of what is called the "Busy Day" (cf. Matt. 12:22 — 13:53; Matt. 8:18-34: and parallels in Mark and Luke). It began in Galilee and continued in Gerasa, with two crossings of the sea of Galilee. The time is shortly past the middle of Jesus' public ministry, in the midst of the Great Galilean ministry.

II. EXPOSITORY MEANING

Matt. 12:24. "Pharisees." Note their increasing opposition to Jesus, due to His growing popularity, and the contrast of attitudes in verses 23-24 (cf. Mark 3:22). "This fellow." "Fellow" is not in the original Greek. Literally, "this one," showing their contempt for Jesus. "Beelzebub." The etymology of this word is difficult. Some suggestions are "lord of a dwelling," "lord of flies," "lord of dung," or "lord of idolatrous sacrifices." Some suggest a play on the name of the Canaanite god, Baal. Obviously a title of contempt applied by the Jews to Satan (cf. Matt. 12:26).

Matt. 12:28. In Matthew 12:25-29 Jesus exposes their hypocrisy and illogical statement. The focal point is verse 28. "Spirit of God" versus Satan, Jesus versus Pharisees, kingdom of God versus kingdom of evil.

Matthew 12:31. "Wherefore." Literally, "because of this." Jesus introduces a conclusion based upon verses 24-30. Note the gravity of Mark's account (3:28). "Blasphemy." This is a compound word meaning harmful or injurious speech.

Matt. 12:32. "Against the Son of man ... against the Holy Spirit." This explains verse 31. Note the contrast. "Neither ... neither . . . ." The Jews said blasphemy against God could be forgiven only by death. Jesus extends unforgiveness into eternity.

III. DOCTRINAL VALUE. This is the unpardonable sin. Jesus here speaks of internal attitude and its serious consequences (cf. Matt. 12:34-35). Involved is the very essence both of good and evil. Prejudice, selfishness, or malice may so cloud a man's judgment as to make, for him, evil good, and good evil. For such there is no hope.

IV. PRACTICAL AIM. To show the serious consequences of a wrong attitude toward the gospel which involves all of the gracious work of God. This includes not only those who knew Jesus in the flesh, but everyone today who responds negatively, either by denunciation or indifference, to the gospel appeal.

V. HOMILETICAL FORM
Theme: "The Unpardonable Sin."

Introduction: That a miracle had been performed the Pharisees could not deny. Before their very eyes a blind and dumb man was made to see and speak. Others saw it, and glorified God. The Pharisees saw it, and blasphemed God. There is no logical argument against evident results. One can either accept them in faith, or else reject them in wilful denial. The Pharisees chose the latter course. The response is the gravest words which ever fell from Jesus' lips. In this passage are words of blasphemy, confirmation, and condemnation.

A. *The Words of Blasphemy* — "cast out devils ... by ... the prince of devils."

A supernatural power had been exerted. But whose? "... the people were amazed ...." The Pharisees were contemptuous. Jesus called this latter blasphemy or the sin against the Holy Spirit.

It was a calculated sin, not one of impulse. The Pharisees' developing attitude toward Jesus may be described as curiosity, indifference, denial, maliciousness, blasphemy, and vengeance.

It was a sin of knowledge. They saw but refused to perceive. The more good Jesus did, the more they opposed Him. When they could no longer deny, they blasphemed.

It was a sin of finality. When they could no longer ignore, they rejected completely. Like John Milton's Satan, they said, "Evil, be thou my good." Jesus had no alternative but to avow their choice.

Some insist that this sin is no longer possible since Jesus is no longer on the earth. But it is not a sin against Jesus (cf. 12:31), but against the Holy Spirit who is in the earth. As such a sin it is the rejection of the very principle of good in favor of evil. In regard to the gospel message it is a final rejection of its claims upon one's soul. To do so is to regard the promised salvation as evil and the work of Satan, rather than good and the work of God. One may do so while living. To die in a state of unbelief is most certainly to do so.

B. *The Words of Confirmation* — "the kingdom of God is come unto you."

This is the inevitable conclusion of Jesus' reasoning (12:25-30). By their own words Jesus condemned the Pharisees. No one in league with Satan would cast out his servants. What about their own claims to cast out demons? How could Jesus overpower Satan if He worked by Satan's power? If, then, Jesus is destroying Satan's kingdom, He is establishing the Kingdom of God. To deny it is to deny the work of God. It is to make a calculated, conscious, and deliberate choice of evil to the rejection of the good.

The works of God continue among us. Wherever the gospel of Christ goes it changes lives and conditions. Many receive it gladly. Many reject it wilfully. One cannot be neutral where Christ is concerned. Either He works by the Spirit of God or by the spirit of Satan. To ignore Him is to reject Him. The greater the knowledge, the greater the sin.

C. *The Words of Condemnation* — "it shall not be forgiven him . . . ."

These are harsh, strange words from One who would forgive all. But there are conditions governing this forgiveness. God cannot ignore sin. He will not violate human personality.

Why did Jesus specify blasphemy against the Holy Spirit as the unpardonable sin? He allowed for differences of opinion regarding Himself. He recognized the binding power of social custom. But the Spirit of God involves every element of goodness. To reject Him is to choose evil for good. It is a fixed state. If evil becomes good, then good is evil.

B. H. Carroll offered the following explanation. If one blasphemes God the Father, there still remain the Son and Holy Spirit. If he blasphemes the Son, there is yet the Holy Spirit. But if he blasphemes the Spirit, there is none left. He has rejected deity altogether. This sin is impossible for the Christian. For the non-Christian it is the end result of a gradual, habitual, and growing enmity against God.

Matthew 13

THE CHURCH OF THE LIVING GOD

13:45. *"Again, the kingdom of heaven is like unto a merchantman, seeking goodly pearls:"*

13:46. *"Who, when he had found one pearl of great price, went and sold all that he had, and bought it."*

I. HISTORICAL SETTING. This is in the afternoon of the "Busy Day." Jesus with a series of parables, taught the multitudes by the sea of Galilee. The parable was one of Jesus' favorite methods of teaching. In all He uttered fifty-two parables. The word "parable" means a casting alongside. Jesus cast spiritual truth alongside a natural one. Someone called a parable an earthly story with a heavenly meaning. Another described a parable as a handle by which to carry a spiritual truth. The parable of the pearl of great price was spoken to the Twelve in the privacy of a home (cf. Matt. 13:36).

II. EXPOSITORY MEANING
Matt. 13:45. "kingdom of heaven." This is not to be distinguished from the "kingdom of God." A comparison of the gospels reveals that the terms are often used interchangeably. "Merchantman." This is a traveling merchant, a drummer. "Seeking." This present participle suggests continuous seeking. "Pearls." The word means purity.
Matt. 13:46. "found." This is an aorist participle expressing the excitement of the merchant at the moment of discovery. "Great price." So because it was large, round, and pure. "Went." Literally he "went away." This aorist participle expresses the immediacy and haste of the act. "Sold." The perfect tense involves a complete, final sale of all that he had accumulated in the past. "Had" is an imperfect tense

69

of continuous action in past time. "Bought." This aorist tense is point action of one definite purchase. It means to buy in the market place. The Greek tenses tell a vivid story here as elsewhere.

III. DOCTRINAL VALUE. Herein is seen the value of the Church and the price paid for it. Note the intensity of God in accomplishing it. The kingdom of heaven excels all other values.

IV. PRACTICAL AIM. To bring to the heart the truth that redemption is a gift of God's grace, not the fruit of man's works. To show how men should regard the Church of Jesus Christ.

V. HOMILETICAL FORM
    Theme: "The Church of the Living God."
Introduction: A parable is intended to teach one truth, not many. To press every detail is to lose its lesson. This series of parables reveals many reflections of light from the gem of the kingdom of heaven. But the parable under consideration has to do with the kingdom itself. The kingdom of heaven is not a political entity. Nor is it outward form. It is an inner condition. It is God's rule in His universe. But specifically, in our Scripture, Jesus sees it as the rule of God in the hearts of men. It involves the merchant, the pearl, and the price.
    A. *The Merchant* — "a merchant man seeking...."
Here is a traveling pearl merchant going to pearl divers and markets, examining their wares, and buying the best. Who is he? Some regard him as man seeking for the kingdom of heaven. In one way or another man is seeking a Utopia. His search involves various avenues of approach, economics, politics, culture, religion. In the last of these is the hunger after God. But the Bible teaches that the initiative is with God, not man (cf. Gen. 3:9; I John 4:9-10). Man's yearning is in response to God's initiative.
    The merchant is Jesus. Jesus sought throughout the universe to find the "one pearl." Finding it He did that which was necessary to procure it. The incarnation finds its mean-

ing in this fact (cf. John 1:11-12). He sought not for Himself, but for another. The finest pearls were worn only by kings. So Jesus is seeking that which is worthy to be presented to the King, even God. Note the earnest purpose in His seeking.

B. *The Pearl* — "...one pearl...."

This pearl is so perfect in shape, pure in substance, and resplendent in beauty as to exceed all others. It is fit to be worn only by a king. The Jews did not so value the pearl, but the Gentiles did.

Jesus likened the kingdom of heaven unto this pearl. The kingdom of heaven suggests the Church of Jesus Christ, composed of all the redeemed of all ages. It is the supreme value of this age (cf. Rev. 21:2).

Jesus discerned the pearl. He found it and revealed it. The pearl is a mystery. The kingdom of heaven is a mystery. The gospel is a mystery (cf. Eph. 3:3 ff.). But its revelation is the purpose of the ages (cf. Eph. 3:11). And it finds its meaning in Christ, the Merchant, discovering and evaluating the "pearl."

C. *The Price* — "...bought it."

The merchant "went and sold all that he had, and bought it." It took all that Jesus had to purchase the "church of God" (Acts 20:28).

Note the excitement of the Merchant in His discovery (cf. Matt. 13:46, "found," aorist participle; Heb. 12:2, "for the joy...."). He "went away" from heaven to procure it. He "sold" (perfect tense, permanent, complete sale) all that He "had" (imperfect tense of continuous action in past time; cf. Phil. 2:6-8; John 17:5). He "bought" (aorist of point action, one transaction; cf. Heb. 9:12; Heb. 10:10). "Once" in both verses means "once for all" — to present to the King (cf. I Cor. 15:24-28). It shall adorn Him and enhance His glory in eternity. The Christian should do so even now.

Matthew 14

THE HUNGRY MULTITUDES

14:15. "... his disciples came unto him, saying ... send the multitude away, that they may go into the villages, and buy themselves victuals."

14:16. "But Jesus said unto them, They need not depart; give ye them to eat."

14:17. "And they say unto him, We have here but five loaves, and two fishes."

14:18. "He said, Bring them hither to me."

I. HISTORICAL SETTING. The time is just one year prior to the crucifixion (John 6:4). The place is near Bethsaida Julias (Luke 9:10) on the eastern shore of the sea of Galilee. This was in the tetrarchy of Philip, a brother of Herod Antipas. Herod Antipas' identification of Jesus as John the Baptist returned from the dead (Matt. 14:2) may have prompted Jesus' withdrawal from Galilee, Herod's domain (cf. Matt. 14:12-13). Actually this is the first of four withdrawals from Galilee during the late spring, summer, and early fall of A.D. 29. The reasons for these withdrawals probably were the enmity of Herod Antipas, the growing hostility of the Pharisees, the fanaticism of the people, the need for privacy to teach the Twelve, and the desire to escape the summer heat to rest. Note that in withdrawal Jesus keeps out of Herod's territory, and He goes each time into the mountains. The feeding of the five thousand is reported by all four gospel writers. It marked the turning point in Jesus' popularity with the people (14:22-23; cf. John 6:14-15).

II. EXPOSITORY MEANING
Matt. 14:15. "evening." This is probably the first of two

"evenings," about 3:00 P.M. "Desert." This was an out-of-the-way place with only villages nearby. "Send... away." This is an aorist imperative. "Send away immediately." "Go." The word renders an aorist participle, "going away immediately." Time is short. "Buy themselves." "Buy" is an aorist subjunctive, "they may buy immediately." "Themselves" is stated, and so emphatic.

Matt. 14:16. "But" contrasts Jesus' attitude with that of the disciples. "Not" is emphatic in the Greek. "Give" is an aorist imperative, the same as "send away" in verse 15. The disciples said, "Send them away." Jesus countered with "Give ye them to eat." Literally, "Give to them you to eat." Note the emphasis in "them you."

Matt. 14:17 "And" is better translated "but," with the same effect of contrast as in verse 16. In verse 14 "and" is one word (*kai*). Verses 15-18 are introduced with another word (*de*) "but." It is an adversative of contrast. "Say" is a present tense, they "keep on saying." "Loaves... fishes." These were thin barley cakes and little dried fishes.

Matt. 14:18. "Bring." This is an imperative, and so a command. "Them" refers to the food, not to the people.

III. DOCTRINAL VALUE. This incident bears witness to the responsibility placed upon the followers of the King. They are to feed the hungry multitudes. Note the hesitant helplessness of the disciples and the competency of Jesus.

IV. PRACTICAL AIM. To convict minds and hearts as to the failure of Christian people in their ministry to the multitudes. Jesus does not excuse them but rebukes them. Our little in Jesus' hands is enough.

V. HOMILETICAL FORM
Theme: "The Hungry Multitudes."
Introduction: When Jesus' little boat put out to sea, the crowds, sensing His destination, ran around the northern end of the lake and met Him on the other side. In compassion He "healed their sick" (14:14). This was a miraculous ministry worked by Jesus. But the people needed another ministry. They needed to be fed. This suggests their deeper

need for spiritual food. The subsequent situation may be described as concern, hesitancy, and sufficiency.

A. *The Concern of the Twelve.* "... his disciples came to him ...."

No one can deny the genuine concern of the disciples. They shared Jesus' compassion (14:14). The people were hungry, and they wanted them fed. The place and time demanded that something be done. So they brought the problem to Jesus. But they did not ask Jesus for instructions. They instructed Jesus instead. Note the imperative verb "send ... away." Rather than ask Jesus they commanded Him.

Christian people share a general concern for the fainting multitudes. They want them to be saved and fed. But too often they come with their own ideas rather than following the commands of God's Word. "Why doesn't God do something?" they ask. Too seldom do they ask, "What can we do?" Less seldom do they ask, "Lord what wilt thou have me to do?" The answer has already been given. But the question is not forthcoming.

B. *The Hesitancy of the Twelve.* "We have here but ...."

The Twelve hesitated because they failed to realize the means at their disposal. Therefore note their suggestions and Jesus' reply.

(1) "... send the multitude away ...." Away from them, away from Jesus. Let them look elsewhere for sustenance. They sought to be rid of their responsibility.

(2) "... that they may go into the villages ...." This suggests other sources of help: political, civic, cultural, economic, and psychiatric. These have their place, but they are not sufficient for man's deepest needs.

(3) "... buy themselves victuals." This suggests self-help apart from the ministry of Jesus or His followers.

(4) "They need not depart; give ye them to eat." At the disposal of the church of Jesus Christ is ample provision to minister to the spiritual hunger of men. The command of Jesus is that churches shall discharge their duty.

C. *The Sufficiency of Christ.* "Bring them hither to me."

What they had they brought to Jesus. By His power it was enough and more than enough (14:19-21: cf. Isa. 55:1-2).

Apart from Jesus no one is sufficient. But in Him all things are possible (cf. Phil. 4:13). One plus God is equal to every situation and need. Note the order of the service (14:19 f.). (1) They brought what they had to Jesus. (2) Jesus blessed it and apportioned it. (3) He gave the portions to the several disciples (cf. I Cor. 12). (4) The disciples gave to the people. (5) The people ate and were filled. (6) The residue exceeded even that with which they began. The more religion one gives away, the more he has.

Matthew 15

THE KINGDOM STANDARD OF VALUE

*15:2. "Why do thy disciples transgress the tradition of the
elders? for they wash not their hands when they eat bread."*

*15:3. ". . . Why do ye also transgress the commandment of
God by your tradition?"*

*15:11. "Not that which goeth into the mouth defileth a
man; but that which cometh out of the mouth, this defileth
a man."*

I. HISTORICAL SETTING. The time is late summer in
A.D. 29. The place is Galilee, specifically the land of Gennesaret (Matt. 14:34), and probably in Capernaum. Jesus has
returned from the eastern side of the lake where He fed
the five thousand. The Pharisees from Jerusalem press their
opposition to Jesus. Note the growing boldness of these
critics. Already they have been joined by the Herodians (cf.
Matt. 12:14; Mark 3:6). Soon the Sadducees will join their
arch enemies in their efforts to put Jesus to death (Matt.
16:6). The differences of these three groups are resolved in
their common hatred for Jesus.

II. EXPOSITORY MEANING
Matt. 15:2. "transgress." This means to step by the side of
or deviate. The present tense suggests repeated action. They
accuse Jesus of allowing His disciples to sin. "Traditions."
This means that which was handed down by the "elders" of
the past, speaking *ex cathedra*. The reference is to the oral
law or Mishna. This washing of the hands was not for physical cleanliness, but it was a religious ritual of outward righteousness. The elders said that a demon, Shibta, sat on men's
hands while they slept. Not to wash their hands meant that
the demon was transferred to their food and thence to their

bodies. No such teaching is found in the Old Testament.

Matt. 15:3. "commandment of God." Note the contrast.
Jesus accuses the Pharisees of sin in replacing God's commandment with the oral law. In their practice the latter
superseded the former.

Matt. 15:11. "defileth." The word means "common." Here
it is used in the bad sense of uncleanness (cf. Acts 10:14).
Jesus contrasts unclean food with unclean words or attitudes.
Defilement was a serious matter with the Jewish ceremonial-
ists. This verse and following were spoken to the crowd
(15:10).

III. DOCTRINAL VALUE. In this passage is contrasted
ceremonial righteousness and true righteousness. A man may
be outwardly correct and inwardly wrong. The traditions
of man should never supersede the commandments of God.

IV. PRACTICAL AIM. To impress upon the hearers the
nature of kingdom righteousness as opposed to man's righteousness. Man looks on the outward appearance, but God
looks into the heart.

V. HOMILETICAL FORM
Theme: "The Kingdom Standard of Value."

Introduction: The religion of Jesus was in direct contrast
with the religion of the Pharisees. His refusal to compromise
His teaching to theirs figured in the crucifixion. Tradition,
in the evil sense, always conflicts with spiritual religion. They
are based upon two different things: the one upon the customs of man, the other upon the commandments of God.
The one is outward, the other is inward. This contrast may
be set forth in the words custom, conflict, and cleanliness.

A. *The Power of Custom.* "tradition of the elders...."

Man is a creature of habits, customs, or traditions. These
may be good (cf. I Cor. 11:2 where "ordinances" means traditions) or they may be bad (cf. Matt. 15:3). Many activities
progress from act to habit to custom to tradition. Within
themselves they may be good or bad. Sometimes, as here, they
spring from superstition. In any segment of society these may
be found. They are essentially *taboos.* Such often take on

the aura of religion. In such cases they become binding to the suppression of a genuine spiritual experience. Because "everybody's doing it" does not make it right. More likely it is wrong. If tradition is the only basis of an act, even good within itself, it may rightly be questioned.

B. *The Conflict between Custom and Commandment.* "transgress the commandment of God by your tradition?" The Bible contains many commands of God. Within themselves they are good. But when they are obeyed merely as a custom, they become bad. Satan takes good things and makes them evil. Worship as a custom only is robbed of its essential meaning. Bible reading, prayer, church membership may be viewed likewise. These are but examples of which there are many (cf. John 4:20-24; John 5:39-40).

There is always conflict between tradition for tradition's sake and the vital, spiritual meaning of God's Word. Note the custom of "Corban" (Matt. 15:4-6) and the empty practice of religion (Matt. 15:7-9). In the one God's "commandment with promise" is violated. In the other the whole of worship is nullified. Any type of stereotyped religious practice conflicts with the teachings of God's Word. Outward form is not enough. For religion to be genuine it must reach into the inner springs of the heart and will. The attitude determines the validity of the act.

C. *The True Cleanliness.* "... this defileth a man." The Pharisees regarded that which entered a man as defiling him. Hence their tradition of washing their hands. It was not physical cleanliness but ceremonial cleanliness which concerned them. Basically it was superstition. By a simple illustration Jesus set this aside. True cleanliness is inward.

The attitude of the Pharisees still prevails (cf. Matt. 23:25-28). It is not enough to garnish and adorn the outside. Worshippers go to church or elsewhere carefully groomed, but what of the inner attitude?

That which comes out of a man reveals the inner condition (cf. Matt. 15:18-20).

Matthew 16

THE PERSON OF JESUS CHRIST

16:13. ". . . Whom do men say that I, the Son of man, am?"

16:15. ". . . But whom say ye that I am?"

16:16. ". . . Thou art the Christ, the Son of the living God."

I. HISTORICAL SETTING. This event came during the fourth and last withdrawal. The time is probably late September in A.D. 29. The place is near Caesarea Philippi in the region of Mount Hermon in the northern part of Palestine. This was in the tetrarchy of Herod Philip, hence the name to distinguish it from Caesarea by the sea. Literally, "Caesarea, the one of Philip." The place was originally called Paneas. It was a center of idol worship. Even today one may see the remains of such temples and altars. In this area Herod the Great had built a temple to Caesar Augustus, suggesting the worship of Caesar. Examination time had come for the Twelve. This was a perfect place for such a test.

II. EXPOSITORY MEANING
Matt. 16:13. "say." This is a present tense suggesting varied opinions of Jesus. "Son of man." This was Jesus' favorite designation of Himself. Ezekiel used it repeatedly of himself. Note Daniel 7:13. This is the probable source of this title for Jesus. It is definitely Messianic. Note that in the New Testament it is from Jesus' lips only, save John 12:34 (quoting Jesus) and Acts 7:56.
Matt. 16:15. "say ye." In the Greek "ye" is stated in the emphatic position, and also implied in the verb. Literally, "But ye, whom me do you say to be?"
Matt. 16:16. "answered." This is an aorist participle, one definite avowal. "Thou" is emphatic. It is both stated and the first word of the answer. "Christ." This is Greek for

81

the Hebrew "Messiah," the Anointed One. Note that in Greek there are four definite articles. Literally, "Thou art the Christ the Son of the God the living." Each article makes each of these specific. "The God the living" is in contrast with the dead gods of stone which abounded there.

III. DOCTRINAL VALUE. In this confession is found both the humanity and the deity of Jesus. The Christ is declared to be both man and God. Men's opinions may vary, but the Father's revelation is certain.

IV. PRACTICAL AIM. To present the King as one with man and one with God. In essence He is the God-man, the fulfilment of the hopes which abound in the word "Christ" or "Messiah."

V. HOMILETICAL FORM
    Theme: "The Person of Jesus Christ."
    Introduction: Behind Jesus were the plaudits of the multitudes. Before Him lay the abandonment of the mobs. What is the conviction of the Twelve concerning Him? Will they be able to resist the clamor of these mobs? When they see Him forsaken, beaten, and crucified will they stand firm? The future of Christianity rests upon them. Jesus has taught them, but have they learned the lesson? Did His followers then, yea, do they now, comprehend Him and His mission? In this examination are seen popular opinion, personal conviction, and permanent value.
    A. *The Answer of Popular Opinion.* "... men say ...."
    Probably the Twelve, in holiday fashion, were examining various idols and altars, identifying them one by one. Jesus interrupted their game with a question. "Whom do men say that I ... am?" They replied with varied answers. Note that they thoughtfully withheld such answers as demon and madman. Instead they mentioned the more complimentary ones: John the Baptist, Elijah, Jeremiah and other prophets. Note these as the answers of established government, institutional religion, and public surmise.
    Men saw varied things in Jesus: preaching, fire, lamentation, teaching. This is the error of putting Jesus in specific

categories. Men still emphasize one aspect of Jesus' person to the neglect of all others. In so doing they miss the true portrayal of His meaning and mission.

B. *The Answer of Personal Conviction.* "...whom say ye....?"

Peter answered for the Twelve. They saw the above elements but they saw more. Their *seeing* was not the conclusion of logic but the conviction of divine revelation (16:17). Through intimate association they observed the many facets of Jesus' being. Under God's guidance these added up to the right answer. Objective and casual reason is no substitute for a personal and abiding experience.

C. *The Essence of Permanent Value.* "...The Christ, the Son of the living God."

Note the many facets of the King's person. (1) Son of man: representative man, involving His earthly ministry, passion, and second advent (cf. Matt. 8:20; 9;6; 11:19; 12:40; 17:9, 22; 20:18; 13:41; 24:27, 30). (2) Christ: eternal God, involving the eternal redemptive purpose (cf. Eph. 3:11), the Suffering Servant (cf Isaiah), the eternal Kingdom (cf. I Cor. 15:22-28). (3) Son of the living God: God in the form of man (cf. John 1:1, 14; cf. Matt. 1:21-23). Jesus is not a dead figure of history but the Son of the *living* God.

These abiding truths are as much needed today as in the first century. God cares. He has invaded time for eternal purposes. This invasion is seen in the Christ, Son of man and Son of God. Though men may variously regard Him, He is still the beloved Son of the living God. He is history's origin and goal. He is man's only Saviour.

Matthew 17

THE UNIQUE SAVIOUR

17:2. "And [Jesus] was transfigured before them: and his face did shine as the sun, and his raiment was white as the light."

17:3. "And, behold, there appeared unto them Moses and Elijah talking with him."

17:5. "... This is my beloved Son, in whom I am well pleased; hear ye him."

17:8. "... they saw no man, save Jesus only."

I. HISTORICAL SETTING. It was late September, A.D. 29, just before the Feast of Tabernacles. One week after the event in Matthew 16:13 ff. (cf. Matt. 17:1; Luke 9:28), Jesus took Peter, James, and John up the slopes of Mount Hermon (cf. Mark 5:37; Matt. 26:37). There Jesus was transfigured. After the confession of Matthew 16:16 Peter, and the rest, demonstrated their lack of comprehension as to the cross (Matt. 16:21-23) which was only six months away. Gloom once again settled upon Jesus. G. Campbell Morgan sees a note of estrangement between Jesus and the Twelve during this week. The Transfiguration was given for the benefit of both.

II. EXPOSITORY MEANING

Matt. 17:2. "transfigured." The Greek word is "metamorphosed." It means a change of form. See Romans 12:2 for this word ("be ye transformed"). Note also II Corinthians 3:18. It is used of the shining of Moses' face ("metamorphosed from glory unto glory" cf. Mark 9:2-3; Luke 9:29).

Matt. 17:3. "Moses and Elijah." They are symbols of law and prophecy, the Old Testament revelation. With Jesus, note law, prophecy, and grace. Both Moses and Elijah left this world under extraordinary circumstances. "Talking." This is a present participle of repeated action or conversation. Luke 9:31 says that they talked "of his decease" or exodus (literally) from this world. This includes His death, resurrection, and ascension.

Matt. 17:5. "bright cloud." Such clouds form quickly over Mount Hermon. "Bright" suggests the Shekinah glory or God's presence (cf. Num. 9:15). "My beloved Son...." This is the same confirmation given at Jesus' baptism (Matt. 3:17). "Hear ye him," even when He speaks of His death. It is a sharp rebuke to Peter and the others. "Hear" is a present imperative, a command. "Keep on hearing him."

Matt. 17:8. "no man, save Jesus only." Literally, "no one they saw except Jesus only." Moses and Elijah were gone. Only Jesus remained.

III. DOCTRINAL VALUE. In this passage is seen the supremacy of the King. He alone can save, and that through His "exodus." The old revelation is swallowed up in the new. Jesus stands alone in the arena of redemption as both God and man. It is sinful to align Him with any other.

IV. PRACTICAL AIM. To point out Jesus as perfect God and perfect man fulfilling God's redemptive purpose. All others must give place to Him. Regardless of men's opinion of Him, He is still well-pleasing to God.

V. HOMILETICAL FORM

Theme: "The Unique Saviour."

Introduction: Jesus had reached the point of no return. If the disciples did not understand, Jesus did, and so did heaven. Behind Jesus is the desertion by the multitudes. Present is the density of the Twelve. Before Him is the *Via Dolorosa* to the cross. But events of recent days had clouded the issue. Six months before the crucifixion the disciples are not ready for the event. Once again Satan tries to swerve Jesus from the cross (cf. Matt. 16:23). As God Jesus knows the future. As man He is momentarily discouraged. The Transfiguration was for His benefit as well as that of the Twelve. This event may be summarized as transfiguration, conversation, and confirmation.

A. *The Transfiguration of Jesus.* ". . . transfigured before them . . . ."

In the Transfiguration Jesus appears as both man and God. As man He had a form, wore raiment, and experienced discouragement. As God He was *metamorphosed.* The light was not from without. It was His deity shining forth from within. G. Campbell Morgan says that the wick of His essential deity was suddenly turned up. He was the perfect man. Had He been less, this sudden outrushing of deity would have killed him.

Here is perfect deity and perfect humanity, the God-man. As He was glorified in the "throe of Calvary," so was He glorious in "the glow of Hermon." Here one sees "the glory as of the only begotten of the Father" (John 1:14).

B. *The Conversation of the Saviour and the Servants.* ". . . Moses and Elijah talking with him."

Elsewhere in moments of stress angels ministered to Jesus (cf. Matt. 4:11; Luke 22:43). Why not here? Why Moses and Elijah? Note the relationships of Moses, Elijah, and Jesus: Sinai, Carmel, Calvary respectively; Moses (law), Elijah (prophecy), Jesus (grace). The first two found fulfilment in the third. Moses and Elijah were symbolic of the Old Covenant; Jesus symbolizes the New Covenant. Moses and Elijah epitomize the Old Testament saints who were saved, on credit, looking in faith toward the Christ.

Why did they speak of Jesus' "exodus"? It involved that which Jesus should do for the salvation of all men who trusted in Him. It involved law, sin, and grace. Angels as a-moral beings could not comprehend these things. Hence Moses and Elijah. What did they say to Jesus? They affirmed heaven's plan. If Jesus' exodus were not completed, those who had died in faith would not be saved. Heaven would be emptied and hell filled. Encouraged, Jesus "stedfastly set his face to go to Jerusalem" (Luke 9:51).

C. *The Confirmation of the Father.* ". . . my beloved Son . . . hear ye him . . . Jesus only."

Peter broke into the conversation to propose three tabernacles. It was near the time for the Feast of Tabernacles.

The "mountain-top experience" was glorious. Why end it?

But God's voice interrupted man's thoughts and plans. He rebuked Peter. For his desire to stay in the mountain away from need and suffering? Yes. Too many remain on Hermon to avoid Calvary. But there was more, and particularly so. Peter placed Jesus, Moses, and Elijah on the same plane. This was, and is, sin. Moses and Elijah must fade. But Jesus remains. They are to hear Jesus, not Moses and Elijah, as God's full and final revelation. What Jesus says they are to believe and do. The law or the prophets cannot save. "Jesus only" is the hope of the world. He went through His "exodus" to that end. When "Moses and Elijah" are put in their proper perspective, men see "no man, save Jesus only." This was the needed message of their day — and of every day.

Matthew 18

THE STANDARD OF KINGDOM GREATNESS

18:1. "Who [then] is the greatest in the kingdom of heaven?"

18:3. "Except ye be converted, and become as little children, ye shall not enter into the kingdom of heaven."

18:4. "Whosoever therefore shall humble himself as this little child, the same is greatest in the kingdom of heaven."

I. HISTORICAL SETTING. From Mount Hermon Jesus returned to Capernaum. On the return trip Jesus had repeated His word about the coming crucifixion. The disciples finally understood, and "were exceeding sorry" (Matt. 17:22-23). In Capernaum they were probably in Peter's home (Matt. 17:24-27). Chapters 18-20 involve Jesus' teaching of the Twelve, both in Galilee and on His last journey to Jerusalem. John records an intermediate visit to Jerusalem (John 8-10) which is corroborated by Luke (9:51 – 13:21).

II. EXPOSITORY MEANING

Matt. 18:1. "Who [then] is greatest...?" "Then" is absent from the KJV, but appears in the best manuscripts. "Then" refers back to the events contained in Matthew 16:16-17, 27. Mark and Luke note a discussion among the Twelve as to position in the kingdom (Mark 9:33-34; Luke 9:46). Jesus' teaching (Matt. 16:21; 18:22-23), plus the consideration shown to Peter, James, and John, had upset their fixed ideas about the kingdom order of prominence.

Matt. 18:3. "ye be converted." This is an aorist passive subjunctive. It expresses a condition unfulfilled but possible of fulfilment. The action is something done to them one time by another. The verb means to turn about and is akin in

meaning to the Greek word for "repent," a change of mind
or attitude.

Matt. 18:3. "become." This is a second aorist middle subjunctive with the same condition as above. The middle voice
suggests something done to themselves. The verb basically
means to come into being. The aorist tense suggests the definite beginning. These words "converted" and "become"
may be called justification and sanctification respectively.

Matt. 18:3. "little children." Maybe the "child" was Peter's.
Here Jesus passes from the child to those who are "converted"
and "become." "Ye shall not enter." In the Greek this verb
is preceded by a strong, emphatic double negative.

Matt. 18:4. "humble himself." This verb means to depress
one's pride. A. B. Bruce (*The Expositor's Greek Testament*)
calls this "the most difficult thing in the world for saint as for
sinner."

III. DOCTRINAL VALUE. This chapter relates the true
nature of the kingdom of heaven and its citizens. It reveals
kingdom standards in contrast to earthly standards. Conversion is the prime requisite for citizenship, and proper devel-
opment is necessary for achieving greatness in the kingdom of
heaven.

IV. PRACTICAL AIM. To impress upon the hearer the
false standard of greatness in contrast with Christ's standard
and the consequences of each. The latter calls for a turning
back and a new beginning. Both involve man's submission
and God's power.

V. HOMILETICAL FORM
  Theme: "The Standard of Kingdom Greatness."

Introduction: The Twelve were products of their age.
They envisioned Christ's kingdom as one of pomp, power,
and splendor. But they are no isolated group. Despite Jesus'
teachings to the contrary their standard of values has plagued
Christendom through the ages. It does so today, not only in
hierarchical systems but in every local church. The example
of the little child is needed perhaps more today than in the
first century. It is certainly as difficult to follow. Indeed,

apart from the Spirit of God it is impossible. In this chapter are seen contrast, conflict, and consequences.

A. *The Contrasting Standards*. "Who [then] is the greatest...? ... as this little child, the same is greatest...."

The disciples were having a rough time. Their dreams of glory had been shattered by Jesus' words about His death. The consideration shown to Peter, James, and John apparently did not help the situation. The failure with respect to the demon-possessed child punctured their egos. The tax-collector only aggravated the situation as he singled out Peter to the neglect of the others. If their concept of greatness was wrong "who then is greatest...?"

Note the paradox in Jesus' acted parable. He called a little child, probably playing nearby and oblivious to their problem. Here was the symbol of kingdom greatness. Note the characteristics of a child: comparative innocence, simplicity, forgiving, trusting, and possessed of almost infinite possibilities.

Furthermore note the words in verse 3 — "be converted, and become...." From their selfish adult attitudes they must return to the attitudes of childhood. This involves the new birth. From there they must "become." This suggests the process of sanctification (cf. Matt. 11:28-30; Eph. 4:13). Such greatness is the result of human submission and consecration plus divine power (cf. Phil. 2:12-13).

B. *The Conflicting Standards*. "Whosoever therefore shall humble himself...."

This is "the most difficult thing in the world for saint as for sinner." It involves conflict. (1) Within one's self as to the standard of values. Note the value of a child (18:6, 10) and of one lamb (18:12-14). See further the conflict between physical and spiritual well-being. (18:8-9). By oriental hyperbole Jesus drives home His point. (2) Within one's relations with other church members (18:15-20). Note that Jesus Himself is present as the Mediator (18:20). (3) With respect to forgiveness (18:21 ff.). A child soon forgets and forgives. Peter thought he was generous. The Rabbis required only three times, Peter suggested seven. Note Jesus' answer which amounts to infinity. Only a "converted" and *becoming* man can resolve these conflicts. This chapter is a commentary on Matthew 16:24-25.

C. *The Consequences of Failure.* "Except."

To do less than "be converted" is to miss the kingdom altogether. Not to "become" is to miss its greatness. Only a childlike spirit can receive a "child," which is to receive Christ (18:5-6). Physical death or maiming is to be preferred to missing this spirit (18:6-9). Not to show the childlike spirit of forgiveness is to suggest that one is not "converted" (18:17, 34-35). One may be a child, yet not develop the childlike spirit. Hence the importance of *becoming*. It is not realized in a day. But it can be begun in a split second. The *becoming* is the work of a lifetime.

Matthew 19

THE DEMAND OF THE KING

19:16. "And, behold, one came and said unto him, Good Master, what good thing shall I do, that I may have eternal life?"

19:20. "The young man saith unto him, All these things have I kept from my youth up: what lack I yet?"

19:22. "But when the young man heard that saying, he went away sorrowful: for he had great possessions."

I. HISTORICAL SETTING. On His final journey to Jerusalem Jesus is in Perea, "the coasts of Judea beyond Jordan" (Matt. 19:1). He was following the customary route from Galilee to Jerusalem. The Jews crossed the Jordan to avoid Samaria. It is the spring of A.D. 30, just a matter of days before the crucifixion. As Jesus journeys He ministers along the way.

II. EXPOSITORY MEANING
Matt. 19:16. "one came." The "one" is identified by Luke as a ruler (18:18). According to Matthew 19:22 he was also rich. He was a Jew prominent in position, possessions, and purity.
Matt. 19:16. "Master." This is the word *teacher*, like schoolmaster. "Good" is not in the best manuscripts of Matthew, but is genuine in Mark and Luke. They probably report the full salutation.
Matt. 19:16. "what good thing." Literally, "what good shall I do?" Verse 17 indicates that Jesus regarded his concept of "good" as inadequate. He thought of outward goodness as did the Pharisees.
Matt. 19:16. "may have eternal life." The verb is an in-

gressive aorist, "may come to have" or "acquire." "Eternal life" is "life of the ages" or "age-abiding life."

Matt. 19:20. "young man." This Greek word refers to one in the prime of life. "All these things" refer to the Ten Commandments. He had observed them faithfully.

Matt. 19:20. "what lack I yet?" The word "lack" means to fall short or to be defective. What more could he do than external things? A. T. Robertson suggests either proud complacency or pathetic despair. It was probably some of both.

Matt. 19:22. "sorrowful." Mark says "his countenance fell." Luke says that he was "exceedingly grieved." He went away grieved. Perhaps he thought that Jesus asked too much. "Great possessions." This could mean property or real estate. His high hopes lay in the dust.

III. DOCTRINAL VALUE. The point here is external righteousness versus internal righteousness. A person may be outwardly correct but inwardly wrong. There is a difference between negative and positive goodness. One may observe the letter of the law, yet break the spirit of it. Basic sin is in the inner attitude, not merely in the overt act.

IV. PRACTICAL AIM. To impress the hearer with the fact that Jesus' demands go beyond rote observance of religious rules. Such cannot satisfy the deepest longings of the soul. There can be no reservation in following the King. That which comes between a man and Jesus is his god.

V. HOMILETICAL FORM
Theme: "The Demand of the King."

Introduction: Apart from the crucifixion scene there is scarcely a more pathetic picture in the Gospels than this. A young man in the prime of life came to Jesus expectantly, yet went away disappointed. He came with a smiling face, and went away with a fallen countenance. He rushed up to Jesus with a joyful heart, yet went away exceedingly sorrowful. One may well ask why. For this scene has been repeated times without number. The story may be described as hope, emptiness, and despair.

A. *The Hope of Youth.* "... that I may have eternal life?"

Hope is characteristic of vigorous, ambitious, idealistic youth. It was especially true of this young man. He was rich, prominent, promising, and pure. What a life to bring to Jesus! "And Jesus looking upon him loved him ..." (Mark 10:21).

But these things were not enough. He wanted age-abiding life. What the words "eternal life" meant to him one cannot say with certainty. But surely there was an intangible idealism which longed for realization. His concept of goodness was far short of Jesus' goal (Matt. 19:17). He thought of goodness as quantitative instead of qualitative. Jesus did not rebuke him for it, but sought to lead him to a full understanding of it. Jesus never quenches a smoking flax, but endeavors to fan it into a flame. This is the *hope* of the hope of youth.

B. *The Emptiness of Youth.* "... what lack I yet?"

Despite his outwardly pure life, he was not satisfied. There was a defect in his life which a mere keeping of the commandments could not mend. His life was an empty shell, perfect on the outside but hollow on the inside.

Note again the things possessed by this young man: youth, wealth, authority, position, character, idealism. Yet his life was empty. It fell short of its possibilities.

Modern youth may well study this picture. With so much of the tangibles, youth often lacks in the realization of the intangibles. The greatest youth problem is not deliquency. It is frustration. The average youth possesses idealism far beyond that of his elders. His problem lies in the fulfilment of this hunger for a better life. Lacking the proper guidance or example from their elders, they end up in the blind alley of cynicism. The unsettled state of world affairs leaves youth in a quandary. So many say, "What's the use?" But despite everything else, this young man still cherished his ideals. When youth loses them all is lost. The greatest need of youth is a noble, spiritual purpose.

C. *The Despair of Youth.* "... he went away sorrowful ...."

Why did he go away? "For he had great possessions." Not merely because he had them, but because they had him (cf. Luke 12:20). Jesus made demands upon him which he was not willing to meet. Although he claimed to have kept all the commandments, actually he had broken the first one. His possessions were his god (cf. James 2:10). This teaching of Jesus does not necessarily call for a vow of poverty. Instead it calls for a right use of property. In effect Jesus told the young man to get rid of that which stood between him and a right relationship with God and His will. The King demands absolute love and obedience.

Jesus does not command every person to sell his property and give the receipts away. It may be other things. A dime can be held so close to one's eye as to shut out the entire landscape. Whatever shuts out God must be removed. It may be intellect, doubt, pride, prejudice, cynicism, companions, occupants, or leisure. Each must examine his own life.

Because the young man was wedded to his possessions, he went away from Jesus. "... he went away sorrowful ..." — but he went away. No further record of him is found. One may hope that he returned to Jesus. But all that the Bible says of him is that he sought to save his life here-and-now, and in the process lost the age-abiding life. His despair should warn others. Thus it will become their hope and assurance.

Matthew 20

A STUDY IN GREATNESS

20:25. "But Jesus called them unto him, and said, Ye know that the princes of the Gentiles exercise dominion over them, and they that are great exercise authority upon them."

20:26. "But it shall not be so among you: but whosoever will be great among you, let him be your minister."

20:27. "And whosoever will be chief among you, let him be your servant."

20:28. "Even as the Son of man came not to be ministered unto, but to minister, and to give his life a ransom for many."

I. HISTORICAL SETTING. Jesus was moving ever closer to Jerusalem and the cross. This burden weighed heavily upon Him. The event under consideration occurred probably in Perea, shortly before Jesus crossed the Jordan river near Jericho. Repeated incidents had served to focus attention upon the demands of the King. In response the Twelve inquired as to the reward; Jesus thought in terms of service. This is ever the conflict between human and divine standards. The request of James and John, through their mother, and the indignation of the other disciples, served to bring the matter into focus.

II. EXPOSITORY MEANING
Matt. 20:25. "them." This refers primarily to James and John, but includes the other disciples. "Know" is more than experiential knowledge. It involves inner perception. "Princes." They are those in places of rulership. This is a contrast with the disciples' request (20:21). "Gentiles" are pagan people. "Exercise dominion." The verb means to lord it over one. In the Greek it is an intensive form. "Great."

Literally, "the great ones or grandees." "Exercise authority" means "to play the tyrant." Another intensive form. The Greek word means authority out of the nature of one's being, with no outside restrictions. Its root form is used of God's power (cf. Matt. 28:18).

Matt. 20:26. "not." This word is first in the Greek sentence, so emphatic. "Among you" in contrast with pagan rulers. "Great among you" in contrast with "great ones" of verse 25. "Minister." This is the word for deacon *(diakonos)*. Thayer forms this word out of *dia* (through) and *konis* (dust), one who raises dust in hurrying to minister. More frequently it applies to ministers of the gospel (cf. I Cor. 3:5).

Matt. 20:27. "chief." Literally "first." "Servant." This is the word for bond slave. Note the contrast of highest and lowest dignity.

Matt. 20:28. "came not." In Greek "not" is first, and so emphatic. The very purpose of Jesus' coming. "Ministered unto, but to minister." These verbs are the root of *diakonos* (minister). The first is passive; the second is active. Both are aorist tenses of point action, referring to the whole of Jesus' ministry. "Ransom." This word was used in the papyri for the price paid for a slave in order to set him free. Some see difficulty in the suggestion that God had to pay Satan a ransom. Not so. God paid the ransom to Himself (cf. Rom. 3:23-26). This is Jesus' only use of the word (cf. parallel in Mark 10:45).

III. DOCTRINAL VALUE. Here is the contrast between worldly and heavenly standards of greatness. Service is the criterion of true grandeur. The perfect standard is Jesus Christ. He went through the cross to the throne.

IV. PRACTICAL AIM. To enable the hearer to see that one's service is more to be regarded than one's servants as an estimate of Kingdom position. Christ, not human rulers, is the pattern for successful Christian living. Faithfulness unto the point of dying should be the goal of every follower of Christ. Service, not selfishness, is the goal.

V. HOMILETICAL FORM

Theme. "A Study in Greatness."

Introduction: The very air was charged with expectancy. The words and mood of Jesus indicated a rapidly approaching climax to His ministry. Naturally the Twelve related this to the establishing of the Kingdom. Still unable to identify it with the cross, they thought in terms of some divine fiat from which would emerge the rule of Christ. This concept resulted in a scramble for positions of privilege. Maybe relying upon natural kinship, John and James, through their mother, waxed bold to request places of first and second power next to Jesus. Resentment flared through the others. Once again the patience of Jesus was sorely tried. Another lesson was in order. It may be outlined with three words: false, true, ideal.

A. *The False Standard of Greatness.* "the princes of the Gentiles . . . ."

The pagan world placed great emphasis upon "the great ones," lords and tyrants. The political scene reeked with avarice, greed, oppression, and power. From Caesar down to the local petty officials one standard prevailed, lording it over or playing the tyrant. Felix, a liberated slave, was said to exercise the power of a king with the disposition of a slave (cf. Acts 23:24 ff.).

The Twelve were obsessed with the same idea. They thought in terms of an earthly kingdom with its hierarchy of power. Such an idea has plagued Christianity through the ages. Like a poisonous fog it hovers over every denomination, church, and individual Christian. The thirst for prominence and power nullifies Christian usefulness and negates spiritual power. Political standards and materialistic measures have no place in spiritual endeavors. Jesus forever separated them (cf. Matt. 22:21). What God has put asunder, man should never join together.

B. *The True Standard of Greatness.* ". . . not be so among you . . . let him be your minister."

With one emphatic negative Jesus brushed aside the false to emphasize the true. Lords and tyrants have no place in the Kingdom of God. The standard of Kingdom greatness is service. Not the number of one's servants but the number whom one serves is the Christian criterion. Note the contrast: "great ... minister ... chief ... servant." The servant is a slave. The minister is a slave hastening to serve. Pagan society may scorn, but God is well pleased.

Position in the Kingdom is to be neither asked nor demanded. It is achieved and deserved. God is sovereign in giving His rewards (cf. Matt. 20:1-16). Man is free to fail or achieve. God has "proposed" greatness for those who fit themselves for it (cf. Matt. 20:23). In losing his life for Christ's sake man finds it in Christ's service. The highest plaudit is not the acclaim of the crowd, but the "well done" of the Christ. The final verdict is not one's fame or fortune, but "What did you do with Jesus?"

C. *The Ideal Standard of Greatness.* "... the Son of man ...."

"Let this mind be in you ...." (Phil. 2:5-11). King of kings and Lord of lords — yet He became a servant raising dust in His haste to serve. He trod the dusty road that led even to the cross. Herein is the explanation of the incarnation. He became everything that man is, that man might become, everything that He is. He bore man's grief that man might bear other's burdens, and "so fulfil the law of Christ" (cf. Gal. 6:2). One standard of judgment is the Christian's service toward others. (cf. Matt. 25:31-46; Luke 16:8.)

Matthew 21

WHO IS THIS?

21:10. "And when he was come into Jerusalem, all the city was moved, saying, Who is this?"

21:11. "And the multitude said, This is Jesus the prophet of Nazareth of Galilee."

I. HISTORICAL SETTING. This is Palm Sunday, just five days before the crucifixion. It has been called Jesus' triumphant entry into Jerusalem. In fact it was His last appeal to the city. It was a further fulfilment of prophecy (21:4-5). Here the King offered Himself only to be rejected. Such entries were common in that day. A victorious king entered his capital city riding on a white stallion. Jesus, in meekness and peace, rode upon an ass, a beast of burden. Expectancy was in the air. Those who accompanied Jesus hailed Him as the Messiah (21:9). Doubtless many who cried "hosanna" on Sunday cried "crucify him" on Friday. This demonstration created a sensation among residents of the city and the pilgrims who had come for the Passover.

II. EXPOSITORY MEANING

Matt. 21:10. "moved." This means stirred as by an earthquake or a mighty wind. This is an aorist passive verb from which comes the word "seismograph" (cf. Matt. 27:51; Matt. 28:4). "Who is this?" A question of curiosity, but more. "Who is this to whom you ascribe messianic titles?"

Matt. 21:11. The answer literally reads, "This one is the prophet Jesus, the one from Nazareth of Galilee." Bruce sees this as an answer of pride. Chrysostom regarded it as "a low-pitched answer... as if they were ashamed of their recent outburst of enthusiasm" (Bruce).

Matt. 21:11. "Jesus." To them this was a common name. Note that they did not say "Christ." "Prophet." His vocation, but just one among many. "Nazareth." A despised town of Galilee (cf. John 1:46). "Galilee." Regarded with scorn by the Judeans (cf. John 7:52-53).

III. DOCTRINAL VALUE. This question involves the entire scope of the person and work of Jesus Christ. It echoes the hunger of men's minds and hearts. The answer is the tragedy of failure in Christian witness. Truth watered down is no truth at all.

IV. PRACTICAL AIM. To impress upon the friends of Jesus the necessity of a bold, complete witness as to the person and purpose of the King. Because those who know Jesus best fail to reveal Him at His best, opportunity is lost. Furthermore cities, nations, and souls are lost.

V. HOMILETICAL FORM
   Theme: "Who Is This?"
Introduction: What a scene! It began with hope but ended in despair. It was born in witness but was buried in denial. What promised to be a coronation became a crucifixion. Jerusalem's greatest hour soon became her final hour.

The time and place may change, but the principles are ever the same. No nation or man can confront Jesus and ever be the same again. Different people see different things in Jesus. The Roman soldiers saw the scene. A triumphant procession? No king, stallion, army, or trophies of victory. Instead a lowly man, a beast of burden, and a laughing, shouting mob. "Who is this?" they asked. The Jews saw a procession. Messianic shouts, torn garments, broken palm branches, and Galilean peasants? "Who is this?" they asked. The scene involves a question, an answer, and an examination.

   A. *The Question.* "Who is this?"
It was an honest question. Few residents of Jerusalem knew Jesus by sight. The pilgrims probably did not know Him at all. This fact, plus natural curiosity, produced the question. In their hearts was a hunger for the Messiah. The Passover was regarded as a possible time for His manifestation. Perhaps this was He.

This question, uttered or silent, is in every heart. Though

He is the desire of all nations, many do not know Him, indeed have never heard of Him. This question is seen in the unrest of men and nations. It is involved in the attempts of art, science, culture, even theology to meet the manifold hungers of men everywhere. Jesus Christ is the mystery of all mysteries. He is the answer to every need. Hence the repeated question, "Who is this?"

B. *The Answer.* "... Jesus the prophet of Nazareth of Galilee."

Before an eager audience this answer was a tragedy. There were many men called Jesus, and many prophets. Nazareth was a despised village. "No prophet came from Galilee," said they. In effect, the crowd replied, "He's a nobody." So they melted away, only to reassemble to cry, "Crucify him!"

The answer was true. But there was so much more truth which they did not speak. They said nothing of the "Christ." Outside the city He was the "Son of David." Intimidated by the cynical city they said, "He is Jesus." To modern man that is definite. To them it said nothing.

This tragedy is repeated daily. In the heart He is the Christ. In the outward expression He is a nobody. Business, pleasure, politics, scholarship, and fear of scorn are only a few of the reasons why the friends of Jesus give the wrong answer. They lose their opportunity. What is worse — others lose their souls.

C. *The Examination.* "Who is this?"

The question is repeated. History, art, literature, architecture, music, poetry, prose, philosophy, and psychology have sought to answer it. But each falls short of its goal. The answer is found in the Bible. It is God's answer to man's question: (1) pre-existent (John 1:1); eternal (Heb. 13:8); divine (John 1:1; Luke 4:9; John 17:11); Creator (John 1:3, Col. 1:16-17); virgin-born (Matt. 1:21-23); sinless (John 8:46; Matt. 27:4; Luke 23:14; II Cor. 5:21); wonderful (Matt. 4:23; Mark 1:22; John 7:16; 11:1-46); vicariously died (Isa. 53:4-6; II Cor. 5:21); resurrected (Matt. 28:5-6); ascended (Acts 1:9); returning (Acts 1:11). The true answer is not merely historical but personal. "What think ye of Christ?" (Matt. 22:42).

Matthew 22

A CITIZEN OF TWO WORLDS

22:17. "Tell us therefore, What thinkest thou? Is it lawful to give tribute unto Caesar, or not?"

22:20. "And he saith unto them, Whose is this image and superscription?"

22:21. "They say unto him, Caesar's. Then saith he unto them, Render therefore unto Caesar the things which are Caesar's; and unto God the things that are God's."

I. HISTORICAL SETTING. It was later in the day on Tuesday. The Herodians, along with the disciples of the Pharisees, came to Jesus with a tricky political question. Both groups, while differing in their politics, were opposed to the Roman rule. They objected to Roman taxation. The Pharisees sought a return to the theocratic nation. The Herodians advocated the return of kingship to the house of Herod. Had Jesus sided with them He would have brought the wrath of Rome upon Him. Had He advocated Roman taxes, the people would have turned upon Him. The question actually turned upon Roman law and Messianic law. According to their concept the latter forbade the former. To have rejected the latter would, in their eyes, have been to renounce His Messianic claims. Jesus supported neither side of the question, but spoke an eternal truth as to the relationship between Church and State.

II. EXPOSITORY MEANING
   Matt. 22:17. "lawful." The reference is to theocratic or Herodian rule versus Roman rule. "Tribute" was a head tax or *tributum capitis* paid with a silver coin. "Caesar." The reigning Caesar was Tiberius who reigned A.D. 14-37.

In the larger sense "Tiberius" refers to government as an institution.

Matt. 22:20. "image and superscription." A Roman coin with Caesar's image on one side and the inscription *"Tiberiou Kaisaros"* on the other.

Matt. 22:21. — "render." This is an aorist imperative of the verb to give back or to recompense. It was a term for paying tribute money. Literally, "the things belonging to Caesar . . . the things belonging to God."

III. DOCTRINAL VALUE. This is the basic word as to the relationship between Church and State. It shows the Christian's obligation to both. Implied is the higher obligation owed to God. When both Church and State recognize their respective places in God's plan, there need be no conflict.

IV. PRACTICAL AIM. To set forth the proper attitude of Kingdom citizens toward the Kingdom of God and varying political systems under which they live. To attempt to resolve the conflict in divided loyalties. Jesus had little, almost nothing, to say about politics. He dealt with guiding principles.

V. HOMILETICAL FORM
   Theme: "A Citizen of Two Worlds."
   Introduction: Although the Herodians and the Pharisees' disciples acted with an ulterior motive (22:18), they posed a problem which calls for serious consideration. How can a person be a citizen of the Kingdom of God and a citizen of an earthly kingdom at the same time? Does the Chirstian conscience conflict with one's civic duties? If so, where does his loyalty lie? The truth is that he is a citizen of two worlds. In each he has responsibilities. He cannot be a good Christian and a bad citizen. Nor may the reverse be true. In dealing with this matter three words are noted: conflict, consequence, and complement.
   A. *The Conflict.* "Is it lawful . . .?"
   Behind this *loaded* question was a real conflict. Should the advocates of a theocracy submit to pagan rule? Could the champions of Herod be subject to Caesar? The problem was both religious and political.

This is especially true for the Christian. Does loyalty to Christ precede obedience to law? Should the Church control the State, or the State the Church? Are religion and politics to be mixed? When the State makes demands contrary to religious conscience, what must the Christian do? Are extreme positions in either case ever justified? Is there a possibility of resolving these conflicts?

B. *The Consequence.* ". . . this image and superscription?" Jesus did not answer with a coin of His own or of His disciples. He asked for their coin. It was not Jewish but Roman. Its use implied their subservience to and dependence upon the Roman government. Jesus neither condoned nor condemned the Empire and its rule. He simply recognized an evident fact.

Christianity exists under many varied forms of government. The New Testament approves the institution of government (cf. Rom. 13:1 ff.). Christians are exhorted to be law abiding (cf. I Peter 2:12-17). Even when persecuted they are to endure it willingly as a testimony unto the Lord (cf. I Peter 3:14-15).

The Christian is a part of society in which he lives. He is not to live a monastic life, but is to flavor life with his witness (cf. I Cor. 5:9-13). Where laws are wrong he is to use his influence to change them. But he is to abide by them, unless they involve a matter of Christian conscience (cf. Acts 4:19-20). Always he is to be a Christian (I Peter 3:15).

C. *The Complement.* ". . . unto Caesar . . . unto God. . . ." Jesus sided with neither question. Instead He declared a principle of conduct. Some things belong to Caesar, others to God. Each is to be rendered in its own sphere. The Christian is a citizen of two worlds. Each entails obligations.

In Jesus' answer is the ideal. Neither State nor Church is bodily to control the other. In this ideal neither should fear the other. They complement each other. (cf. Rom. 13:5-10). It is under such an ideal that both State and Church have realized their greatest potential.

Matthew 23

THE JUDGMENT OF GOD

23:2. "The scribes and Pharisees sit in Moses' seat."

23:3. "All therefore whatsoever they bid you observe, that observe and do; but do not ye after their works: for they say, and do not."

23:13. "But woe unto you, scribes and Pharisees, hypocrites! . . ."

23:38. "Behold, your house is left unto you desolate."

I. HISTORICAL SETTING. This event occurred probably about mid-afternoon on Tuesday of Passion Week. It climaxed the "day of controversy." The place was probably in the court of the temple. Already Jesus had denounced the Pharisees (Luke 11:42 ff.). Here the denunciation is completed. These are the most scathing words which ever fell from the lips of Jesus. Some have criticized Jesus for lack of self-control. But this ignores the elements involved. Through this outburst of righteous indignation runs a sobbing compassion (cf. 22:37). Here are seen both sides of the nature of Deity, compassion and wrath.

G. Campbell Morgan notes an interesting comparison between "blessed" in Matthew 5 and "woe" in Matthew 23 (*The Gospel According to Matthew,* Revell, *in loco*). There are seven beatitudes, excepting the double beatitude in Matthew 5:10-11 (cf. 23:34-36). There are also seven woes. Verse 14 is not found in the best manuscripts. But note parallels in Mark 12:40 and Luke 20:47.

II. EXPOSITORY MEANING
Matt. 23:2. "Moses' seat." They were regarded as the interpreters of the Mosaic law.

109

Matt. 23:3. "whatsoever they bid." The Mosaic law, not their multitude of rote rules of conduct. "Say, and do not." These are present tenses. "They keep on saying, and keep on not doing."

Matt. 23:13. "woe." This is an interjection. With the definite article it means "calamity" (cf. Rev. 9:12; Rev. 11:14). "Hypocrites." This word is the transliteration of a word meaning "play actor," one who plays a part. Note that it was spoken not to outward sinners but to pretenders after righteousness void of inward character.

Matt. 23:38. "house." Probably a triple meaning: temple, city, and nation. "Left desolate." This verb means to send away or dismiss. The passive form means to desert, depart from, to leave alone. Jesus gave up on the Jewish nation. In A.D. 70 judgment will fall!

III. DOCTRINAL VALUE. This chapter sets forth in frightening fashion the wrath of God against sin. It teaches the compassion of God for the sinner. Here is seen the "righteousness of the scribes and Pharisees" (cf. Matt. 5:20) or hypocrisy, the most condemned of all sins. Jesus authenticates the Mosaic code, but abhors its misuse.

IV. PRACTICAL AIM. To point out the judgment of God upon man's righteousness which ignores the righteousness of God in Christ. God is a God of wrath as well as a God of grace. The judgment of God is not an arbitrary one. He only recognizes the evil character produced. When such is fixed even God Himself can only declare it. It is left desolate.

V. HOMILETICAL FORM
Theme: "The Judgment of God."

Introduction: If Matthew 23 seems harsh, it is just that. To understand it properly one must view it against the backdrop of the preceding chapters. The King had patiently sought the Jewish nation. The more He pleaded with them the greater their rebellion. It was only after every means had failed that Jesus pronounced judgment. This is always God's way. Patience, love, mercy, compassion, and grace, when scorned, can only rebound in judgment. Such lies at the very basis of the moral structure of the universe. Man reaps what he sows. Herein is a lesson for every man. It suggests commendation, condemnation, and consummation.

A. *The Word Commended.* ". . . Moses' seat . . . observe and do . . . ."

Jesus never took one jot or tittle from the Old Testament, the Bible of His day. It was binding; it was good. Higher critics may seek to separate the chaff (?) from the wheat. But Jesus never questioned one word of this recorded revelation of God. Note His repeated quotations from it.

This revelation of God is basic in the moral structure of the universe. Note the Ten Commandments. They are not right because they are in the Decalogue. They are there because they are right. No man or group of men can ignore God's Word without paying the penalty.

Jesus said, "All therefore whatsoever they bid you observe, that observe and do." "Observe" means to take note of it as to its intrinsic value. "Do" means to make obedience to it the habit of one's practice. Jesus commends both right teaching and right practice insofar as God's Word is concerned.

B. *The Deed Condemned.* ". . . do not after their works . . . they say, and do not."

"They keep on saying, and they keep on not doing." Jesus condemns such. *Orthodoxy* and *orthopraxy* should go hand in hand (cf. James 2:10-20).

What did Jesus condemn in the Pharisees? (1) A dog in the manger attitude (23:13). (2) Purposeless enthusiasm unto evil results (23:15). (3) Rote rules which evade essential Christian character (23:16-22; cf. Exod. 20:7; Matt. 5:33-37). (4) A meticulous letter-of-the-law attitude which ignores the true spiritual meaning (23:23-24). (5) Outward honesty but inward "extortion" (robbery) and "excess" (greed) (23:25-26). (6) Outward purity and inward impurity (23:27-28). (7) Abhorring the sins of others while practicing greater sins in God's sight (23:29-33). Note that these were the sins of the religious leaders of Jesus' day. Everyone who aspires to deal with sacred things should beware!

C. *The Result Consummated.* ". . . your house is left unto you desolate."

Here is cause and effect. It is the verdict of history, of eternity. Jesus saw the holocaust of A.D. 70. But more, He recognized the present tragedy (cf. Rev. 3:1). The nation and its leaders had proved their refusal to be used of God. So only this judgment remained. God went away from Israel to build a people who at that time was not a people (cf. Hosea 1:6; I Peter 2:9-10). God was not inextricably bound to one nation or people then. Nor is He now. The judgment of Matthew 23 has been repeated often. It may be again and again.

If this judgment applies to nations, it includes individual persons also. God has commended His Word. He condemns its abuse. The same result may be consummated in a man as in a nation. The word "hell" in verse 33 is "Gehenna," Jesus' word for the place of eternal punishment. No hell, some say? Whose word will one follow? The critics or the Christ?

Matthew 24

THE SECOND COMING OF CHRIST

*24:3. "And as he sat upon the mount of Olives, the disciples
came unto him privately, saying, Tell us, when shall these
things be? and what shall be the sign of thy coming, and of
the end of the world?"*

*24:4. "And Jesus answered and said unto them, Take heed
that no man deceive you."*

I. HISTORICAL SETTING. This was late afternoon on
Tuesday of Passion Week. The "day of controversy" was over.
Jesus and the Twelve had left Jerusalem, and were on their
way to Bethany. Passing through the temple area the Twelve
had pointed out to Jesus the magnificence of the temple.
Jesus, in turn, prophesied its destruction which came in A.D.
70 at the end of the Jewish War (A.D. 66-70). Probably stop-
ping to rest somewhere on the Mount of Olives, the Twelve
(Mark 13:3 identifies Peter, Andrew, James, and John) came
to Jesus with three questions: the destruction of Jerusalem;
the second coming; and the end of the world. Matthew 24-25
is the answer to these questions. It is difficult to follow these
answers, for Jesus dealt with first one and then another. This
is the most difficult passage in the Synoptic Gospels. But a
clear picture may be discerned if one keeps the three questions in mind. It is well to remember that Jesus is using
apocalyptic language which relied upon imagery to express
prosaic truth.

II. EXPOSITORY MEANING
Matt. 24:3. "when shall these things be?" This question refers to the destruction of Jerusalem and the temple which
occurred in A.D. 70. "Coming." This translates a Greek word
parousia, used in the papyri of the visit of an emperor. Literally it means "presence." It is used in the Gospels only here

and in Matthew 24:27, 37, 39, but is found often in the Epistles (cf. Phil. 2:12; II Thess. 2:1). "The end of the world."
Literally, "the consummation of the age." Like *parousia* this
phrase occurs in the Gospels only in Matthew. In the New
Testament these were technical terms for the second coming
of Christ.

Matt. 24:4. "take heed." This Greek verb could be either
an indicative or an imperative, probably the latter here. "Deceive" means to lead astray or cause to wander. This warning
runs through the entire discourse. It was needed then. It is
needed now.

III. DOCTRINAL VALUE. This passage involves the second coming of Christ. It also deals with the destruction of
Jerusalem. The warning as to false messiahs and as to misin-
terpretation of world events is quite evident. The refrain running throughout is that of readiness for the return of the
Lord.

IV. PRACTICAL AIM. To seek to interpret Jesus' great discourse in the light of the questions posed by the disciples.
Extreme and dogmatic positions should be avoided. Jesus set
no timetable of events, nor should anyone else. The fact He
declared. That is sufficient. The time element should be left
with God. Readiness is the key throughout — for one's self
(24:44) and for the whole world (24:14).

V. HOMILETICAL FORM
Theme: "The Second Coming of Christ."

Introduction: No words of Jesus have been subjected to a
more careful scrutiny. Nor have any others been the basis of
a greater diversity of interpretation. But the "blessed hope"
inspires students of God's Word to seek their teaching. Only
as one keeps in mind the three specific questions which Jesus
answered may one hope to approximate the meaning of Jesus'
words. Three words may help in revealing the content of this
passage: warning, description, and declaration.

A. *The Warning of Jesus.* "Take heed that no man deceive
you."

This is a needed caution. Jesus foresaw the pandemonium

which would accompany this "blessed hope." It is obvious that Jesus had in mind at this point all three questions. Note the warnings. (1) As to false Christs (24:5). This relates to all three questions. False Christs abounded just prior to and during the Jewish War (A.D. 66-70). They have continued through the ages. (2) As to cataclysmic world events (24:6-7). But these are not a sign of the *Parousia*. They are parts of world history. (3) As to persecution (24:8-13). "The beginning of sorrows" refers to the persecution of Christians, not to the approaching end of the age. This began in widespread scope about A.D. 66-70 as a policy of the Roman Empire. (4) The one sure sign (24:14). Through tribulation the gospel will be spread through the ages until the end of the age.

This warning is needed today. False messiahs have dotted the pages of history. Political, economic, philosophical, theological, and theosophical messiahs repeatedly present themselves. Note modern cults. Jesus said, "Do not go after them" (24:23-26). Every great disturbance among governments, in nature, and in society produces its cries, "The end is near." But life goes on.

B. *The Description by Jesus.* "When shall these things be?" Matthew 24:15-22 answers this first question. The "abomination of desolation" refers to the fall of Jerusalem. "Abomination" refers to a nausea caused by a stench. Idolatry is described as a stench in God's nostrils. When Jerusalem fell the Romans offered heathen sacrifices at the eastern gate of the city near the temple area.

Note Jesus' warnings in this regard. "Get out of Jerusalem when you see the armies gathering" (cf. Luke 21:20 ff.). Eusebius says that at that time many Christians fled to Pella, a town in the mountains about seventeen miles south of the sea of Galilee. Those with child or nursing children could not run. Winter would produce added hardships. A sabbath day's journey would not allow them to escape. Had the carnage of the fall of the nation continued, no one would have escaped. For the Christians' sake God shortened the days of it.

Such an experience would produce false messiahs and prophets. Ignore them. When the Christ appears all will see Him (24:27). To Him His own will gather (24:28).

This is Jesus' prophecy of what today is recorded history. It serves as a warning to all ages, including ours, not to be deceived by world events about us. This does not mean that His *Parousia* is not near. It is always imminent. Modern man's responsibility is not to chart events and fix speculative dates. He is to be ready, and busy getting others ready (24:14).

C. *The Declaration of Jesus.* ". . . the sign of thy coming . . . the end of the world."

Verse 29 ff. deals with these questions. Verses 29-31 are apocalyptic language commonly used in connection with the coming of the Christ or of some other cataclysmic intervention of God in history. The sign? "The Son of man in heaven" or in the sky (24:30). Those unprepared will mourn. His own will rejoice (24:31). "This generation" probably refers to the destruction of Jerusalem, a literal fact. In just forty years it occurred. "But the day and the hour" of the second coming is known only to God (24:36). There it should remain. Life will go on its way until the end (24:37-39). Some will be ready, others will not be (24:39-41). But Christian people are to "watch" in service (24:42). Lost people are to prepare through faith in Christ (24:43). "Therefore be ye also ready: for in such an hour as ye think not the Son of man cometh" (24:44).

Matthew 25

THE INTERIM RESPONSIBILITY

25:14. "For the kingdom of heaven is as a man travelling into a far country, who called his own servants, and delivered unto them his goods."

25:19. "After a long time the Lord of those servants cometh, and reckoneth with them."

25:29. "For unto every one that hath shall be given, and he shall have abundance: but from him that hath not shall be taken away even that which he hath."

I. HISTORICAL SETTING. The scene is the same as in Chapter 24. With a series of parables (24:45–25:46) Jesus points out various aspects of the time between His ascension and second coming. The import of all is that in the Lord's return character will be revealed and rewarded or condemned accordingly.

II. EXPOSITORY MEANING

Matt. 25:14. Literally, "For as a man travelling into a far country called his own servants...." "Travelling into a far country." This is one word, a participle, meaning to be away from one's home or country. He was about to go abroad. Note Jesus' ascension, etc. "His own servants" or slaves. This corresponds to Jesus' own followers. Paul called himself a slave of Jesus Christ (cf. Gal. 1:10). "Goods" are "belongings," all that he had of earthly goods.

Matt. 25:19. "After a long time" or much time. Note that no date is specified. This suggests a delay. "Reckoneth." Two Greek papyri and one ostracon have this as a business idiom. Literally, "He makes a reckoning."

Matt. 25:29. Literally, "For to the one having, all things shall be given, and he shall be overflowing all the edges

117

around [as a bowl overflows which cannot contain its contents]; but from the one not having, even what he has shall be taken away from him." Opportunity used and rewarded; opportunity neglected and lost.

III. DOCTRINAL VALUE. This is a lesson in stewardship, not merely of money, but of the Christian life and its opportunities. God has placed Kingdom affairs in the hands of His people. He will demand a reckoning upon His return. Ability and faithfulness, not results, will be the determining factors in judgment. One's fruits prove the true Christian character or lack of it.

IV. PRACTICAL AIM. To bring each person face to face with his responsibility as a Christian. Each has the same opportunity. Not all give the same response. God does not look for excuses but results. Fruitless church members may well question their Christian experience.

V. HOMILETICAL FORM

Theme: "The Interim Responsibility."

Introduction: In the crucifixion and resurrection God completed His work of redemption. Henceforth, under the guidance of the Holy Spirit, He will propagate it among men. Jesus is going away, and will some day return. What of the interim? This is the burden of the parable of the talents. Its message may be described as bestowal, reckoning, and reward.

A. *The Bestowal of Responsibility.* ". . . delivered unto them his goods."

Five, two, one "to every man according to his several ability." "His own servants" refers to each Christian individually and to the Church collectively. He has committed to His people the things of the Kingdom, His revelation of God and man, His redemptive work, His call to repentance, His gospel, the "power of God unto salvation to every one that believeth." To each Christian He has committed according to his ability. Happily, some are faithful. Sadly, some are untrustworthy. They waste their Master's goods. Are these latter Christians at all (cf. Matt. 7:16-29)?

B. *The Reckoning.* "... reckoneth with them."

Those who propose to do business for God have business with God. Responsibility is not bestowed by God and then forgotten.

Note that each of the first two servants reported the same increase. They doubled that which was entrusted to them. God holds man responsible for what he has, not what he has not (cf. II Cor. 8:12). Success is determined by endowment. He does not demand an "A" out of a "B" student. Nor is He satisfied with a "B" from an "A" student. A Church or a Christian is judged by its faithfulness to opportunity.

Note further the third servant. He is not condemned for not producing, but for not trying. Jesus condemned him with his own words (25:24-27). He had not wasted his master's goods. He had buried them. Fear became his master, not Jesus. He served out of fear, not love.

The reports of the servants are most revealing. The first two used sixteen words to report their successes. The third needed forty-three words to explain or alibi his failure. God is not interested in excuses but in results. This applies to churches as well as individuals.

C. *The Reward.* "... good and faithful ... wicked and slothful ...."

One should never belittle the matter of rewards as a Christian incentive. Jesus magnified them repeatedly. There are degrees of reward in heaven as there are degrees of punishment in hell (cf. I Cor. 3:8, 14-15; Luke 12:47-48).

Note that the first two servants received the same reward. The same is true of churches and individuals. In God's sight there are no little churches and big churches, or little Christians and big Christians. Each is little or big as it chooses to be. God recognizes the result.

The third servant lost what he had. It is a law of life. Note "wicked and slothful." Laziness is wickedness in God's sight. Not only did he lose his opportunity. He lost his soul (25:30). He was "unprofitable." This word means "garbage" (cf. Rom. 3:12, verb form of noun "unprofitable" in 25:30). He was fit only for the garbage dump (cf. Gehenna, hell). This does not mean falling from grace. He was never in grace. His "wicked and lazy" attitude only proved the true character which he had (cf. Matt. 25:31-46). One may question as to whether the third was a Christian.

Those who claim to follow Christ should beware of mere lip service (cf. Matt. 7:21-23). Works alone do not save. But works, or their lack, do declare the quality of faith which does save (cf. James 2:14-20). If one is faithful in his opportunity, God will see to the results.

Matthew 26

A STUDY IN LIGHT AND SHADOWS

26:7. "There came unto him a woman having an alabaster box of very precious ointment, and poured it on his head, as he sat at meat."

26:8. "But when his disciples saw it, they had indignation, saying, To what purpose is this waste?"

26:15. "And said unto them, What will ye give me, and I will deliver him unto you? And they covenanted with him for thirty pieces of silver."

I. HISTORICAL SETTING. This event took place on Tuesday night in Bethany at the home of Simon the leper. After a hard day Jesus was the guest of a friend, maybe one whom He had healed of leprosy. According to John Lazarus was present. Martha served. The anointing was done by Mary (John 12:1-3). The disciples complained of Mary's "waste." John notes that Judas did this. Probably the others joined in. Some identify this event with Luke 7:36 ff. But the differences between the events are quite evident. There is no reason why both could not have happened. Note that John supplies details omitted by Mark and Matthew. When he wrote the characters probably were dead, and so could be named with impunity. John identifies the woman whose good deed became a memorial to her. He also shows the immediate reason for Judas' betrayal (cf. John 12:4; Matt. 26:14-16).

II. EXPOSITORY MEANING

Matt. 26:7. "woman." John identifies her as Mary of Bethany (John 12:3). "An alabaster box of very precious ointment." This flask got its name from the town in Egypt where the material was found. It was used to contain precious ointments. The ointment was "exceeding precious," of weighty

121

value or a great price. "An alabaster of nard (*murou*) was a present for a king" (Bruce). Herodotus lists it as one of five presents sent by Cambyses to the King of Ethiopia. "Poured it on his head." Literally, "poured down." John says that she "anointed the feet of Jesus." She did both in a great act of love.

Matt. 26: 8. "disciples." John singles out Judas as the leader in this complaint (John 12:4). "Waste." Literally, "a total loss." Just so much "sentimental aroma" (Robertson). "She was a poet and they were somewhat prosaic" (Bruce).

Matt. 26:15. "give me." Literally, "what do you will to me to give." Their price, not his. Note the contrast between Mary and Judas. "And I" is one word (*kagō*). "I," even one of His disciples. "Deliver." This means to hand over (cf. Matt. 27:26 b.). "Covenanted." Literally, "they weighed" as in balances. "Coined money was in use, but the shekels may have been weighed out in antique fashion by men careful to do an iniquitous thing in the most orthodox way" (Bruce). "thirty pieces of silver" (cf. Zech. 11:12). Less than twenty-five dollars, the current price of a slave.

III. DOCTRINAL VALUE. This incident shows the different reactions to Jesus, love and hate. Spiritual deeds are a waste to unspiritual people. Virtue has its reward. Note the final disastrous end to wrong spiritual attitudes. Judas' deed was not one of passionate anger but of calculated greed.

IV. PRACTICAL AIM. To show the outward fruit of inward attitudes. Love will find a way. The love of money is the root of every kind of evil. Profit and loss cannot be measured by man's balances but by God's.

V. HOMILETICAL FORM.
    Theme: "A Study in Light and Shadows."
Introduction: The deed of Mary was an island of love in a sea of hate. It was a ray of light shining through the lowering clouds of the storm which was about to burst upon Jesus (26:2-5). The result is one of the most meaningful stories in the life of our Lord. It is all the more so since it is painted

against the ugly background of greed and hatred. This scene may be described as realization, reaction, and result.

A. *The Realization.* "...a woman...his disciples...."
In all probability Mary and Judas were the first of Jesus' disciples fully to realize that He was going to the cross. Jesus' announcement (26:2) made it certain. Possibly Judas even knew about the meeting of the Sanhedrin (26:3-5).

Neither could prevent the crucifixion. Upon realizing that the end was near, each asked a question. Mary: "What can I do for Jesus?" Judas: "What can Jesus do for me?" Why this difference? Each had had equal opportunities to know the innermost heart of Jesus. But with far different results. The one was a true believer. The other was merely a *joiner* for selfish reasons. He was an unregenerated devil (cf. John 6:70-71).

In any generation those gathered about Jesus may be divided into the Marys and the Judases. One is Christ-centered. The other is self-centered. One asks, "What may I do?" The other asks, "What must I do?" The one asks, "What service may I render?" The other asks, "What is there in it for me?" Through the one Christ is glorified. Through the other He is crucified .

B. *The Reaction.* ". . . very precious ointment . . . this waste."

Mary's answer was sympathetic love and understanding. She did what she could to alleviate His suffering. She gave to Him her very best. It was her gift to the King.

Judas' answer was carping criticism of her act. He despised Mary because he despised Jesus. Note how his act even contaminated the very elect (disciples). If Mary eased the heart of Jesus, Judas broke it. Note further that his criticism of Mary was intended to cover up his own sin of thievery (cf. John 12:6). Under the hypocritical guise of charity he sought to further his own gains. Trouble makers in the church usually have an ulterior motive. They may fool the disciples, but not the Lord. Crass materialism always regards spiritual investments as "waste," a waste of time and money. But the Lord accepts it as a gracious and eternal service (26:10-13).

C. *The Result.* "a memorial unto her ... what will ye give me ...."

Mary's was a selfless act, but it redounded to her eternal glory. Judas' was a selfish deed, but it brought to him eternal shame. Mary received that which she did not seek. Judas lost that which he sought (cf. Matt. 27:3-10), even his life (cf. Matt. 27:5), yea, his soul.

Judas sold out too cheaply. Note that the Sanhedrin set the price (Matt. 26:15a). "The wages of sin is death..." (Rom. 6:23). The devil drives a hard bargain.

Through the centuries Mary's name is breathed with reverence. Judas' name is uttered with a curse. Men name their lovely daughters after Mary. They do not even name their dogs after Judas. The only thing named Judas is the goat which leads sheep to the slaughter. Mary's timeless monument is the preaching of the living Word. Judas' name adorns a potter's cemetery. Amen.

Matthew 27

THE KING ON TRIAL

27:11. "And Jesus stood before the governor: and the governor asked him, saying, Art thou the King of the Jews? And Jesus said unto him, Thou sayest."

27:17. "Therefore when they were gathered together, Pilate said unto them, Whom will ye that I release unto you? Barabbas, or Jesus which is called Christ?"

27:22. "Pilate saith unto them, What shall I do then with Jesus which is called Christ? They all say unto him, Let him be crucified."

I. HISTORICAL SETTING. It is early Friday morning in Jerusalem. Shortly after midnight Jesus was arrested by the temple police, and brought before Annas. Annas was a former high priest who still ran the office through his son-in-law Caiaphas. The Jewish trial comprised three parts: (1) preliminary examination before Annas (John 18:12-14, 19-23); (2) informal pre-dawn trial by the Sanhedrin (Matt. 26:57, 59-68 and parallels in Mark, Luke, and John); (3) formal condemnation before the Sanhedrin (Matt. 27:1; Mark 15:1; Luke 22:66-71). By Jewish law it was illegal on most every count.

Since the Sanhedrin could not pronounce the death sentence, they brought Jesus to Pilate, the Roman Governor. Here again the trial may be divided into three phases: (1) before Pilate the first time (Matt. 27:2, 11-14 and parallels in the other three Gospels. John 18:28-38 gives the most details here); before Herod Antipas (Luke 23:6-12); before Pilate the second time (Matt. 27:15-26 and parallels. Again John furnishes the longer account). Despite the Roman pride for justice, here again many illegalities are found.

125

Matthew's account involves parts of both appearances before Pilate. For convenience it may be treated as one. Jesus is still in control as He proceeds to die as a King.

II. EXPOSITORY MEANING

Matt. 27:11. "governor." Pilate, the Roman provincial governor. He was a *legatus Caesaris* or procurator who ruled over one of the lesser provinces. "Art thou the King of the Jews?" Literally, "You are the King of the Jews?" The Sanhedrin had so charged that He made this claim. Note their subtlety in giving "Christ" a political connotation (cf. Luke 23:2). Pilate's question invited an affirmative answer. "Thou sayest." Jesus turns the answer on this thought. Jesus confessed that He was their King (cf. John 18:36-37). The Jews had charged Jesus with this claim (cf. Luke 23:2-3), but gave it a political flavor. Note that Jesus did not reply to the Jews. Nor did He do so to the direct questioning of Pilate. Note Matthew 27:14. Literally, "He did not answer to him up to even one word." Jesus had established His Kingship. That was all that He wanted.

Matt. 27:17. "gathered together." They were now before Pilate the second time. "Will ye." A choice of the will, not a passing desire. "Release." This custom (cf. 27:15) is mentioned only here and in Josephus (Ant. XX. 9, 3). "Barabbas." This means in Aramaic "son of father." Mark 15:7 describes him as an insurrectionist and a murderer. The very kind of messiah which Jesus refused to be. Some manuscripts call him "Jesus Barabbas." Note the sharp contrast with "Jesus the one being called Christ" (literal reading).

III. DOCTRINAL VALUE. The doctrine which runs through this passage is that of the Kingship of Jesus Christ. Pilate thought that he sat in judgment upon Jesus. The opposite was true. Cowardice still allows Jesus to be crucified. Men still choose Barabbas and crucify Jesus. Wrong may be on the throne, but not forever.

IV. PRACTICAL AIM. To see in the trial of Jesus the trial of every man. God offers alternatives, but man must live and/or die with his choice. Through all the shouts of greed and hate Jesus still reigns as King.

V. HOMILETICAL FORM

Theme: "The King On Trial."

Introduction: This is one of the most dramatic moments in history. The King of kings standing before the rulers of earth. It is also one of the most sordid scenes. For here the legal justice of both Jew and Gentile stands condemned. History records that Jesus was on trial before them. But the final verdict of history records that they were on trial before Him. The one is convicted of venomous pre-judgment. The other stands condemned of cowardly surrender to material opportunism. Justice has often been nailed to a cross for such reasons. So the courtroom in Pilate's hall blends into the halls of history where wrong upon the throne has repeatedly nailed truth to the scaffold. The timely and timeless lesson is revealed as conviction, choice, and consequence.

A. *The Conviction.* "You are the King of the Jews?" (literal translation).

Jesus' answer turned the tables on Pilate. Whether he actually believed Jesus to be a King may be open to question. But there is solid evidence that he suspected as much (cf. Matt. 27:19; John 18:33-38). Certainly he judged Jesus as innocent of political charges. Jesus' Kingdom was in the realm of truth. Pilate's references to Jesus as a King were scorn for the Jews, but there could have been more. As in the mockery of the soldiers (Matt. 27:28-29), so here, God causes the wrath of man to praise Him.

Jesus stands before every man as a King. Some may deny it for various reasons: Sanhedrin (prejudice); multitudes (indifference); Pilate (moral cowardice); soldiers (spiritual hardness). Finite minds put Jesus on trial, but the ages have vindicated Him. The burden of proof is upon him who would question the Kingship of Jesus. The time will come when every knee shall bow, and every tongue shall confess Him as Lord (cf. Phil. 2:11).

B. *The Choice.* "... Barabbas, or Jesus ...?"

The choice was greater than any of the choosers realized. Origen reports having seen a manuscript of Matthew's Gospel wherein Barabbas is called "Jesus Barabbas." This height-

ens the contrast. "Jesus son of father" versus "Jesus the Son
of His Father." "Jesus" means "Jehovah is salvation." Jesus
Barabbas offered political salvation. Jesus Christ offered
spiritual salvation. The one proposed insurrection. The other
promised regeneration. The former offered the nation political freedom through the shedding of their blood. The latter
proffered spiritual freedom through the shedding of His own
blood. The one would establish a kingdom among men. The
other came to establish the Kingdom of God within men.

The multitudes, spurred on by selfish leaders, chose Barabbas and rejected Jesus. They chose the material over the
spiritual. Thus Barabbas was turned loose to pursue his evil
ways. Jesus was nailed to a cross. Pilate's question is the question of all (cf. Matt. 27:22). He had Jesus on his hands. An
analysis of the trial indicates his many efforts to dispose of
him: ignore him (John 18:31); praise Him (Luke 23:4);
shift responsibility to another (Luke 23:6-12); substitute
another (Matt. 27:21); wash his hands of the whole matter
(Matt. 27:24). But he still had Jesus on his hands — and on
his soul. Men still make the same attempts with the same results. Still the question remains. "What shall I do then with
Jesus which is called Christ?"

C. *The Consequence.* ". . . crucified."

This was the cry of the multitude incited by the Sanhedrin.
Where were the "Hosannas?" Where were the friends of Jesus?
Fled or following afar off. Many who cried "hosanna" on Sunday cried "crucify" on Friday. The fickle nature of popular
acclaim!

Who crucified Jesus? Pilate, the Sanhedrin, the soldiers,
the multitude? The story is told by the superscription over
the cross. Roman law required this. "JESUS OF NAZARETH,
THE KING OF THE JEWS" (John 19:19). John notes that
it was written in Hebrew (language of religion), Latin (language of government), and Greek (language of culture).
These represented the great divisions of people of the Empire. Institutional religion condemned Jesus. Governmental
power crucified Him. Pagan culture rejected Him. There is
guilt enough for all (cf. Matt. 27:25). There were crucifiers

then — there are crucifiers now. All stand in judgment before God (cf. Luke 23:28-31).

"Men, brethren, what shall we do?" (Acts 2:37; literal translation). "Repent . . ." (Acts 2:38).

Matthew 28

THE COMMISSION OF THE KING

28:18. "And Jesus came and spake unto them, saying, All power is given unto me in heaven and in earth."

28:19. "Go ye therefore, and teach all nations, baptizing them in the name of the Father, and of the Son, and of the Holy Ghost."

28:20. "Teaching them to observe all things whatsoever I have commanded you: and, lo, I am with you alway, even unto the end of the world."

I. HISTORICAL SETTING. The Gospel of Matthew ends in a blaze of glory. In compliance with Jesus' instructions the Eleven came to a mountain in Galilee. Along the way others joined them so that above five hundred were assembled there (cf. I Cor. 15:6). The mountain is not specified. Was it the same one on which Jesus delivered His "Manifesto" (cf. Matt. 5-7)? It is an intriguing thought. At any rate sometime during the forty days between the resurrection and the ascension the event took place. Matthew does not record the ascension, but closes his Gospel with the Great Commission. It is a fitting finale. Here the King looks at all the world and down all ages to the end of the age. Satan had proposed his method of taking the world. Here Jesus gives His plan. The King goes forth to claim His Kingdom.

II. EXPOSITORY MEANING

Matt. 28:18. "All power." The word "power" translates a word meaning "out of being." It means *authority* springing from the nature of one's being. "Is given." This is a timeless aorist tense encompassing all future time. "Me." The risen Christ, "Heaven . . . . earth." Cosmic, absolute power, enhancing "all power."

Matt. 28:19. "Go." This is a participle, not an imperative. Literally, "going" or "as you go." "Teach." This is the only imperative in the Commission. It means "make disciples" or "disciple." This is suggestive of the new birth (cf. Matt. 11:29). "All nations." Both Jews and Gentiles. "Baptizing." This is another participle. After *discipling* comes baptism. "Name." This refers to authority. "Father . . . Son . . . Holy Ghost" [Spirit]. Not trine immersion, but one, in the name of the Trinity.

Matt. 28:20. "teaching." This is a different word from "teach" in verse 19. It refers to the process of instruction after the new birth and baptism. "Observe" means to practice. "I am with you." "I" is stated, and so emphatic. "I, the risen Christ, am with you." "Always" or "all the days," suggesting a long period of time. "The end of the world." Literally, "The consummation of the age."

III. DOCTRINAL VALUE. The doctrine taught here is missions or evangelism in its larger sense. It includes the new birth, but also involves baptism, and growth in grace, knowledge, and service, or sanctification. The presence of Christ in the interim and His second advent are clearly set forth. "The consummation of the age" suggests also glorification.

IV. PRACTICAL AIM. To set forth the duty imposed upon all Christians, and the means of fulfilling that duty. Evangelism does not end with conversion or baptism. It extends throughout one's life and through every generation. The evangel does not strive alone, but is assured of the presence and power of the King through His Spirit.

V. HOMILETICAL FORM

Theme: "The Commission of the King."

Introduction: The work of God in Christ for man's redemption is finished. Henceforth it rests with His people as they strive in the power of the Holy Spirit. The King sends forth His emissaries. No script writer would have the audacity to reproduce this scene. A band of peasants with no worldly authority, treasure, or army pitted against the might of a pagan world. Yet history records that in less than three hundred years, they so succeeded that the emperor of that world found it politically expedient to espouse their cause. Whence came this achievement? The answer may be seen in three words: Person, program, and presence.

A. *The Person of the King.* "All power is given unto me...."

It is the risen Christ speaking. He is King in fact as well as in name. The word "power" means "out of the nature of being." So as the Risen Christ, out of that very nature, He commands. What a sublime picture! He sends the five hundred forth in world conquest armed only with spiritual weapons. "According to the spirit of holiness" (Rom. 1:4) He had conquered. He sends them to do the same in the same Spirit. And, what is even more remarkable, He convinced them that they could do it!

The Risen Christ still stands upon every mountain and before every "five hundred." In His authority they have crossed seas, stormed the citadels of sin, and changed the course of the rivers of history. Pagan cultures still defy Him. But King Jesus has never been driven from the field. The arena of battle is the hearts of men. They do not fall before carnal weapons. But they do succumb to the Sword of the Spirit. The battle has been joined, and must be pressed until the flag of the King flutters in the breeze above every heart, every nation. It may be in joyful surrender, or it may be in coerced submission. But "He must reign, till he hath put all enemies under his feet" (I Cor. 15:25). He is reigning now in His mediatorial Kingdom. He will reign supreme in all of eternity.

B. *The Program of the King.* "Go... disciple... baptizing ... teaching...."

The King did not leave His work to chance. He spelled out the details. He did not even imply that His people would not go. Hence no command to do so. "Going" or "as ye go...." Then the command. "Disciple all nations." They were to go purposefully. Plant the flag of the King in their hearts. "Baptizing." Lead them to an open declaration of allegiance to Him. "Teaching." To the end that they may become obedient, useful citizens of the Kingdom.

Tragic is the result of ignoring this program: unregenerate church members; *mavericks* with no brand, no local church or denominational allegiance; idle, untrained, useless Christians. Evangelism is more than winning a person to Christ. It does not end with conversion any more than a full life ends with birth. It is only the beginning. Enrolling as a pupil is the beginning not the end. True evangelism involves regeneration, sanctification, and glorification. All are found in the Great Commission.

C. *The Presence of the King.* "I am with you . . . ."

This is Matthew's equivalent of John 14-16. For the King spoke not of bodily but of spiritual presence. "With you" in power, guidance, comfort, courage, understanding, and victory. The disciples needed this promise. And they found it fulfilled times without number.

Men often express the wish that they might have been with Jesus in bodily presence when He walked the earth. But the modern Christian has more. Then Jesus was *with* them. Now He is *in* them. Then He was in only one place at one time. Now He is omnipresent. Then He was present only for a few years. Now "I am with you alway, even unto the end of the world."

BIBLIOGRAPHY

Broadus, John A., *Commentary on the Gospel of Matthew*, American Baptist Publication Society, Philadelphia, 1886.

Bruce, A. B., *The Gospel According to Matthew*, The Expositor's Greek Testament, Vol. I, Eerdmans, Grand Rapids, 1951.

Edersheim, Alfred, *The Life and Times of Jesus the Messiah*, Vol. I and II, Eerdmans, Grand Rapids, 1953.

Henry, Matthew, *A Commentary on the Whole Bible*, Vol. V, Revell, New York.

The International Standard Bible Encyclopaedia, Vols. I-V, Eerdmans, Grand Rapids, 1949.

Lange, John Peter, *The Life of the Lord Jesus*, Vols. I-IV, Zondervan, Grand Rapids, 1958.

Morgan, G. Campbell, *The Crises of the Christ*, Revell, New York, 1936.

————, *The Gospel of Matthew*, Revell, New York, 1929.

————, *The Parables and Metaphors of our Lord*, Revell, New York, 1943.

Robertson, A. T., *A Harmony of the Gospels*, Broadman, Nashville, 1950.

————, *Word Pictures in the Greek New Testament*, Vol. I, Sunday School Board of the Southern Baptist Convention, Nashville, 1930.

Spurgeon, Charles H., *Sermons on the Miracles*, Zondervan, Grand Rapids, 1958.

————, *Sermons on the Parables*, Zondervan, Grand Rapids, 1958.

PREACHER'S HOMILETIC LIBRARY

PROCLAIMING THE NEW TESTAMENT

The Gospel of Mark

The Gospel of Mark

by
Ralph Earle

BAKER BOOK HOUSE
Grand Rapids, Michigan

Copyright © 1961 by
Baker Book House Company

Reprinted, January, 1972

Library of Congress Catalog Card
Number: 61-11088

ISBN: 0-8010-6912-2

Preacher's Homiletic Library
ISBN: 0-8010-6916-5

Photolithoprinted by Cushing-Malloy, Inc.
Ann Arbor, Michigan, United States of America

Dedicated
to
My faithful partner in proclaiming
the New Testament
with
all my sincere gratitude for her
love and patience

Author's Introduction

According to ancient tradition the Gospel of Mark reflects the preaching of Peter. He was the man who had three thousand converts at the close of his first sermon. We can afford to listen to him today.

There is a freshness about this Gospel that inspires good homiletics. Here we find rapid action, vivid detail, picturesque language. Many a preacher might be jolted out of his rut — another name for long grave — by letting the impact of Mark really hit him.

It is hoped that the present volume will be at least a lure to further study and finer preaching in the Gospel of Mark. The suggestions contained herein are just signposts, pointing the way to a richer, more rewarding ministry of the Word.

Ralph Earle

Contents

Mark 1

THE GOSPEL OF JESUS CHRIST

1:1. "The beginning of the gospel of Jesus Christ, the Son of God."

I. HISTORICAL SETTING. Mark was writing in Rome for Romans. He wished to present Jesus Christ as the Mighty Conqueror and at the same time as the Suffering Servant of Jehovah. So he omitted the genealogy of Jesus (found in Matthew and Luke), as well as the Infancy Narratives. Romans were interested in a man's deeds rather than his descent. Mark gives us little of the words of Jesus, but concentrates on His deeds and death.

II. EXPOSITORY MEANING. "Gospel" means "good news." It is not a proposition to be debated nor a doctrine to be defended. It is news to be proclaimed. "Of Jesus Christ" is objective genitive, not subjective. So the verse might be translated: "The beginning of the glad tidings about Jesus Christ, the Son of God." This first verse is probably the heading for the book of Mark, though some apply it only to the ministry of John the Baptist. "Jesus Christ" was accepted and used as a proper name by the time Mark wrote his Gospel. Originally it was "Jesus the Christ"; i e., the Messiah.

III. DOCTRINAL VALUE. Commonly *Mark* has been thought of as the historical Gospel, in greatest contrast to *John,* which is spiritual and theological. But increasingly it has been recognized in recent years that Mark's Gospel has a strong theological purpose. Mark, as well as John, is presenting Jesus as the Son of God. In line with this the tendency now is to accept the last phrase "son of God" as genuine, even though it is missing in some of the early Greek manuscripts. It is included in the Revised Standard Version (1952) and also

11

in the New English Bible (1961). It is defended by F. C. Grant in *The Interpreters Bible* (VII, 648).

IV. PRACTICAL AIM. Mark's primary purpose was to introduce men to Jesus Christ as Son of God and Savior. That is the first responsibility of every preacher. All men need a divine Savior.

V. HOMILETICAL FORM

Theme: "The Gospel of Jesus Christ."

Introduction: Long the world had waited. For dreary centuries sin had multiplied, with its consequent sorrow and suffering. Tear-stained eyes looked heavenward, sometimes it seemed in vain. But at last came the joyful proclamation: The Messiah, the Savior, has come!

A. *The Beginning of the Gospel*

Too often we have thought of the gospel as a creed, of the Bible as a textbook in systematic theology. But the Old Testament begins with history: the record of God's dealings with His chosen people. Also the New Testament begins with history: the account of Jesus' earthly life, death and resurrection, and the spread of the early church following Pentecost.

Likewise the gospel begins with history. It is preëminently "His Story." Mark describes this beginning of the gospel. He gives the story of the Conquering Christ and Suffering Servant who thereby became the Savior of mankind.

B. *The Gospel of Jesus Christ*

The noun *euangelion*, "gospel," is a favorite with Paul. He uses it sixty times in his epistles. In contrast it occurs only four times in Matthew's Gospel, eight times in Mark's, and not at all in Luke's or John's. But the verb *euangelizo*, "preach the gospel" is used by Luke ten times in his Gospel and fifteen times in *Acts*. The gospel is not a credal formula to be buried in a theological tome. It is glorious good news to be proclaimed. It is something to *evangelize*.

Apart from Jesus Christ there is no gospel. The so-called "social gospel" is a misnomer. Other religions began with a sage who promulgated a philosophy of life. Christianity began with a divine Savior. It is more than a creed or an ethic. Christianity is Christ. That is the gospel.

C. *The Son of God*

The deity of Jesus is the foundation of the gospel. Unless the Son of God had come to earth there would be no good news to proclaim. It is a striking fact that no other great world religion claims that its founder was divine. Moses, Confucius, Gautama, Laotze, Mohammed — all were mere men. Jesus Christ is the eternal Son of God. Therein lies the utter uniqueness of Christianity. It alone is a true religion of salvation, because it alone has an adequate Savior.

To deny the deity of Jesus Christ is to remove the foundation of our religion. No building can stand when its foundation is gone. Christianity without a divine Christ is no longer Christianity. And it is certainly no gospel.

Mark 1

THE HIGHEST CALLING

1:17. "And Jesus said unto them, Come ye after me, and I will make you to become fishers of men."

I. HISTORICAL SETTING. After His public inauguration (the Baptism) and His private initiation (the Temptation) — both of which took place in the southern part of Palestine — Jesus went north to Galilee. Here He made Capernaum the headquarters of His great Galilean ministry. Walking along the lakeshore nearby He saw four fishermen and called them to follow Him.

II. EXPOSITORY MEANING. "Come ye after me" means "Be my disciples." The rabbis of that day had disciples who "came after them." So these four fishermen were to go to school to Jesus, that He might teach them how to become fishers of men.

III. DOCTRINAL VALUE. Jesus is shown here as the Master of men. He said, "Come," and men forsook all to follow Him. He still speaks with divine authority, and people are still hearing and heeding His call.

IV. PRACTICAL AIM. To challenge each Christian to a life of consecrated stewardship. All of us should be fishers of men. Only by following Christ can we learn the secrets of successful soul-winning.

V. HOMILETICAL FORM
Theme: "The Highest Calling."
Introduction: The highest calling is that of being a soul-winner. This surpasses the most exalted political position, the supreme social recognition, even the special office of the ministry. There is no greater task on earth. And every Christian is called to this task.

A. *The Divine Call.* "Come ye after me."

Soul-winning is an art. It must be learned. Jesus is the master Teacher. He invites every Christian to follow Him, to sit at His feet, to learn of Him. It is at once our greatest privilege and responsibility.

This call is more than an invitation; it is a command. It is in the imperative mood. We have no choice. If we refuse to follow, we are disobeying the King. He calls; we must come.

"Come ye after me" means "Come, follow me." One cannot be a Christian and choose his own path. He must follow Christ.

For these four fishermen, following Christ meant forsaking everything for full time service. While this is not literally true for every Christian, there is a very real sense in which everyone who would follow the Master must forsake all. There has to be a surrender of our will to His will. That is the price of discipleship.

B. *The Divine Concern.* "I will make you."

Two things this verse suggests. The first is that unless we follow Jesus we cannot become fishers of men. There is no way by which He can make us such except by His own example. There are some things in life which cannot be learned from books; they come only by personal contact. No amount of inspiration and instruction from human sources can take the place of fellowship with the supreme Soul-winner. Only as we catch His passion for souls, His spirit of compassionate love, can we become soul-winners. There are no short cuts to success in this field.

The second thing this verse suggests is that if we really follow Jesus we *shall* become fishers of men. We have His promise for it. If we are not winning souls to Christ, it is because somehow we are failing to follow. Fellowship with the Master will "make" us fishers of men. The challenge is ours.

C. *The Divine Commission.* "fishers of men."

Detailed assignments differ. One is called to the foreign field, another to labor at home. Some are designated as pastors, others are commissioned as evangelists. But all are called to win souls. This is the commission that comes to every Christian.

Successful fishing demands skill. That is also true of fishing for men. It is the most exacting work; but at the same time the most rewarding. It requires patience as well as knowledge. Nothing in life is more important. Christ is still calling His disciples to be fishers of men.

On the phrase "fishers of men" the sainted Bishop Ryle wrote: "It is the oldest name by which the ministerial office is described in the New Testament. . . . The minister who does not strive to live up to this name, has mistaken his calling."

Mark 1

THE PRICE OF PRAYER

1:35. "And in the morning, rising up a great while before day, he went out, and departed into a solitary place, and there prayed."

I. HISTORICAL SETTING. Jesus had just had an extremely busy day in Capernaum. At the synagogue service in the morning He not only taught the assembled crowd but also cast an unclean spirit out of a man. When He and His disciples returned to Peter's house for dinner they found that apostle's mother-in-law bedridden with a sudden, severe fever. Again the Master met the need. As soon as the Sabbath ended at sunset, so that burdens could be carried, multitudes thronged to Him, bringing those who were diseased and demon-possessed. Mark records Peter's observation that "all the city was gathered together at the door." Yet this healing service after sunset was followed by a prayer meeting before sunrise.

II. EXPOSITORY MEANING. Mark uses three adverbs to make more graphic and vivid the fact that Jesus rose very early to pray. The first means "early" or "in the morning." The second means "at night." The third means "very" or "exceedingly." Put together, the phrase indicates: "very early in the morning, while it was still night."

Likewise three verbs (one a participle) describe Jesus' action. All three are in the aorist tense, suggesting prompt, immediate movement. Literally the Greek reads: "having risen he went out and went away." He lost no time in getting to prayer.

"Solitary" is literally "desert" or "wilderness." It means primarily an uninhabited area. The idea here is of a lonely spot.

III. DOCTRINAL VALUE. If Jesus Christ the eternal Son of God needed fellowship with His Father, how much more do

17

we! The true humanity of Jesus is reflected in His prayer life. Though filled with the Spirit, He needed to pray.

IV. PRACTICAL AIM. To show how utterly essential prayer is to every Christian. Also the price of prayer: self-discipline.

V. HOMILETICAL FORM

Theme: "The Price of Prayer."

Introduction: Prayer is the breath of the soul. Paul exhorted: "Pray without ceasing." When we stop breathing we die physically. When we stop praying we die spiritually. There is no substitute for prayer. To the one who walks close to God prayer is as natural as breathing.

A. *The Priority of Prayer.* "And in the morning, rising up a great while before day . . ."

Jesus had had a very strenuous day. Probably the healing service had lasted to a late hour. The Master had every excuse for lying abed the next morning. He needed sleep.

Instead He rose to pray. Not just any time, but "in the early morning, long before daylight" (Moffatt). With Jesus prayer had the highest priority.

Almost all those who have prayed successfully have found that the best time for prayer is early in the morning. There are many reasons for this. One needs to pray before his mind becomes cluttered with the many cares and duties of the day. Usually the mind is clearer and fresher at an early hour. Not least important is the quiet atmosphere that is essential to the highest communion with God. It is much more difficult to pray when one is caught up in the bustle and hustle of the distracting daylight hours. If we would have the dew of heaven on our hearts we must seek it early. In most lives prayer either comes first or not at all — except perhaps for a meaningless perfunctory performance at bedtime.

B. *The Place of Prayer.* "he went out, and departed into a solitary place."

Next in importance to the time of prayer is the place of prayer. Real "private devotions" require being alone with God. Ideally this means isolation. If that cannot be found, then extra insulation of heart and mind is needed.

In the modern home it is very difficult to find a lonely spot. One cannot hope to pray with radio or television blaring away. In some homes the only escape may be an early hour before others rise and turn on their radios. The earnest seeker after the sense of God's presence will be willing to pay the price of self-discipline to find the time and place for solitary communion with his Lord. Only those who do so at least in a measure really keep alive spiritually.

C. *The Practice of Prayer*. "and there prayed."

The only way to learn to pray is to pray. Reading books on prayer helps. But one can as quickly learn to ride a bicycle by reading about it as one can learn to pray thus. Perfection comes only through much practice.

It is possible to be in a solitary place at an early hour and yet fail to pray. The time and place are no guarantee against a wandering mind. Jesus really prayed. In this, as in all else, we are called to follow Him.

Mark 1

LOVE'S WILLINGNESS

1:40, 41. "If thou wilt, thou canst make me clean . . . I will; be thou clean."

I. HISTORICAL SETTING. After His sunrise prayer meeting Jesus refused to return to Capernaum for another great healing service, though the crowds clamored for Him. Instead He announced that He must go to other towns to preach (lit. "proclaim"). It was for this reason He came forth from heaven (v. 38). So He made a tour of Galilee, preaching (proclaiming) in the synagogues and casting out demons (v. 41). Somewhere along the way a leper came to Him, asking to be cleansed.

II. EXPOSITORY MEANNG. "Came" (v. 40) is in the Greek "comes." Mark loves to use the historical present to add greater vividness to his narratives, to give it the sense of immediacy. A "leper" has always been looked upon as unclean. Scholars seem agreed that the leprosy of Bible times was a skin disease, which differed from the leprosy of today. But it made its victim ceremonially unclean. Luke the physician says the man was "full of leprosy" (5:12).

"Moved with compassion" is an aorist passive participle. To bring out the force of the aorist tense it might be better to translate it "gripped with compassion." This was Jesus' immediate reaction to human sorrow and suffering. The word "compassion" is from Latin, "sympathy" from Greek — words with exactly the same connotation. To have real compassion or sympathy we must suffer with sorrowing hearts. Jesus did.

"I will" is not the future tense of the word "to be." The Greek verb *thelo* means "will" or "wish," expressing an activity of the will. So the two phrases (vv. 40, 41) could be translated: "If you are willing . . . I am willing." "Be thou clean" is the aorist passive imperative. It means: "Be thou (right here and now, immediately) cleansed."

III. DOCTRINAL VALUE. Again the deity of Jesus is emphasized. He was able to cure instantaneously the disease of leprosy. Also we have the beautiful, comforting truth that God's power is matched by God's love. When power is controlled by love, we are safe.

IV. PRACTICAL AIM. To show the willingness of Jesus to meet our every need, if we only ask Him. Whatever the nature of our need, He is always willing to help.

V. HOMILETICAL FORM
   Theme: "Love's Willingness."
   Introduction: The commonest concept of God is that He is the all-powerful, eternal Being who created the heavens and the earth. In this atomic age we are just beginning to realize something of the terrifyingly tremendous power that is built into the structure of our universe. The outstanding revelation of God in nature is that of His infinite power.
   Yet nowhere in Scripture do we read, "God is power." Instead we find twice "God is love" (I John 4:8, 16). God has power. He displays His power. But His essential nature is *love*. That is the lesson taught by our text.
   A. *The Man's Fear.* "If thou wilt."
   Fear is always an evidence of lack of faith. How awful to say to Divine Love Incarnate, "If you are willing"! Love is always willing. The leper had seen Jesus' *power* demonstrated. But somehow he had failed to see His love disclosed. How little he understood the real Christ. Sadder still, how little we understand Him! Too often we doubt divine love. The disconcerting truth is that the reason we doubt divine love is that we do not know well enough the divine Lover. When we become sufficiently acquainted with some saints down here, we never question their willingness to do the thing that is right and kind and generous. Why should we doubt Christ's willingness to help us at the place of our deepest need?
   B. *The Man's Faith.* "Thou canst make me clean."
   About the Master's power the man had no question. "You

are able," he said. His faith in Jesus' ability was unwavering. He had seen the mighty Conqueror meet disease and demons, and defeat them both. What he had failed to sense was that Christ's healing ministry was as much an evidence of divine love as it was of supernatural power. It was power impelled and propelled by love. Power controlled by selfish hate is the most dangerous thing in the world. Power controlled by unselfish love is the greatest blessing mankind can know. In this day of discovery of the secrets of fission and fusion God grant that our world may learn that lesson before it is too late!

We cannot doubt God's power. Let us not be guilty of doubting His love.

C. *The Master's Fulfilment.* "I will; be thou clean."

Only two words in the original: *thelo, kathāristheti.* It takes six in English to translate them: "I am willing; be thou cleansed."

The Master's response was immediate. No chiding the man's unbelief. No holding off his hesitating heart. No reproof for his half faith. What comfort in that word, "I am willing"! God forgive us for ever doubting divine love.

The Master fulfilled the man's faith. But He did more. He went the second mile and banished his lingering fear. Have you ever noticed how often in the Scriptures the Divine confronts the human with the words "Fear not"?

Not only did Jesus say to the anxious leper, "Be thou cleansed," but "as soon as he had spoken, immediately the leprosy departed from him, and he was cleansed" (v. 42). He spoke, and it was done. No word of God shall be without power. It was so in creation (Gen. 1:3, 6, 9, 11, 14, 20, 24, 26). It is still true today.

Mark 2

THE FAITH THAT WORKS

2:5. "When Jesus saw their faith, he saith unto the sick of the palsy, Son, thy sins be forgiven thee."

I. HISTORICAL SETTING. Jesus had spent some time evangelizing the villages of Galilee (1:39). As a Jewish rabbi He could go into any synagogue on the Sabbath Day and be invited to say whatever He wished. This custom of the day was of tremendous advantage to Christ, as it was later to Paul.

Finally Jesus returned to Capernaum, where He was making His headquarters. It was heard (*ekousthe*), "He is at home." Immediately the great crowds thronged once more to Him to be healed. But true to His mission, "He was speaking to them the Word" (so the Greek).

II. EXPOSITORY MEANING. "One sick of the palsy" (v. 3) is one word in the Greek — *paralyticon*. Today we would say, "a paralytic." The term "press" (v. 4) has no reference to newspapers! It is simply the common Greek word *ochlos*, which means "crowd." "Uncovered" is literally "unroofed." "Bed" is "pallet," probably nothing more than a heavy quilt. It acted as a stretcher.

"Thy sins be forgiven thee" (v. 5) is a bad mistranslation. It sounds like an expressed wish — "may they be." The Greek, however, is an assertion. Manuscripts differ between the present and perfect tenses, but both in the indicative. The former would be, "Your sins are forgiven"; the latter, "Your sins have been forgiven." "Reasoning" (v. 6) is the verb *"dialogizomai."* It might be translated "debating" or "arguing." The "scribes" were those who studied and taught the Scriptures.

III. DOCTRINAL VALUE. Jesus demonstrated His deity not only in healing the paralytic instantly but also in forgiving his sins. The latter is a divine prerogative, as the scribes recognized. Since they did not accept Jesus as the Son of God they charged Him with blasphemy for claiming the authority to forgive sins. But Jesus made good His claim by healing the man.

IV. PRACTICAL AIM. To show that Jesus can forgive sins and also heal the paralysis of sin, freeing one to walk in the newness of life. But someone must work to get the sinner to the Savior.

V. HOMILETICAL FORM
   Theme: "The Faith That Works."
   Introduction: James wrote in his Epistle (2:18) : "Show me your faith apart from your works, and I by my works will show you my faith" (literal translation).
   "When Jesus saw their faith." How did He see it? By their works! They demonstrated their faith by bringing the paralytic to Jesus. They believed the Master could heal him. Faith produced action. The faith that works (succeeds) is the faith that *works*.
   A. *The Setting.* "It was heard, 'He is at home.' "
   Probably the paralytic had heard about the momentous day in Capernaum when Jesus had healed so many. It began with delivering the demoniac in the synagogue from his affliction (1:21-28) . Then came the healing of Peter's mother-in-law (1:29-31) , followed by the great sunset healing service (1:32-34) . Somehow the poor paralytic was left out. Perhaps no friends appeared to take him to Jesus.
   We can imagine him saying to himself: "Well, I can wait until tomorrow. Then somebody will see that I reach the Healer." But the next day Jesus was gone! After an early prayer meeting he had gone elsewhere. The man's hopes were all dashed to the ground. Days of disappointment followed.
   Then suddenly came the exciting news, "He is home again!" Four sympathetic friends came hurrying to the paralytic's side. Each grabbed a corner of the padded quilt and quickly they carried the helpless man to the Master.
   B. *The Scene.* "When they could not come nigh ... they uncovered the roof."

Eagerly the stretcher-bearers hurried to the house where Jesus was teaching. But already a crowd had gathered. The place was packed so tightly with people that it was impossible to reach Jesus. At least so it seemed.

But, "all things are possible to him that believeth." The four friends showed their faith by their works. Up an outside stairway they carried the paralytic to the flat roof of the one-story home. Vigorously they attacked the job of digging away the hard-packed dirt and tearing a wide hole in the branches laid on cross beams. Before the startled gaze of those who sat below they lowered the paralytic on his pallet right down in front of Jesus. They had succeeded. They had done their part. The rest was up to the Master.

We might call these four friends Prayer, Persistence, Patience, and Perseverance. Doubtless they encouraged each other in overcoming the apparently impossible obstacles in the way of getting the paralytic to Jesus. Together they did the job. What would happen today if four people would dedicate themselves unitedly to the task of winning one helpless sinner to Jesus?

C. *The Sequel.* "Thy sins be forgiven thee. . . . Arise, and take up thy bed."

The man's first need was forgiveness. His paralysis was a symbol of his sin. It may possibly have been due to a serious guilt complex. In any case, Jesus first forgave the man his sins.

The scribes were horrified. This was blasphemy. But Jesus proved He had authority to forgive sins by healing the man instantly.

The four friends gained more than they had planned for the paralytic. He was healed both physically and spiritually. What a celebration they must have had at his house that day.

Thousands around us are paralyzed by sin. They seem helpless to do anything about it. But prayer, persistence, patience, and perseverance can bring them effectively to the Great Physician.

Mark 2

JESUS AND THE SABBATH

2:28. "The Son of man is Lord also of the sabbath."

I. HISTORICAL SETTING. In the section 2:1—3:6 we find Jesus five times in conflict with the Pharisees. The first controversy was over His claim to forgive sins (2:1-12), the second because of His eating with publicans and sinners (2:13-17), the third about the matter of fasting (2:18-22), the fourth because the disciples plucked some heads of wheat on the Sabbath Day (2:23-28), and the fifth because he healed the man with a withered hand on the Sabbath (3:1-6). The last two may well be treated together, since they are concerned with the same subject — keeping the Sabbath.

II. EXPOSITORY MEANING. "Corn fields" (2:23) should be "grainfields" in an American translation. In England wheat is still called "corn." But to the American reader "corn" connotes something very different. So "ears of corn" should be "heads of grain." We cannot be sure whether this was barley harvested earlier and eaten by the poor people or wheat (ripe in May).

The mention of Abiathar the high priest (2:26) poses a little problem. The Old Testament account indicates that his father Ahimelech was high priest when this incident took place (I Sam. 21:1-8). The best solution is that "in the days of Abiathar the high priest" should be interpreted as meaning during the lifetime of Abiathar, who became the outstanding high priest of that period. "Shewbread" is better translated "bread of the Presence" (Hebrew). The Greek literally says, "loaves of the presentation." Fresh loaves of bread were placed before the Lord in the Holy Place each Sabbath (Lev. 24:5-9).

"Watched" (3:2) is a strong word in the Greek. Literally it means, "They kept watching him closely." Wycliff (first

THE GOSPEL OF MARK

English version of the Bible) translated it, "Thei aspieden Hym." That conveys the correct meaning. The Pharisees (Luke 6:7) were spying on Jesus, hoping to catch Him in a trap.

"When he had looked round about" (3:5) is all one word in the Greek, an aorist participle. On the other hand "being grieved" is a present participle, indicating continuing action or state. The momentary flash of anger was accompanied and followed by an abiding feeling of deep grief (an intensive compound is used in the Greek). That is the test of Christian anger. Is it like that of Christ? "Hardness" is better rendered "hardening." It indicates moral insensibility. A good English equivalent is "callousness." The Greek word was used for the formation of a hard substance on the bones. The Pharisees had become brittle in their rigid legalism.

III. DOCTRINAL VALUE. The sovereignty of the Son of Man is strongly asserted in the text. The compassion of Christ for human need is also highlighted in this passage (2:23 — 3:6).

IV. PRACTICAL AIM. To seek to understand Jesus' attitude toward the Sabbath as giving us guidance for Sabbath observance.

V. HOMILETICAL FORM
   Theme: "Jesus and the Sabbath."
   Introduction: Five times in little more than a chapter (2:1— 3:6) we find Jesus in conflict with the Pharisees. The last two times it had to do with keeping the Sabbath. Our present text lies between these two incidents (2:23-27 and 3:1-6) and ties them together. It gives us Jesus' conclusion of the matter.

   A. *The Controversy.* "Behold, why do they on the sabbath day that which is not lawful?"
   It was not a question of stealing. The Mosiac law specifically permitted the plucking of grain to eat from another's field (Deut. 23:25). The complaint was that in picking the heads of wheat, rubbing out the kernels in their hands, and blowing away the chaff the disciples were harvesting, thresh-

ing, and winnowing grain. This is a typical example of the legalists' habit of making a mountain out of a mole hill. To use Christ's own figure, the Pharisees were straining out a gnat and swallowing a camel!

Jesus defended His disciples by calling attention to the example of their hero king. David in an emergency had taken the sacred bread of the Presence, which only the priests had a right to eat. Actually, the rabbis struggled over this problem and came to the conclusion that a man was justified in eating the sacred loaves rather than starving. God's laws were given that men might live, not die. With this Jesus agreed.

B. *The Conflict.* "They watched him . . . that they might accuse him."

Jesus came into still sharper conflict with the Pharisees over the question of healing on the sabbath day. Noting in the synagogue a man with his hand all dried up (perfect passive participle), they rightly judged that the compassionate Christ might wish to heal him. So they watched Him narrowly.

Healing on the Sabbath Day came under the category of forbidden labor. The rabbis drew fine distinctions in these matters. It was permitted on the Sabbath to give medication that might ease pain. But a poultice could not be placed on a boil, for it would draw the pus and this would be work! Actually, all that Jesus did was to speak to the man. When he obeyed the Master's command to stretch out his hand, it was healed.

The fury of the Pharisees is seen in that they, the religious leaders, went out and plotted with the politicians (Herodians) "how they might destroy him" (3:6). It was wrong for Jesus to heal a man on the Sabbath, but it was perfectly all right for them on that day to conspire to murder Him! What did Jesus say about wanting to take a speck out of your brother's eye when you have a log in your own?

C. *The Conclusion.* "The sabbath was made for man, and not man for the sabbath."

Legalists are interested in precepts. God is interested in persons. Legalists must protect their pet prejudices and private opinons, no matter what the cost in human personality. What matters if souls are offended and forever lost as long as we preserve intact our rigid regulations? Against this divine love reacted.

What is proper on the Sabbath or Lord's Day? God provided the Sabbath for man's welfare and highest good — physically, mentally, and spiritually. He who made us knows we need to rest and worship one day in seven. We flout His law to our own detriment.

On the Lord's Day we should do what we sincerely feel is pleasing to the Lord of the Sabbath. No honest heart will go far astray at this point. To please Christ is to be a Christian.

Mark 3

SUCCESS IN SUCCESSORS

3:14. "And he ordained twelve, that they should be with him, and that he might send them forth to preach."

I. HISTORICAL SETTING. Jesus had already called several disciples to follow Him. John 1:35-51 tells of the first five or six — six if John also brought his brother James. Mark has recorded the call to full time service that came to the four fishermen on the shores of Galilee (1:16-20), as well as to Levi (Matthew), the tax collector (2:14). But now something new takes place. Jesus selects twelve of His disciples to be apostles, His chosen messengers or missionaries. Appropriately this event took place on a mountain (v. 13).

II. EXPOSITORY MEANING. "Ordained" is better rendered "appointed." The former suggests an ecclesiastical ceremony which is probably not a correct picture. The Greek simply says "made." After "twelve" the two oldest manuscripts add: "whom also he named apostles." It would seem that twelve were chosen to represent the twelve tribes of Israel. "Canaanite" (v. 18) should be "Cananaean." Luke (6:15) interprets this as "the Zealot." This could mean simply that he was a very zealous individual, or it might indicate that he was a member of the party of Zealots who became prominent later.

III. DOCTRINAL VALUE. Again the sovereignty of Christ as Lord is emphasized. He summoned those He wished as His ambassadors, and they came to Him. The doctrine of divine healing is also suggested (v. 15).

IV. PRACTICAL AIM. To emphasize the importance of the ministry for the carrying on of the work of the kingdom.

V. HOMILETICAL FORM

Theme: "Success in Successors."

Introduction: A man's success is measured not so much by what he actually accomplishes in his own lifetime as by what provision he makes for posterity. Success cannot be properly gauged except in terms of the long view. Not a meteor-like flash across the sky but a permanent deposit of benefit for the future. Only in these terms can Jesus' brief span of life be accurately assessed. He did not travel widely, nor did He head a great movement. But He left twelve apostles who did, after Pentecost, project a movement that has circled the globe and reached every nation of the world. This is the true measure of Jesus' success.

A. *The Preparation.* "That they should be with him."

A call to preach implies a call to prepare. Before the apostles could go out to represent Jesus they must spend time with Him and learn His spirit.

In these days when most professions demand years of preparation, it is difficult to understand how so many can take lightly a call to the ministry. If one would be a lawyer he must go not only to college but to law school. Is winning souls to Christ less important business than winning cases in court? One who chooses to be a physician or surgeon must submit to a very expensive, sacrificial period of training in medical school. Is the cure of souls less important than the cure of bodies? One who takes seriously his call to the ministry will give careful attention to the matter of adequate preparation. For the Christian ministry the seminary is equivalent to what the schools of law and medicine are for those professions.

It should not be overlooked, however, that the most important preparation is a close and enriching fellowship with Christ himself. Nothing else will take the place of this.

B. *The Preaching.* "And that he might send them forth to preach."

What is preaching? To answer that question one would have to note the different Greek verbs translated "preach" in English. One is *euangelizo,* which means "announce good news." Our word "evangelize" is simply a transliteration of it. So in one sense preaching is evangelizing.

The word in our present text is *keryssein*. In the ancient armies of Greece and Rome the *keryx* was the herald who was sent out before the troops to make important proclamations. The word was also used for the herald of the emperor or king.

To the first readers of Mark's Gospel, then, *keryssein* would mean "proclaim." The twelve apostles were to be the heralds of Jesus, going out to proclaim His message. They were the official heralds of the King, making the proclamations that He gave them. They were not representing themselves, but Him. This is what every minister must remember. He is but a herald, speaking for another. It is not his own message he gives, but the King's. What a privilege and what a responsibility!

C. *The Power.* "And to have power to heal sicknesses, and to cast out demons."

Many today would discount the reality of demons. But missionaries working in darkened pagan lands testify to the fact of demon-possession in our time. Some have given reliable reports of casting out demons in the name of Jesus. Where this is needed we cannot doubt that divine authority is available for the situation.

Divine healing has been largely neglected by the church of Christ in modern times. But of late there has been a considerable revival of interest in this subject, even among the leading denominations in the British Isles and the United States. Clergymen in the Anglican Church and the Church of Scotland are reporting miraculous cases of divine healing.

There is another important aspect of which we have only recently become aware. Now that doctors are claiming that perhaps more than half the illness today is psychosomatic, it is being increasingly recognized that the physician needs the services of the minister in the healing of mankind. Here is a great field where the alert pastor can exercise a helpful ministry to the sick.

Mark 4

A QUARTET OF HUMAN HEARTS

4:9. "He that hath ears to hear, let him hear."

I. HISTORICAL SETTING. After Jesus' selection of the Twelve He was so beset with crowds that He and His disciples could not even find opportunity to eat. His relatives said, "He's gone crazy." The scribes had another verdict: "By the prince of demons he is casting out demons." Jesus warned them that they were blaspheming against the Holy Spirit, and thus committing the unpardonable sin.

Meanwhile His relatives had arrived to take Him home and see that He got something to eat. But Jesus met their demands by asserting that His real family consisted of those who "do the will of God" (3:35).

II. EXPOSITORY MEANING. "Sea" in the Gospels almost always means the Lake of Galilee. To those who lived on its shores and fished its waters it was "the sea." "Ship" should be "boat," as any Navy man would be quick to point out! Jesus sat in a small fishing boat, while the crowds gathered on the gentle slope along the shore. It was His favorite setting for teaching.

"Stony" (v. 5) is better rendered "rocky." It refers to thin soil on a ledge of rock, not to ground covered with small stones. "Thorns" may be translated "thistles." "Offended" (v. 17) means "caused to stumble" (*skandalizo*), or "fall away." "Lusts" should be translated "desires." The Greek word does not, of itself, carry any bad connotation.

III. DOCTRINAL VALUE. The emphasis of this parable is on the fact that the effectiveness of the message depends to a great extent on the attitude of the listener. All the seed is good. It is the difference in the kinds of soil that is the point of the parable. For this reason it is sometimes called The

Parable of the Soils. Also one notes the clear implication that some may receive the word and "endure for a time" (v. 17) or even grow up (v. 7) and yet finally be choked out. It is a solemn warning against *a false sense* of "eternal security" that breeds a fatal attitude of complacency in the Christian life.

IV. PRACTICAL AIM. There are two main lessons suggested in this parable. One is that many hearers of the Word receive no profit because of their carelessness (roadside) or callousness (rocky ground), while others grow, but finally allow *things* (thorns) to choke out the spiritual life. The second lesson is that even the good ground brings forth in varying degrees (v. 20). It is a challenge to bear abundant fruit (cf. John 15:2, 5).

V. HOMILETICAL FORM
   Theme: "A Quartet of Human Hearts."
   Introduction: Every human being catalogs himself. He chooses his own place in the classification of men. There is only one thing we cannot choose — to remain unclassified.

   One day a great crowd gathered on the shore of the Lake of Galilee. So dense was the throng that Jesus had to embark in a boat. In keeping with the Jewish custom of His day, He sat while He taught.

   Perhaps at that very moment a man strode across a field nearby, taking handfuls of seed from a bag slung over his shoulder and scattering it broadside with wide sweeps of his arm. Pointing to this familiar sight, Jesus said to the crowd on the hillside: "Listen! See! The sower went out to sow." As the crowd turned to look, He called attention to what was happening to the seed. Some fell along the path, some on rocky ground, some among thorns, and some on good soil. "This," said Jesus, "is what is happening to my teaching."

   A. *The Stolid Heart.* "Some fell by the way side."
   We need to guard against letting our hearts become beaten down into a hard road by the deadly monotony of daily living. We must fence our lives around with care and prayer lest they be trodden and trampled by the legitimate things of

life until we lose that receptivity to the Word of God and
sensitivity to the presence of the Spirit which alone can save
us. There is a great deal of traffic traveling over us every day.
Even church services, if we do not keep our hearts responsive,
can leave us increasingly insensitive to spiritual things.

B. *The Shallow Heart.* "Some fell on rocky ground."
Some people respond to the message with emotional enthusiasm. But they do not put down their roots in deep repentance, based on a godly sorrow for sin. They live thin lives
spiritually. These rootless Christians, with shallow souls,
under tribulation or persecution, fall away. Sometimes the
people who shed the most tears and show the most emotion
are the least stable. Moral endurance is more important than
emotional enthusiasm.

C. *The Strangled Heart.* "Some fell among thorns."
1. The cares of this world ("the anxieties of the age").
The cluttering cares of our daily doings can strangle the
spiritual life. This is the greatest threat to every Christian.
Too busy to pray, too busy to take time to be holy. Choked,
starved, dead!
2. The deceitfulness of riches.
Most Americans think that money spells happiness. But
riches are deceitful. We spend all our time and energy accumu-
lating them, and they sell us short. Very few wealthy people
are happy. Too many say: "When I have made some money,
I'll take time for God and the church." But they do not!
3. The desire for other things.
This is the greatest threat to the average Christian. We may
allow our lives to become over-crowded with *things* until they
choke out the consciousness of God. The radio, the telephone,
television, neon signs — all clamor constantly for our attention.
Luccock tells of a schoolboy reading a list of causes of death.
He recognized heart failure, cancer, etc., but the last he
could not pronounce. So he spelled it out. It was "miscella-
neous"! Too often that is the cause of spiritual death.

D. *The Steady Heart.* "Other fell on good ground."
Note the difference in fruitbearing: 30-60-100. Are we func-

tioning at our full capacity? Are we bearing "more fruit" and even "much fruit" (John 15) ?

Where do we find ourselves in this fourfold classification of human hearts?

Mark 4

LITTLE IS MUCH IF GOD IS IN IT

4:30, 31. "The kingdom of God . . . is like a grain of mustard seed."

I. HISTORICAL SETTING. The Gospel of Mark has only four parables, as against fifteen in Matthew and nineteen in Luke. (John has none.) Three of these parables are found in the fourth chapter, and they are all related to sowing seed. After the parable of the sower (4:1-20) comes that of the seed growing secretly (4:26-29). "Of herself" (v. 28) is *automate,* from which we get "automatic." The lesson of this parable is that we must trust the Word of God, when faithfully sown, to take root and grow automatically. We are not to dig up the seed to see if it actually is growing, but trust God's promise: "So shall my word be that goeth forth out of my mouth: it shall not return unto me void, but it shall accomplish that which I please, and it shall prosper in the thing whereto I sent it" (Isa. 55:11). It is possible for Christian workers to get too impatient and not give the seed time to grow.

II. EXPOSITORY MEANING. The third parable is that of the mustard seed, which we are now studying. "With what comparison shall we compare it?" is literally "With what shall we place it in a parable?" The word parable is from the Greek *parabole,* used here. It comes from *para,* "beside," and *ballo,* "throw." So it means something thrown beside another for the purpose of comparison. "Fowls" is better rendered "birds." Today we use the term "fowl" mainly for a domesticated creature with wings, although there is a holdover of the earlier usage in such names as waterfowl.

III. DOCTRINAL VALUE. God is the author of all life. Scientists can analyze the chemical properties of a seed and assemble a synthetic one. But it is doubtful if they will ever

37

be able to put into that artificial seed the germ of life that
will make it grow. God is the author of all life. Man can make
marvelous things that would seem sheer miracles only a few
years ago. Men can make machines. But only God can make
a man. That is what our proud age needs humbly to recognize.

IV. PRACTICAL AIM. We need to recognize the importance
of sowing the seed and then trusting God for the harvest from
our sowing. We also need to believe that small beginnings
can produce great results.

V. HOMILETICAL FORM
    Theme: "Little Is Much if God Is in It."
    Introduction: This old proverb finds striking illustration in
the parable of the mustard seed. The least of all seeds becomes
the greatest of all plants. This has been demonstrated thousands of times in the history of the Christian church. We need
to believe that it can still be true in our day and in our
particular situation.

    A. *Lost in the Soil.* "When it is sown in the earth."
    Seed cannot grow unless it is sown. It can be left indefinitely
in a dry atmosphere without germinating. Only when it is
placed in the ground does it come to life.

    So it is with the Word of God. The Bible may lie on the
living room table for years without having any effect on the
home. But let someone begin to read it with an open mind
and honest heart, and something is bound to happen. This has
taken place many times both in so-called Christian homes
and in pagan lands. Cases are on record of nationals, who had
never seen a white missionary, purchasing a Bible from a
native colporteur, reading it, and becoming wonderfully saved
from sin without ever hearing a Christian sermon.

    Jesus said: "Except a corn of wheat fall into the ground and
die, it abideth alone: but if it die, it bringeth forth much
fruit" (John 12:24). His own death on the cross is the greatest illustration of this truth. He did not win many faithful
followers during His lifetime. But His crucifixion has produced a crop of millions of redeemed souls.

    In a very real sense this must be true of us as Christian
workers. We must die to self that we may be fully alive to

God. We must lose ourselves in sacrificial service if we would
find ourselves in the saving of souls.

B. *Least of the Seeds.* "Less than all the seeds."

The mustard seed is not the smallest seed known to bota-
nists. But it was the smallest in common use among the Jews.
Already it had become proverbial for something tiny (cf.
Matt. 17:20).

The beginnings of the Christian church seemed hopelessly
small. Twelve apostles; one hundred twenty Spirit-filled
disciples — how could these conquer the world? But within
thirty years the gospel of Jesus Christ had swept around the
Mediterranean from Jerusalem to Rome. Within a century
it compassed the Roman Empire.

Other small beginnings could be cited: the Protestant
Reformation in the town of Wittenburg, the Evangelical
Revival in the Aldersgate Street experience of John Wesley,
the great foreign missionary movement in the courage and
faith of William Carey, the American missionary enterprise in
the famous haystack prayer meeting. These are only a few
among many. We need to trust God that our tiny mustard seed
of faith will grow into a great plant of fulfilment.

C. *Largest of the Herbs.* "Greater than all herbs."

Mustard plants have been known to grow to a height of
twelve feet or more — all from a little seed. What a parable
of the Christian Church! From a despised crowd of "heretics"
it has become the greatest enterprise on earth, invading every
continent and country for Christ. The kingdom of God has
today become the greatest single force on earth, even though
seriously threatened by Communism and paganism. Its influence reaches into every nation of the world. Who can recount
its conquests?

The individual experience of every Christian also demon-
strates this truth in miniature. From the small beginnings of
repentance and faith the seed of God's Word grows into a
large, beautiful plant of Christian character.

Mark 4

WITH THE MASTER ON BOARD

4:39. "And he arose, and rebuked the wind, and said unto the sea, Peace, be still. And the wind ceased, and there was a great calm."

I. HISTORICAL SETTING. After recounting three parables of Jesus on seed sowing, Mark notes that He spoke "many such parables" to the people (v. 33). At this time He apparently used the parabolic method exclusively with the crowds, reserving for the disciples the explanation of meanings (v. 34).

That evening Jesus decided to get away from the crowds and cross to the east side of the Lake of Galilee (v. 35). There He and His disciples could hope to find the solitude they needed after the busy days near Capernaum. So they entered a boat (not "ship"!), probably Peter's fishing craft, and set out for the other side. This is the first of five withdrawals of Jesus described by Mark.

II. EXPOSITORY MEANING. "Storm" (v. 37) is a strong term in the original. It means "hurricane." The verb "beat" is in the imperfect tense. The waves "were crashing" into the boat. "Full" is obviously a mistranslation. If the boat were actually full, it would have sunk! No boat can be full of water and still stay on the surface. The Greek here clearly says "already filling," which is quite another matter. "Hinder part" (v. 38) is one word, as our "stern." The "pillow" was probably the cushion on the oarsman's seat. Small boats were steered by an oar, as can still be seen on the Nile River. "Master" is literally "teacher." "Arose" (v. 39) might be translated "having been fully wakened." It is a compound of the simple verb "awake" in verse 38. "Peace" is literally "Be silent!" The command "be still" is a strong word. The full meaning is "Be muzzled and stay muzzled" (perfect tense). It would be equivalent to our saying "Shut your mouth and keep it shut!" Perhaps the simplest English translation is, "Keep still!"

III. DOCTRINAL VALUE. All of these miracles of Jesus were demonstrations of His deity. He who created the elements can control them.

The tendency today is to give more credence to Jesus' healing miracles, explaining them often in terms of psychotherapy. That is, it is said that Christ possessed a superior understanding of the psychosomatic nature of most illnesses and cured them by powerful suggestion. At the same time, His nature miracles are called into question. The present one, for instance, is explained as a quieting of the disciples' fears by His firm faith in the care of a loving heavenly Father.

The crux of the problem of miracles is the acceptance of the deity of Jesus and the fact of the Incarnation. Granted that He was the eternal Son of God, no serious problem exists. The Incarnation was the great miracle which makes all lesser miracles not only possible but natural.

IV. PRACTICAL AIM. The Master who stilled the storm on the Lake of Galilee can quiet the tempest in the human heart. Conversely, if we have experienced this stilling of the storm within, we have no difficulty in believing that Jesus could calm the winds and waves of the lake.

V. HOMILETICAL FORM
Theme: "With the Master on Board."

Introduction: Jesus was weary, almost worn out, with his much work on the west side of the Lake of Galilee. Day after day, week after week, the throngs had crowded around Him. He had been constantly busy with teaching, preaching, and healing.

So one day He said to His disciples: "Let us go to the other side of the lake." On the east side it was quiet, relatively uninhabited. There amid the silent hills they could find rest, relaxation, refreshment of body and mind.

A. *The Storm.* "There arose a great storm."

As the little fishing boat pulled out from the western shore Jesus lay down on the steerman's cushion in the stern. There He was soon sound asleep. The measure of His weariness is shown by the fact that He did not even waken when the wind began to blow and the water became rough.

At first it was just a gentle breeze. Then suddenly the storm struck. Wind off the highland plateau on the east side of the lake rushed down the canyons which acted as funnels, hitting the surface of the water with terrifying fury. Quickly the fishermen furled their sail and tied it tightly to the mast. But the waves were breaking over the bow and the boat was filling fast. Finally, afraid for their lives, these hardy sailors rushed back to Jesus, shook Him awake and cried: "Teacher, is it not a care to you that we are perishing!"

B. *The Sternness.* "And he arose, and rebuked the wind, and said unto the sea, Peace, be still."

Jesus' reaction was immediate and mighty. The Master of earth and sea and sky stood to His feet. Looking into the teeth of the howling hurricane He uttered just two words: "Silence! Keep still!"

From anyone else's lips that would have been sheer insanity. But when God — Father, Son, or Holy Spirit — speaks, the word has divine authority and infinite power. This was not an empty gesture. It was the act of the Creator who was conscious of control of His own creation.

The sternness with which Jesus "rebuked" the wind is noted. It was as if He said: "What do you mean by terrifying my disciples while I am resting? Hush up! Put the muzzle on and keep it on! Not another sound out of you!"

What a comforting thought! When Jesus is on board our frail bark we never need to fear. He is the Commander who can take us safely across life's sea to our eternal harbor home.

C. *The Stillness.* "And the wind ceased, and there was a great calm."

The winds ceased their raging, and the waves stopped their rolling. As they sank to restful slumber, a dead calm ensued. To one who has had the storm of sin stilled in his soul there is no problem in believing that Jesus could quiet the tempest on the lake. The former is a greater miracle than the latter.

No matter how furious the storms of life that may beset us, if we turn to the Master we can always hear His quieting command, "Peace, be still."

Mark 5
PUBLIC ENEMY NO. 1

5:3-5. "had his dwelling among the tombs ... neither could any man tame him ... crying, and cutting himself with stones."

I. HISTORICAL SETTING. When Jesus and His disciples arrived on the east side of the lake they expected to find a quiet place of rest. Instead they found a raging maniacal demoniac. Jesus had to perform another miracle, stilling the storm in this deranged man's mind. But He was equal to the occasion.

II. EXPOSITORY MEANING. There is a bit of problem about the variant readings (v. 1) : Gadarenes, Gerasenes, and Gergesenes. The first would refer to the largest city nearby, Gadara, which was half a dozen miles from the southern tip of the lake. Gerasa and Gergesa may both stand for the village of Khersa, the ruins of which have been discovered on the eastern shore of Galilee. "Crying" (v. 5) does not mean weeping but "crying out" or screaming. "Devils" (v. 12) should be "demons." The Greek always makes a clear distinction between one devil (*diabolos*, always singular) and many demons (*daimonia*). The difference should be maintained in English.

III. DOCTRINAL VALUE. The main problem that confronts us here is the doctrine of demonology. The tendency today is to dismiss the idea as merely a superstitious way the ancients had of explaining the phenomena of insanity. It is true that demon-possession and insanity are often linked together in the Gospels. Most demoniacs were maniacs. But this solution is too simple to be true. Many modern scholars are feeling that the happenings in our world today can be explained only on the basis of unseen forces of evil at work in human beings. The Bible calls them demons, and the evidence of their existence is abundant and obvious.

44

IV. PRACTICAL AIM. No matter how sad and seemingly hopeless a man's condition, divine power can set him completely free from the awful bondage of sin. What men need is to meet Jesus. He can cure every case.

V. HOMILETICAL FORM
   Theme: "Public Enemy No. 1."
Introduction: Jesus and His disciples beached their boat on the eastern shore and stepped out on solid ground. Now they would enjoy the quiet rest they sought.

But suddenly the silence of the solitude was shattered by piercing shrieks. Looking up the hill they saw an awful apparition — half man, half monster. Naked, disheveled, dirty, he came rushing down upon them, while his horrible screams rent the air.

The disciples turned to run to the boat and push out from the shore for safety. But seeing the same stern look on Jesus' face with which He had faced the raging storm on the lake a short time before, they paused and watched. When the demoniac's eyes met the Master's, he stopped, and then fell trembling on his face. Then it was that Jesus commanded the unclean spirit to come out of him.

In the description of the Gadarene demoniac we have a vivid picture of sin, which is public enemy number 1. We might note some of the lines of that portrait.

A. *Sin is Suicide.* "Had his dwelling among the tombs."
This man was literally living in the place of death, and liking it. He felt more at home there.

Everyone who is not believing in Jesus Christ as his Savior is dwelling in the place of death (John 3:36). The person who keeps on sinning is slowly but surely committing spiritual suicide. The Bible declares: "The wages of sin is death" (Rom. 6:23). Every time a man deliberately disobeys God he is driving another nail into the coffin of his eternal doom.

B. *Sin is Insanity.* "Neither could any man tame him."
When the maniac had his quieter moments the men of the nearby village would seize him, fasten his hands with chains behind his back, then quickly tie ropes tightly around his

ankles. But soon the demoniac forces within would assert themselves. He would tear the chains apart, kick the fetters off his feet, and rush at his captors with murderous fury.

Sin is *unbindable*. You can bind it down in one place, and it will break forth in another. You can conquer one habit, and another will get the best of you. You cannot conquer sin! Only Christ can.

Also sin is *untamable*. It is a wild monster which no man can tame. Only God can solve the problem of sin. It is claimed that a bear is the most treacherous creature in the north woods. You cannot trust it. You may think you have it tamed, and it will turn on you. Sin is like that.

C. *Sin is Self-destruction.* "And always, night and day, he was in the mountains, and in the tombs, crying out, and cutting himself with stones."

Wandering among the tombs, the demoniac would pick up the sharp stones of the hillside and slash himself, until the blood was running down his naked body and caking with the filth and perspiration there.

What a sordid sight! But no worse than that of the sinner who slashes his soul. We can see the effects outwardly of such sins of the flesh as drunkenness. The sunken cheeks, hollow eyes, red nose, trembling fingers, staggering step, weakened will — all these tell their sad tale of self-destruction. But the sins of the flesh are no less damaging. Anger, hate, jealousy, pride — they, too, take their toll. These destroy the finer fiber of the soul just as truly as the sins of the flesh destroy the body. All sin is self-destruction.

Mark 5

FAITH RECEIVING

5:34. "thy faith hath made thee whole."

I. HISTORICAL SETTING. After he had been healed the Gadarene demoniac wanted to follow Jesus. This was a natural expression of his gratitude. But instead the Master commanded him to go home and tell his friends what had happened to him. The man gladly obeyed, and so the news of Jesus' power spread throughout the Decapolis. Thus the way was prepared for Jesus' later ministry there (7:31).

By boat Jesus and His disciples returned to the west side of the lake. There a synagogue ruler named Jairus asked Him to hurry to the bedside of his dying daughter. On the way there occurred the incident of our present study.

II. EXPOSITORY MEANING. "Issue" (v. 25) means "flowing." "Press" (v. 27) is "crowd." The word for "garment" is *himation,* the outer garment or robe. "Whole" (v. 28) is literally "saved." The verb *sozo* is used of physical healing in the Gospels and spiritual salvation in the Epistles. In Acts it is used both ways. "Virtue" (v. 30) is "power" (*dynamis*). It is interesting to note that Jesus was conscious of power having gone out of Him in response to the woman's faith. "Thronging thee" (v. 31) is literally "pressing you together." In verse 34 the first "whole" is "saved" (*sozo*). But the second is an entirely different word, *hygies,* from which comes "hygiene." In the Pastoral Epistles this word is translated "sound" (e.g., sound doctrine).

III. DOCTRINAL VALUE. The deity and humanity of Jesus are beautifully blended here. The Master was conscious that divine energy had gone from Him to heal the woman. Yet He asked, "Who touched my clothes?" and kept looking around to see who it was. When she had confessed, He as-

47

sured her that her faith had resulted in her healing, and He bade her go in peace.

IV. PRACTICAL AIM. To show that if we come to Jesus in simple, child-like faith we know He will meet our need. Also, to suggest the importance of testifying to what Christ has done for us.

V. HOMILETICAL FORM

Theme: "Faith Receiving."

Introduction: We have here a unique incident in the Gospels: two miracles dovetailed in together. Jesus starts for the house of Jairus to heal the latter's daughter. On the way the woman touches Him, receives healing, and testifies to it. Then Jesus continues on to the synagogue ruler's house and raises his daughter. We have a suggestion, in symbol, of two necessary phases of soul-winning. Some sinners will come to the church and be saved. But others will have to be reached in their homes, or not at all. Again, some sinners come to Jesus for help, while others seem helpless to make a move toward Him. As in the case of Jairus' daughter, they must have the Master brought to them.

A. *The Woman's Affliction.* "An issue of blood twelve years."

The life is in the blood. When one's blood is constantly flowing, life and strength are ebbing away. This had gone on in the woman's case for twelve long years.

The situation was aggravated by the fact that her condition was apparently hopeless. With the uninhibited frankness of a layman, Mark records the sad story: She "had suffered many things of many physicians, and had spent all that she had, and was nothing bettered, but rather grew worse" (v. 26). Luke the physician describes it in a way that protected his profession. He admits she "had spent all her living upon physicians," but adds "neither could be healed of any" (8:43). In other words, hers was an incurable case.

Mark's statement that she had "suffered many things from many physicians" finds ample illustration in what we know about Jewish doctors of that day. The rabbis had a saying: "The best physician is worthy of Gehenna." It is still the

custom in some places of the East to call in as many physicians as possible, with sad results for the patient. The methods
used were often both cruel and useless. For a further description of Jewish medicine in that day see Adam Clarke (V, 304)
or Vincent's *Word Studies* (I, 189). Mark has not expressed
the matter one bit too strongly. Her medical treatment had
caused untold suffering and not benefited her at all. She was
discouraged, with all hope gone.

B. *The Woman's Faith.* "If I may touch but his clothes, I
shall be whole."

In her helpless, hopeless condition the woman heard about
the healing miracles of Jesus ("heard of Jesus" is in the best
Greek text "heard the things concerning Jesus"). Hope sprang
up within her. Perhaps He can heal me too! So she came as
fast as her weakened condition would permit. Her loss of
blood had naturally made her timid and easily embarrassed
in public. So she slipped through the crowd as unobtrusively
as possible, came behind Jesus, and reached out to touch His
garment.

C. *The Woman's Fortune.* "She was healed."

It was just that quick! "Straightway" the flow of blood was
stopped. She knew she was well. With what a thrill of joy
she must have turned to leave. She would escape as unnoticed
as she had come.

But Jesus wanted to confer upon her an added blessing, one
that could only come as she met Him face to face and thanked
Him. No blessing is quite complete without the response of
gratitude. It was not heartless cruelty that caused Jesus to
make the woman identify herself and testify publicly. It was
His love that wanted to lift her to a higher level. No longer
need she sneak around out of sight, ashamed to be seen in
public. Hers was to be a new life, and He wished her to begin
it right then and there. It was worth it all to hear from His
own lips, "Go in peace." Her heart, as well as her body, was
healed that day.

Mark 5

FAITH THAT KNOWS NO FAILURE

5:36. "Be not afraid, only believe."

I. HISTORICAL SETTING. It is altogether possible that Jairus' daughter had become ill while Jesus was across the lake in the country of the Gadarenes. If so, we may well imagine the eager concern with which the distressed father awaited the return of the great Healer. As soon as he heard that Jesus had arrived on the west side of the lake he hurried out to the shore to meet Him. By now the crowds had gathered (v. 21). But Jairus pushed his way forward to the Teacher and begged Him to come immediately to his home.

II. EXPOSITORY MEANING. The "other side" (v. 21) means Capernaum (Matt. 9:1). Jesus was back home again in "his own city." A ruler of the synagogue (v. 22) was the president, who presided but did not teach or preach. This was done by the rabbis. The synagogue president, as today, was a layman. "Lieth at the point of death" (v. 23) might more literally be translated: "is at her last gasp." "Heard" (v. 36) is in the best Greek text "ignored" (*parakousas* instead of *akousas*). The latter is the common meaning of the compound (cf. ASV). "Be not afraid" (v. 36) is literally "stop being afraid" (present imperative). "Only believe" is "just keep on believing" (also present imperative). "Tumult" (v. 38) means "uproar." "Make ye this ado" (v. 39) is the same root as "tumult" (v. 38). So we might better render it "make an uproar." That will show the connection of the two words in the Greek. "Talitha cumi" (v. 41) is Aramaic, the language of the common people of Palestine in that day. "Straitly" (v. 43) is simply "much."

III. DOCTRINAL VALUE. As in the healing of the woman with a hemorrhage, dovetailed in between the two sections of the raising of Jairus' daughter, we observe both Jesus' love and His power in action. His acts of power were always expressions of His nature of love. It is still so today. There is the further suggestion that God always honors faith.

IV. PRACTICAL AIM. To learn that love never lets us down; that though our faith may be tested, it is for our highest good; that when things seem to be getting worse, God can get greater glory in the victory that finally comes.

V. HOMILETICAL FORM
Theme: "Faith That Knows No Failure."
Introduction: The position of Jairus as president of the synagogue made him one of the most respected members of the community. In view of the attitude of the Jewish leaders toward Jesus, it may not have been an easy thing for him to seek out the help of the prophet from Nazareth. But desperation knows no barriers, and love has no limits. So the ruler came and fell at Jesus' feet in abject humility and earnest supplication. He "besought him greatly" (v. 23) to come and heal his daughter.

A. *Faith Trying.* "Come . . . that she may be healed."
Real faith always produces action. Without works, says James, faith is dead. Jairus showed his faith in Jesus' healing power by coming to Him in his hour of greatest need. The rabbis of his own synagogue could give no help, but he believed that Jesus could.

His faith is shown not only by his action but also by his words. He asked Jesus to come and lay His hands on the little girl "in order that she may be saved and live" (literal translation). He would not have asked had he not believed.

B. *Faith Tried.* "Be not afraid, only believe."
As Jesus and the anxious father hurried toward the house where the little girl lay dying, the people thronged around them and impeded their progress. We can imagine Jairus already getting impatient at being slowed down.

But the worst was yet to come. A woman touched Jesus' clothes and was healed. The Master stopped, turned around, and asked who touched Him. Why was that necessary? Not only that, but He kept on looking around, seeking to discover who had touched Him. Finally the woman came forward and gave a full testimony to what had happened. Jesus gently assured her that her faith had made her whole, and bade her go in peace.

Meanwhile some messengers from Jairus' house hurried up to him and said — so Jesus could hear! —"Your daughter has died; why bother him? He doesn't care! If he had, he would not have been fooling around talking to this woman. If he cared anything about your daughter, he would have come straight to the house without delay. It's too late now!"

Imagine how Jairus felt. Could he have any more faith in Jesus now? But the Master, ignoring the slurring tones of the messengers' voices, quietly commanded: "Stop being afraid; keep on believing." It was Jairus' darkest hour. But faith met the test. He did not angrily turn away from Jesus, but led Him to the house.

C. *Faith Triumphant.* "The damsel arose."

When Jesus arrived at the home, He found a confused uproar. The hired professional mourners were already making a loud noise weeping and wailing — the louder the better they were paid. It was no kind of an atmosphere for the exercise of faith.

So Jesus put them all out. Taking the father and mother and His inner circle of three disciples, He entered the room where the girl lay dead. Taking her by the hand He spoke in the familiar Aramaic perhaps the very words with which the mother was in the habit of calling her daughter in the morning. The girl opened her eyes, got up, and walked. Faith had not failed! What a joyous victory celebration it was for Jairus. But the parents must feed the restored life. Divine miracles do not rule out human responsibility.

Mark 6

A KING'S UNEASY CONSCIENCE

6:16. "It is John, whom I beheaded."

I. HISTORICAL SETTING. After Jesus had raised Jairus' daughter he left Capernaum and came into "his own country" — Nazareth. Here He taught in the synagogue on the Sabbath. His fellow townsmen were astonished at His teaching and miracle-working power, but they stumbled ("offended," *skandalizo*, v. 3) over the fact that He was known to them as the village "carpenter." The sad thing was that Jesus was hindered from blessing them with His healing ministry, because of their unbelief.

The Master then sent out His twelve apostles on a preaching mission throughout Galilee. Their proclamation (*kerysso*, v. 12) was that men should "repent." Herod heard of Jesus' miraculous ministry, and immediately his conscience began to trouble him.

II. EXPOSITORY MEANING. Herod is called "king" (v. 14). Actually he was only a tetrarch, ruler of Galilee and Perea. His father, Herod the Great, had been king of all Palestine. But at his death the kingdom was divided among his sons. However, Herod Antipas was popularly called "king." In fact, the Romans — and Mark was writing in Rome — tended to call all Eastern rulers kings. Matthew and Luke give him his more correct title of tetrarch. Herod Antipas ruled from 4 B. C. to A. D. 39.

While on a visit to Rome, Antipas stayed in the home of his brother Philip. There he fell in love with his brother's wife, Herodias (v. 17). She forsook her husband and accompanied Antipas to Galilee. But John the Baptist cried out against this ungodly situation. The result was that Herodias "had a quarrel against him" (v. 19) . The Greek literally says, "had it in for him."

"Observed" (v. 20) is more accurately translated "was keeping him safe" — from Herodias' attempts to asassinate him? For "did many things" the oldest manuscripts have "was much perplexed." The "charger" (v. 25) was not a horse, but a "platter." The meaning of "by and by" is just the opposite today from its use here (KJV) . The Greek word means "immediately." "Sat" (v. 26) is "reclined." The custom in those days was to recline on cushioned couches while eating and drinking. "Executioner" (v. 27) means one of Herod's body guard. "His disciples" would be the followers of John the Baptist (cf. John 1:35) .

III. DOCTRINAL VALUE. Two doctrines are illustrated in this lesson: the awful depravity of the human heart, and the conscience as monitor of the soul.

IV. PRACTICAL AIM. To show that one cannot escape the voice of conscience speaking within. Also that God may allow seeming tragedy to take place, but will cause it all to work out for the progress of His kingdom.

V. HOMILETICAL FORM

Theme: "A King's Uneasy Conscience."

Introduction: Herod had killed the preacher. But he found he still had a powerful preacher inside, whose voice he could not silence. Conscience rose up to haunt him with memories from the past. He found that while he could get rid of John he could not escape himself. He had to live with himself as the bloody murderer who had killed a righteous man.

A. *Cutting Conscience.* "It is John, whom I beheaded."

When Herod Antipas heard about the miracles Jesus was performing, his conscience took a sudden twist, cutting him to the quick. "It is John," he cried out, "John whom I beheaded."

Superstitious as he was, Antipas did not doubt that John the Baptist had "risen from the dead." No one else could be doing the things that Jesus was doing. It must be John.

Herod was a weak, vacillating character. That is indicated

by the correct reading of verse 20. He was "perplexed," upset, at his wit's end. But like Jezebel with her Ahab, so Herodias cast her evil spell over Herod and led him on to his doom.

Criminals pay an awful price for their crime. The worst penalty is not the fine or prison sentence, but the gnawing accusation of conscience. What a wonderful blessing to live with a conscience "void of offense"!

B. *Crafty Conniving.* "Herodias had it in for him."

There is nothing in the world more cruel than a crafty woman. One is reminded of Madame Defarge in *The Tale of Two Cities,* knitting away while she plotted against scores of men and saw them sent to the guillotine.

They say that a woman never forgets. Herodias never forgave John the Baptist for implying that she was an adulteress. She made up her mind to get him. And she did!

She found "a convenient day" (v. 21) when her husband's birthday arrived. Doubtless she worked hard to make as elaborate preparations as possible. She wanted her revenge on the prophet to be as public as she could make it.

We may be sure that she saw to it that the king drank heavily. It was important that he be drunk enough to fall in with her plans and make a rash promise.

C. *Cruel Compliance.* "The daughter ... danced."

The most important piece of strategy that Herodias planned was this: when Herod and his men were so sodden with drink that their passions could be most completely roused, Herodias' daughter Salome would come in and put on a very sensuous dance in front of the men. Of course it was unheard of that a princess should perform like a common slave girl. But so desperate was Herodias that she was willing to degrade and disgrace her own daughter publicly in order to win her purpose.

The sad thing is that Salome complied. How she must have winced as she took the bloody head on the platter to her mother. But nothing was too low to stoop to if only John could be killed. So the degenerate daughter carried the bloody gift to the murderous mother, and human hate was satiated with the sacrifice.

Mark 6

THE REWARD OF OBEDIENCE

6:37. "Give ye them to eat."

I. HISTORICAL SETTING. The twelve whom Jesus had sent forth (v. 7) now returned (v. 30). They reported the miracles they had wrought (cf. v. 13) and the teaching they had given.

The Master realized that His men needed a vacation after their strenuous preaching mission. There was no opportunity for this on the western shore. In fact, the crowds thronged them so constantly that they could not even find leisure to eat (v. 31). So Jesus said to them: "Come ye yourselves apart into a desert place, and rest awhile." The little group embarked in a boat and headed across the lake to find a quiet spot. But the people recognized Jesus, as the boat pulled out, and hurried on foot around the north end of the lake, reaching the landing place before the disciples arrived.

II. EXPOSITORY MEANING. "Desert place" (v. 35) means deserted place, or lonely spot, not a sandy waste. "Pennyworth" (v. 37) is *denarii*. A denarius was worth about twenty cents, but represented a day's wages. "Sit down" (v. 39) is "recline." The Greek "by companies" is *"symposia, symposia,"* from which our word "symposium" comes. The Greek for "in ranks" is *"prasiai, prasiai."* It means "garden beds" and suggests the orderly arrangement of the people. But it also probably reflects Peter's reaction when he saw the people reclining on the green grass in groups, with their bright Oriental garments of red and yellow. They looked to him like flower beds. Mark has retained the vivid picture for us. "Filled" (v. 42) is literally "grassed." It was used of animals being satisfied after grazing, filled with grass. The twelve "baskets" (v. 43) were probably the lunch baskets of the twelve apostles.

"Men" (v. 44) is not the generic term, but means "males." Matthew adds: "besides women and children."

III. DOCTRINAL VALUE. The deity of Jesus is underscored again. The matter of nature miracles comes in once more. Also the compassion of Christ receives forcible emphasis.

IV. PRACTICAL AIM. To show that when God guides He provides, that when He commands us to do anything He will furnish the enablement. Our part is to obey, His to furnish the power.

V. HOMILETICAL FORM

Theme: "The Reward of Obedience."

Introduction: Sometimes God asks us to do the seemingly impossible. Our only responsibility is to obey. On His part He gives divine enablement for the assigned task.

Jesus asked His disciples to do something utterly impossible — feed a crowd of thousands with a single person's little lunch. But they did it! That is the thrilling fact which holds an important lesson for us today.

A. *The Master's Compassion.* "And Jesus, when he came out, saw much people, and was moved with compassion toward them."

It had been planned as a quiet vacation. Jesus and His disciples had left the western shore to get away from the throngs. But the crowd had hurried around the north end of the lake and was waiting for Him when He landed.

One might expect Jesus to react with resentment at the presence of the people. But instead of being irritated, He was gripped with compassion (aorist tense) and taught the eager people. Weary as He was, He knew they needed His help.

B. *The Men's Confusion.* "Send them away."

As evening drew on the disciples became deeply concerned. They had thousands of guests for supper, and nothing to give them. No wonder they pleaded with Jesus: "Send them away!"

To add to their confusion Jesus replied: "You give them to eat." How utterly preposterous! They had nothing. And even if they had half a year's wages, that would not give every one enough.

We must remember that Oriental custom demanded that hospitality be extended to all who were present. To the disciples it was a very embarrassing situation, and they wanted to get out of it as quickly as possible.

The disciples thought they had nothing. But Jesus asked them to make a careful check. Andrew came up with the information that there was a boy there with a small lunch of five loaves and two small fish (cf. John 6:9). The loaves were just mere biscuits, like a small pancake. The two fish were probably the size of sardines, pickled to preserve them. What could one boy's lunch do for that crowd? The disciples were still confused.

C. *The Multitude's Comfort.* "They did all eat, and were filled."

First, Jesus commanded the disciples to have the people recline on the green grass of the hillside in groups of fifty and a hundred. This would facilitate both the counting and the serving. It took some faith on the part of the disciples to carry out these orders. To set the table, ask the guests to sit down, and then have no food for them! But they obeyed.

Then Jesus took the five biscuits and the two little fish, blessed the food, broke it, and distributed it to the twelve disciples. They in turn served the whole crowd. At the close each apostle filled his lunch basket as a sort of tip for his services. This would give them food for the next day.

The lesson here is clear. Jesus said: "You give them to eat." They could not. But when they obeyed the Master, He enabled them to do exactly that. They did feed the crowd. When Christ commands us to do the seemingly impossible it is ours to obey and He will furnish the means.

Mark 6

A PRESENCE IN THE DARKNESS

6:50. "Be of good cheer: it is I; be not afraid."

I. HISTORICAL SETTING. After the feeding of the five thousand — the only miracle of Jesus recorded in all four Gospels — the Master constrained His disciples to get into the boat and head back across the lake. We learn from John's Gospel (6:15) that the people wanted to make Jesus king. A Messiah who could feed five thousand with five loaves would solve all their economic problems!

But Jesus had not come to set up a political kingdom. He sent away the disciples — who would have been delighted to see their Master made king — and then dismissed the crowd. He himself went up a hill to spend the night in prayer. What He desired for Israel was not a political revolution but a spiritual revival.

II. EXPOSITORY MEANING. The location of Bethsaida (v. 45) has caused some dispute. It seems best to take this as the well-known Bethsaida Julias on the east bank of the Jordan River where it enters the Lake of Galilee. The feeding of the five thousand took place a short distance south of Bethsaida (Luke 9:10). The disciples evidently headed across the bay toward Bethsaida, expecting to pick up Jesus there. Instead the storm drove them out into the middle of the lake. There Jesus came to them, walking on the water, and they continued across to Gennesaret (v. 53). This was a small plain on the west side of the lake.

The "fourth watch of the night" (v. 48) would be from 3:00 A. M. to 6:00 A. M. "Toiling" is hardly strong enough to bring out the force of the Greek word. It meant to "examine by torture." So it could be translated "tortured," "tormented," or "distressed." Although the disciples had been rowing for perhaps eight hours they had covered only three or four miles (John 6:19). They were half way across the lake and having a very difficult time. "Would have passed by them" has raised some discussion. The simplest way is to take this as the point of view of an eye-witness. It seemed to the disciples that the figure meant to pass them by.

III. DOCTRINAL VALUE. Again the deity of Jesus is in the foreground. He could walk on the water with no fear.

IV. PRACTICAL AIM. To show that Jesus always comes to us in the hour of our darkest difficulty and greatest need, even though we may not always recognize Him.

V. HOMILETICAL FORM
Theme: "A Presence in the Darkness."
Introduction: It was dark. The wind was contrary. The waves were rolling high. Not even the moon shone to relieve the gloom of the night.

It seemed too bad they could not have crowned Christ king. Then the Messianic Age would dawn. All would be peace and happiness.

A. *A Sight.* "They saw . . . a spirit."
To the disciples that night it seemed that everything was against them. They were dejected, disappointed, downhearted. Out in the middle of the lake, unable to reach shore, worn out with rowing against the wind — all this instead of a kingdom.

Just then someone spotted something on the water. A figure draped in white, it looked like a ghost. They screamed in fear. It was bad enough to have the elements against them. But now to be tormented by a spirit was more than they could take. This was the last straw that broke their jaded nerves. They were terrified.

B. *A Sound.* "He talked with them."
What a comfort it was when they heard the familiar voice of the Master. It was not a ghost; it was Jesus! His first words to them were: "Be of good cheer: it is I; be not afraid."

How often do we fail to recognize Jesus when He comes to us in the dark hours of life? Sometimes the form in which He approaches us only fills us with greater fear. We do not know Him in the night.

But then He speaks in the still, small voice within our hearts. We hear Him say: "Be of good courage; I am; stop being afraid." Jesus is still walking on the sea of life, visiting us in our distress, and bringing us safely across to the other side.

C. *A Silence.* "The wind ceased."

The raging of the wind, the roar of the crashing waves — all this was gone. Instead there was quiet peace on the Lake of Galilee. We can even imagine that the clouds were pulled back, and the face of the sky could be seen again.

There is nothing more distressing than being tossed and pitched about in a small boat on the water, with no way of escaping. It leaves one with a helpless feeling. On the other hand there is nothing more peaceful than a ship on a quiet sea. In the silence that ensued the disciples felt the comforting presence of their Lord. How they enjoyed the quiet peace of the water as they finished their journey across the lake. We need the storms in order that we may appreciate the calm.

Mark 7

THE SIN OF CEREMONIALISM

7:20. "That which cometh out of the man, that defileth the man."

I. HISTORICAL SETTING. The previous incident in the Gospel is located in the small plain of Gennesaret, on the west side of the Lake of Galilee. Here in villages, cities, and country the people flocked to Jesus again, bringing their sick to be healed, (6:53-56). Presumably the present incident took place in that general area.

II. EXPOSITORY MEANING. "Defiled" (v. 2) is literally "common." To the ceremonially-minded Pharisees common meant unclean. Instead of *pykna* ("oft," v. 3) the best Greek text has *pyme,* which literally means "fist." This has been variously interpreted as "to the wrist" or "up to the elbow." Probably the simplest translation is "diligently" (ERV, ASV). The "tradition of the elders" was a body of oral regulations handed down by the rabbis and later put in written form.

"Washing" (v. 4) is "baptisms." The strict Jews baptized (washed) their cups, pots, and cooking vessels to rid them of all ceremonial defilement. The phrase "and of tables" is not in the oldest manuscripts and should probably be omitted.

The term "hypocrites" (v. 6) comes directly from the Greek *hypocrites* (only here in Mark, 13 times in Matthew, 3 times in Luke, not elsewhere in N.T.). It was originally used for an actor on the stage. Greek and Roman actors wore big masks which concealed small megaphones, in order to be heard by the large audiences. So being a hypocrite means wearing a false face.

The Hebrew word "Corban" means "gift." It was used for gifts devoted to the temple. But in Jesus' day it signified merely an oath or a vow which could not be revoked.

"Purging all meats" (v. 19) is probably an explanation added by the writer of the Gospel (cf. ASV — "This he said, making all meats clean"). That is, the distinction between clean and unclean meats was not to carry over into the Christian dispensation (cf. Acts 10:15).

"Thoughts" (v. 21) is "reasonings" or "designs" (Moffatt). "An evil eye" (v. 22) was the Hebrew phrase for envy. "Blasphemy" is speaking evil of God or man. Probably here it means "slander." The Greek word for pride (only here in N.T.) suggests self-exaltation and looking down with contempt on others. "Foolishness" is more moral than mental. It is the attitude of making sin a joke.

III. DOCTRINAL VALUE. Sin is moral, rather than ceremonial, uncleanness. The latter is the view of most non-Christian religions. It is a false, superficial concept of sin, against which Jesus rebelled deeply. Christianity demands inward and outward rightness. It is the main emphasis of Amos and Micah that true religion is a matter of righteousness, not ritual.

IV. PRACTICAL AIM. To show the importance of inward, moral cleanness.

V. HOMILETICAL FORM
Theme: "The Sin of Ceremonialism."
Introduction: The bane of most religion, including much of "Christianity," is the substitution of ritualism for righteousness. This may be called the sin of ceremonialism — a false righteousness. It was the sin of the Pharisees and Jesus denounced it severely.

A. *The Cleaning of Cups.* "the washing of cups, and pots, brazen vessels."
This was the religion of the Pharisees — at least, to a distressing degree. In the Jewish Mishna thirty chapters are devoted to the cleansing of dishes. Ceremonialism as a substitute for moral cleanness — this was the sin of the Pharisees. Over and over again Jesus emphasized the fact that inward cleansing was more important than outward purifications.

Even the sacrament of baptism can become a meaningless ceremony, with no more spiritual significance than what is here literally called the "baptisms" of cups and pots and pans. Religion must always be a matter of the heart, or it is not true religion.

We find it easy to criticize the Pharisaic obsession with outward things of the flesh. But to keep Christianity today a religion of the spirit is a constant struggle.

B. *The Case of Corban.* "But ye say, If a man shall say to his father or mother, It is Corban . . . he shall be free."

When the Pharisees criticized the disciples for not living (walking) according to the tradition of the elders, Jesus in turn charged them with a far more serious offense — rejecting God's commandment that they might keep their tradition. He cited a specific case. God said, through Moses: "Honor thy father' and thy mother." But the rabbis taught that a man might declare as "Corban" what he should have used to support his parents. Having dedicated the money, he could not give it to his father and mother for their needs. But the catch was that he did not need to give it to the temple either. He could keep it for his own use after his parents' death. Both Christian and Jewish writers agree that this was the actual practice.

C. *The Character of Carnality.* "out of the heart of men, proceed evil thoughts."

The Jews taught that eating unclean meat defiled a man. Jesus said an emphatic "No!" Nothing physical defiles a man's spirit. It is the outflowing, outpouring of his carnal nature that defiles him.

The true character of carnality is shown here in all its black ugliness. A man does not become a sinner by committing murder, theft, or adultery. He does these things because he *is* a sinner. Outward sins are only reflections of inward sin, and the sins of the spirit are equally wicked in God's sight.

Mark 7

THE TENDERNESS OF THE MASTER

7:37. "He hath done all things well."

I. HISTORICAL SETTING. After Jesus' bout with the Pharisees He withdrew for a third time (cf. 4:35; 6:31). This time he went north into the territory of Tyre and Sidon. This is the ancient Phoenicia, modern Lebanon, on the coast of Syria. Here a Syrophoenician woman petitioned him to cast a demon out of her daughter. After testing her faith, Jesus granted her request. Then he returned to the east side of the Lake of Galilee. It is obvious that He was carefully avoiding the territory of Herod Antipas, because the latter wanted to kill Him (Luke 13:31).

II. EXPOSITORY MEANING. "Coasts" (v. 31) means "borders." The "Decapolis" was a region of ten cities (*deca polis*). It included Damascus in the far north and Philadelphia (modern Amman) in the south. "Had an impediment in his speech" (v. 32) is all one word in the Greek. It means "speaking with difficulty." The word "Ephphatha" (v. 34) is Aramaic. "Be opened" is a compound — be opened completely. "String" (v. 35) is "bond." It would seem that he was literally tongue-tied. "Plain" is "straight."

III. DOCTRINAL VALUE. Again we see Jesus' divine power displayed in healing an afflicted body. Also we see the tender compassion of the Great Physician, His love matching His power. In fact, His power was love.

IV. PRACTICAL AIM. To give us an example of how thoughtfully and tenderly we should deal with afflicted souls.

V. HOMILETICAL FORM
   Theme: "The Tenderness of the Master."
   Introduction: We are apt to think of tenderness as weak-

ness. Nothing could be further from the truth! The all-powerful One was All-Love. Because of that, He was infinitely tender in dealing with the needy. To be strong enough to control
our powers and use them only for healing and helping — that
is the evidence of inward strength. Brusqueness, crudeness,
rudeness, roughness — these are signs of weakness. The brag-
ging boaster is usually a coward. True strength is found in a
combination of sweetness and firmness. This Jesus had.

A. *The Man's Trouble.* "And they bring unto him one that
was deaf, and had an impediment in his speech."

One time it was a leper, another time a blind man or a
helpless paralytic. Now it was a deaf mute. But the Great Physician was able to cure every case.

It would seem that the man was physically tongue-tied.
Not being able to hear himself, he perhaps could not know
how pathetic his incoherent mumblings sounded.

Unable to hear a word, not able to make himself understood by others — what a lonely life he led! Jesus had compassion on him and changed everything that day.

B. *The Master's Touch.* "He . . . put his fingers into his ears
. . . and touched his tongue."

Note the tender compassion of the Christ: "he took him
aside from the multitude." A deaf man is naturally embarrassed and easily confused. Graciously, thoughtfully Jesus
took him aside from the crowd.

With this should be compared the healing of the blind man
of Bethsaida (8:22-26), the only other miracle recorded by
Mark alone. The two have much in common. Note how gently
Jesus took the blind man by the hand and led him outside
the city. These men needed to be treated in quiet privacy.
There were emotional as well as physical factors to be considered. Often sinners need to be dealt with alone, away from the
confusion of a public place.

In both cases Jesus touched the affected spot. With the deaf
stammerer it was his ears and tongue. This was a symbol of
the cure that was soon to come and was intended to bolster
his faith. With the blind man it was his eyes. Unique among

the miracles of the Master, this took place in two stages —
"Twice He touched my blinded eyes."

The clear lesson in these two incidents is that Jesus deals
with each of us as individuals. He knows just how to tailor
the treatment to our specific needs and particular personalities.

C. *The Multitude's Testimony.* "He hath done all things
well."

What a tremendous testimony! Jesus earned it. How far do
we?

It should be noted that a man's spirit is the most important
thing. Not one of us will live without mistakes, as Jesus did.
But we can all, by God's grace, show a good spirit all the time.
If we do, people are apt to say that we are doing all things
well. Any reasonable person will make allowances for some
mistakes. But for a bad spirit there is no acceptable alibi.

Certainly those of us who know the Master personally can
join the observers of His day and say: "He has done all things
well."

Mark 8

JESUS THE MESSIAH

8:29. "Thou art the Christ."

I. HISTORICAL SETTING. After the healing of the deaf mute in Decapolis, Jesus fed the four thousand. This second miraculous feeding is recorded only by Matthew and Mark.

Then He crossed the lake again to the west side. Here the Pharisees asked from Him a sign from heaven to prove that He was the Messiah. But Jesus refused to satisfy their unreasonable demand. Instead He once more crossed to the northeastern shore at Bethsaida. There He healed a blind man.

But again He turned northward to escape the crowds and find opportunity for teaching His disciples. His greatest concern now was preparing them to carry on when He would soon leave.

II. EXPOSITORY MEANING. Caesarea Philippi (v. 27) was so called to distinguish it from the Caesarea on the seacoast, built by Herod the Great. This one was enlarged and beautified by Philip, Herod's son, and named in honor of Tiberius Caesar. It was located at the foot of towering Mount Hermon (9,166 feet elevation). The place is called Banias today, after its ancient Greek name Pan, which means "all."

III. DOCTRINAL VALUE. This is the high point doctrinally in the Synoptic Gospels. Jesus asked His disciples for a declaration of their faith in Him, and Peter rose magnificently to the occasion. The longer form of the confession as found in Matthew 16:16 reads: "Thou art the Christ, the Son of the living God." This is the strongest affirmation of the deity of Jesus in the Synoptic Gospels.

IV. PRACTICAL AIM. To challenge our understanding of who Jesus is. Do we believe in Him by hearsay or by actual experience?

V. HOMILETICAL FORM
Theme: "Jesus the Messiah."

Introduction: The place was propitious. Called Pan by the Greeks, it was situated at the foot of majestic Mount Hermon. Here the Jordan River leaped from a rocky cleft to begin its long journey southward to the Sea of Galilee and onward to the Dead Sea.

Right here at the shrine of the ancient Greek All-God, Jesus called forth the confession of His messiahship. He, not Pan, was the divine Supreme Being.

A. *The Common Question.* "Whom do men say that I am?"

No man could have the miraculous ministry that Jesus did without causing men to ask, "Who is he?" Doubtless that question was on the lips of hundreds of people in Galilee. They had seen Him heal the sick, cast out demons, feed the multitudes. They heard that He had even raised the dead, and stilled the storm. Who could this be?

First the Master asked His disciples what men were saying about Him. They furnished a variety of opinions that were going the rounds. Some, like Herod (cf. 6:16), thought that John the Baptist had come to life again. Others, remembering that Elijah had performed miracles and that Malachi (4:5) had predicted the reappearance of the old prophet, identified Jesus with Him. Others simply said, "One of the prophets." Surprisingly, no one suggested that He might be the Messiah.

B. *The Crucial Question.* "But whom say ye that I am?"

It is important to know what others are saying about Jesus. But the crucial question is our own belief about Him.

The Greek is very emphatic: "But you (pl.), who do you say me to be?" For many months the disciples had been with Jesus. They had eaten, slept, traveled and talked with Him. They had seen Him under all sorts of conditions and circumstances. He had been equal to every occasion. Whether confronted by disease, death, demons, or the stormy deep, He had always been the mighty Conqueror. What was their conclusion concerning Him?

There is no more important question in the world than, "What think ye of Christ?" The answer to that determines our character here and our destiny hereafter.

C. *The Confident Confession.* "Thou art the Christ!"

Peter was one of the first four fishermen called to follow the Lord. He had had enough faith in Jesus to forsake his business and follow this new Leader. He had witnessed the many miracles of the Master. He was one of the inner circle of three who had seen Jairus' daughter raised from the dead. What effect had all this had on him? The answer is found in his ringing declaration: "Thou art the Christ."

"The Christ" is Greek for "the Messiah" (Hebrew). The prophets of old had foretold the coming of the Messiah, the "hope of Israel." Long centuries had waited. At last He had appeared!

It took courage for Peter to declare openly that Jesus was actually the Messiah. But his courage was born of conviction, which in turn was based on growing consciousness of a divine Presence. The only way today that we can really know that Jesus is the Christ is through personal experience of His divine Person and Power.

Mark 8

THE PATHWAY TO LIFE

8:34. "Whosoever will come after me, let him deny himself, and take up his cross, and follow me."

I. HISTORICAL SETTING. The first thing that Jesus had to do after the confession at Caesarea Philippi was to straighten out the distorted concept of the Messiah held by the Jews of His day. They looked for a coming king, a son of David who would overthrow their enemies, free them from foreign domination, and rule over Israel and the world in glory and splendor.

But first must come the Cross. So Jesus made the first prediction of the Passion (v. 31). This forms the background for His call to the disciples to accept the Cross also for themselves.

II. EXPOSITORY MEANING. "Will save" (v. 35) is not the future tense of the verb, as this tranlation might suggest. The Greek says: "Whoever wishes to save." The word "life" (twice in v. 35) is the same in the Greek (*psyche*) as "soul" in verses 36 and 37. In the King James Version it is translated "soul" 58 times, "life" 40 times, "mind" 3 times, and once each "heart" and "heartily." Twice it is left untranslated. It is of interest to note that not only the Revised Standard Version but also the Berkeley Version uses "life" throughout this passage (vv. 35-37).

III. DOCTRINAL VALUE. The main emphasis of the text is on self-renunciation as the gateway to spiritual life. That must be followed by self-crucifixion, and this in turn by a life of constant obedience. Christ took this path, and if we would follow Him we must take it too.

The value of the human soul is also underscored in the context. It is worth more than all the world. To lose it is to lose all.

IV. PRACTICAL AIM. To show that there is no easy way to follow Jesus. It calls for the denial and death of self. It demands full obedience. It means accepting Christ's pattern of life as ours.

V. HOMILETICAL FORM
Theme: "The Pathway to Life."

Introduction: There are two basic philosophies of life. One is that of Nietzsche, the German philosopher, who said, "Assert yourself!" This helped to produce the superman, Hitler, who drenched the world in blood. The other is that of Jesus Christ, who said, "Deny yourself." He shed His own blood to save a world and bring peace on earth.

A. *Denial of Self.* "Let him deny himself."

Over the doorway to the Christian life are written these words: "Deny yourself, all ye who would enter here." Frankly, that is why so few enter. Self-denial is the price that most people are not willing to pay. They will sacrifice money, time, and energy. But to deny one's self — that is asking too much!

It should be noted that Jesus did not say: "Let him deny himself of this or that." He said, "Let him deny himself"— period! Actual denial of *self* is something far different from popular conceptions of self-denial. The latter may mean only sacrificing a nickel chocolate bar to give to missions. The former demands a self-renunciation that involves rejecting our way to accept Christ's way. It means saying "No" to self and "Yes" to Him.

B. *Death of Self.* "take up his cross."

For many people carrying one's cross means enduring some or less inevitable affliction, such as rheumatism. But Jesus said, "take up his cross." That indicates a voluntary acceptance of something we could reject.

The cross is the symbol of death. It means crucifixion. The New Testament emphasizes strongly the truth that self-crucifixion is the price of power, the secret of victory. Paul said: "Knowing this, that our old man is crucified with him, that the body of sin might be destroyed, that henceforth we should not serve sin" (Rom. 6:6). And again: "I have been crucified with Christ; and no longer do I [*ego*] live, but Christ lives in me" (Gal. 2:20, lit. trans.). The order of the Greek emphasizes vividly the fact that Christ had taken the place of the carnal ego at the center of Paul's being.

Just as Christ carried His cross and then was crucified on it, so every Christian must have his Calvary of self-crucifixion. Only then can we say with Paul: "Not I, but Christ."

C. *The Determination of Self.* "follow me."

"Deny" and "take up" are both in the aorist tense, suggesting the crises of conversion and consecration. But "follow" is in the present tense, signifying continuous action. There must be the constant determination of one's will to follow Christ fully, clear to the end. This is a lifelong assignment.

The setting of this text is very significant. Jesus had just predicted His passion. To follow Him meant to take the Calvary road. As for Him, so for all His followers there is no resurrection without a preceding crucifixion. The resurrection life of victory is possible only to those who have died with Christ.

Mark 9

THE TRANSFIGURED CHRIST

9:2. "He was transfigured before them."

I. HISTORICAL SETTING. The first verse of this chapter probably belongs with the previous chapter (cf. Matt. 16:28; 17:1). The reference could hardly be to the Transfiguration, which took place only one week later. Probably the correct interpretation is that it applies to Pentecost and its postlude — the spread of the kingdom of God in the power of the Spirit.

The "high mountain" where Jesus took the three disciples "apart by themselves" is traditionally identified with Mount Tabor, between Galilee and Samaria. But this is a rather low knoll (1000 ft). Furthermore, there are indications of a military fortress on its summit in Roman times. So most scholars today favor Mount Hermon because of its height and seclusion.

II. EXPOSITORY MEANING. "After six days" (v. 2; Matt. 17:1) is "about an eight days after" in Luke 9:28. Both expressions mean "a week later." "Tabernacles" (v. 5) probably means booths made of tree branches. The "cloud" (v. 7) suggests the Shekinah of the Old Testament. "Beloved" also carries the sense of "only." The reference in verse 13 is to John the Baptist, as Matthew (17:13) explains.

III. DOCTRINAL VALUE. This passage highlights the deity of Jesus more than almost any other in the Synoptics. We find here not only the display of His divine glory but also the definite word from heaven: "This is my beloved Son: hear him" (v. 7). The doctrine of immortality is also suggested, for Moses and Elijah are still alive.

IV. PRACTICAL AIM. To challenge us to live the transfigured life.

V. HOMILETICAL FORM

Theme: "The Transfigured Christ."

Introduction: Every great life is marked by great crises. So it was with Jesus. There was the Baptism, the Temptation, and now the Transfiguration. Most of life is lived on the plain of daily duty. But this must be punctuated at times with mountain top experiences, if life is to take on its larger meanings.

A. *The Meaning of the Transfiguration.* "after six days."

Six days after — after what? After the confession at Caesarea Philippi and the prediction of the Passion that followed. Peter had declared: "Thou art the Messiah!" To him it now seemed the time had come to set up the messianic kingdom in Jerusalem. What a day!

But suddenly everything was shattered. Jesus asserted that He was not going up to Jerusalem for a crown but for a cross, not to reign, but to die. Immediately Peter protested. This must not be. In reply Jesus rebuked the apostle, called him an adversary, and indicated he did not look at things as God does. Then He taught His disciples that they too must take the way of the Cross (8:34). All this left them sad and confused. Was He really the Christ?

The Transfiguration was the answer — at least for Peter, James, and John. They saw the inner divine glory burst through the bonds of flesh, shine through the veil, and show itself in unmistakable brilliance. They caught a glimpse of God's glory in the face of Jesus Christ. He was more than a mere man. He was truly the Son of God!

Thus all haunting fears were dispelled again by faith. The Transfiguration was a confirmation of the confession at Caesarea Phillippi.

But what about the death of their Messiah? The answer came in the conversation with Moses and Elijah (cf. Luke 9:31). It was all a part of heaven's plan for earth's salvation.

B. *The Message of the Transfiguration.* "This is my beloved Son: hear him."

Twice came this voice from heaven: at the Baptism and at the Transfiguration. It was God's exclamation point placed after Peter's confession. It was the divine attestation of the human affirmation.

The second part of the message, "hear him," was probably a rebuke to Peter's suggestion about making three booths. By implication he put Jesus on the same level with the two human prophets. But Christ is utterly unique. He stands alone as Lord of all.

C. *The Moral of the Transfiguration.* "They saw no man any more, save Jesus only with themselves."

Peter had become absorbed with vision and visitors. But all these were to disappear. What was left? Jesus only!

The value of a vision depends on the deposit that remains. That is true of all experiences of ecstasy or emotion. Do they leave us different? Do we find the presence of our Lord more real and precious because we have seen Him in a new light? That is the real test of all religious experience. Unless, at least in a measure, it transforms and transfigures us, it is not a genuine spiritual experience.

How may we live the transfigured life? By letting the divine Presence fill our hearts and flood our personalities, so as to shine out through our lives. Thus shall we re-present Christ to the world.

Mark 9

THE HIGH COST OF CARELESSNESS

9:43. "And if thy hand offend thee, cut it off."

9:45. "And if thy foot offend thee, cut it off."

9:47. "And if thine eye offend thee, pluck it out."

I. HISTORICAL SETTING. The Mount of Transfiguration was followed by the valley of trouble. Jesus could not stay on the mount of heavenly fellowship when there was dire, distressing need below. So He came and healed the boy who was demon-possessed (vv. 14-29). Then He headed down through Galilee, avoiding the crowds, for he wanted to teach His disciples. He told them a second time of His coming passion (vv. 30-32).

Finally they arrived in Capernaum. There He chided them for their dispute as to who should be the greatest (vv. 33-37). He also rebuked their narrow, sectarian spirit (vv. 38-41).

II. EXPOSITORY MEANING. The Greek verb *skandalizo* (cf. scandalize), here rendered "offend," is one of the most difficult in the New Testament to translate. According to one member of the revision committee (RSV) it was the last word on which an official vote was taken. It had baffled the committee for years. The verb comes from the noun *skandalon*, which meant the bait stick or trigger of a trap or snare. So the verb has been rendered "trap" or "ensnare." Perhaps the Revised Versions (1881, 1901) "cause to stumble" represents the meaning best.

"Millstone" (v. 42) is literally "millstone of a donkey"; that is, a large stone turned by a donkey, not one of the small, flat ones turned by women in their homes.

"Hell" is Gehenna. This is from *Ge-Hinnom*, the Valley of Hinnom south of Jerusalem. Here the Israelites offered their children to Moloch, letting them roast to death in the arms of his image (Jer. 7:31). King Josiah had declared the place unclean (II Kings 23:10), and it became the city dump. The lurid flames licking at the garbage and refuse made it a fitting symbol of hell.

Note that "the kingdom of God" (v. 47) is equated with (eternal) "life" (vv. 43, 45).

Verses 44 and 46 are not found in the earliest manuscripts. Evidently they were copied in by some later scribe from verse 48, which is genuine. The "worm" speaks of gnawing memory, one of the torments of hell.

III. DOCTRINAL VALUE. Here is to be found one of the most definite passages on hell in the New Testament. The nature, as well as the fact, of eternal punishment is vividly set forth in verse 48.

IV. PRACTICAL AIM. To warn against any carelessness that might result in being lost forever.

V. HOMILETICAL FORM
  Theme: "The High Cost of Carelessness."
  Introduction: The doctrine of hell is passé. So the sophisticated say. Away with the ecclesiastical distortions that have crept into Christianity. Give us again the simple teachings of the gentle Jesus!

Those who talk that way have not read the Gospels carefully. Actually the strongest teaching in the New Testament on hell as a place of eternal punishment is to be found right here in the earliest Gospel. We cannot accept Jesus' words about lilies and sparrows, about love and light, and reject His plain warnings against eternal torment. They all are equally authenticated in the sacred record.

A. *The Offending Hand.* "If thy hand offend thee, cut it off."

The hand is the symbol of *what we do*. If we find that some activities are proving to be a stumbling block to us, we must cut them off. No matter how much we enjoy doing a certain type of thing, no matter how innocent it may seem of itself, we must deal drastically with it. No price is too high to pay for escaping hell. That is what Jesus was saying.

Of course Christ was not advocating literal mutilation of the physical body. One cannot get rid of sin that way. He was speaking figuratively. One of the best applications of His warning is this: If you have a bosom friend, who seems as close to you as your hand, and yet he is tempting you away from God's best in your life, cut off that friendship immediately and completely! That is the only safe policy.

B. *The Offending Foot.* "If thy foot offend thee, cut it off."

The foot is the symbol of *where we go.* If you are being tempted to go places that will hurt you spiritually, do something desperate about it. A man had better change jobs or even his place of abode than to find himself lured into wrong surroundings. Whatever it is that is causing one's steps to go astray must be cut off, no matter what the cost. Any price is cheap, if it but saves us from hell. Jesus could not have put the matter more vividly and drastically.

C. *The Offending Eye.* "If thine eye offend thee, pluck it out."

The eye is the symbol of *what we see.* It is in many respects the most precious part of the body. Sooner lose a hand or a foot than one's eye.

This warning is particularly pertinent today. A generation ago those brought up in Christian homes were seldom exposed to "the lust of the eyes." But what is the situation now? Sex appeal confronting the eye almost everywhere — billboards, magazine covers at the corner drug store, theater advertising, to say nothing of the ever-present television.

What is the cure? Cut off every appeal that causes us to stumble. Sometimes this means simply shutting one's eyes to tempting sights or turning away.

Mark 10

JESUS ON DIVORCE

10:9. "What therefore God hath joined together, let not man put asunder."

I. HISTORICAL SETTING. Jesus was now on His final journey to Jerusalem, there to be crucified. For the last time He left Capernaum, which He had made His headquarters during His great Galilean ministry of perhaps a year and a half. He now went into "the coasts of Judaea by the farther side of Jordan." This was then called Perea (modern Transjordan), from *peran,* "across." Here the Pharisees came to Him with a question about divorce.

II. EXPOSITORY MEANING. "Tempting" (v. 2) is the verb *peirazo,* the primary meaning of which was "test." But it is obvious that here the Pharisees had a malicious motive. "Cleave" (v. 7) is literally "be glued to." It goes without saying that most modern marriages need more glue (unselfish love) to hold them together.

Verse 12 is not found in the parallel passage in Matthew. The latter wrote for Jews, who did not permit a woman to divorce her husband. But Mark wrote for the Romans, who gave a higher legal status to women and allowed them to divorce their husbands.

III. DOCTRINAL VALUE. The doctrine of creation is emphasized here, as well as the suggestion that man, made in the image of God, should live a godly life. It is clearly indicated that God's ideal for human marriage was monogamy.

IV. PRACTICAL AIM. To discover what Jesus had to say on the very important matter of divorce.

V. HOMILETICAL FORM

Theme: "Jesus on Divorce."

Introduction: There is hardly any other single question that plagues modern society more than that of divorce. It confronts us on every side. Even the churches are seriously afflicted with it. What is to be done about it?

For the Christian the highest authority must always be Christ. What did He say about it? That is the most important question for us to ask. The passage before us gives the answer. Jesus did not evade this perennial problem.

A. *The Catch Question.* "Is it lawful for a man to put away his wife?"

This question is as old as time. It is not just a matter of what the law says about it. The Greek verb means, "Is it permitted? Is it proper?"

By asking this question the Pharisees hoped to get Jesus into trouble. Perea was under the rule of Herod Antipas. He had put John the Baptist to death for condemning his adulterous marriage to Herodias. If the Pharisees could trap Jesus into making some strong statement against divorce, perhaps Antipas would execute Him and they would no longer have to endure this rival. At least it was worth trying.

B. *The Counter Question.* "What did Moses command you?"

On more than one occasion Jesus met a catch question with a counter question. That is a wise way to answer those who ask "loaded" questions, seeking to get us into trouble.

The Jews held Moses as their highest authority. So this question was altogether logical and pertinent.

In reply the Pharisees answered that Moses allowed a man to write a certificate of divorce and dismiss his wife. Therefore was not divorce all right? But Jesus explained that it was because of the hardness of their hearts that Moses made this concession.

The point that should be noted is that Moses' action was intended not to encourage divorce, but to discourage it. He was seeking to make it harder, not easier. By requiring a man to engage the services of a paid scribe and set forth in writing the reasons for his action, he hoped to prevent the spread of this plague of easy divorce.

C. *The Conclusion.* "What therefore God hath joined together, let not man put asunder."

What is God's attitude toward divorce? It may be summed
up in one brief statement: He is against it! As Jesus pointed
out, He showed this in creation — one man, one woman. That
is still God's will for humanity.

In marriage the two become "one flesh." That is why it is
a sin to separate them. It is something far different from a
business partnership or any other relationship of life. Not even
parents and children, or brothers and sisters, sustain the close
relation of husband and wife. Therefore it should be treated
with utmost sacredness.

This is the basic secret of successful marriage. When it is
thought of as something sacred, it can become a veritable sacrament of spiritual grace. But when lust takes the place of
love, when selfishness corrodes love until it no longer deserves
that name — then the marriage is headed for serious trouble.

By the very nature of marriage it is obvious that self-
centered individuals clearly cannot be one in a happy union.
There is no earthly relationship that more fully demands unselfish love than marriage. Only as each puts the other first can
both find their highest happiness in seeking to make the other
happy.

Mark 10

TRUE GREATNESS

10:45. "For even the Son of man came not to be ministered unto, but to minister, and to give his life a ransom for many."

I. HISTORICAL SETTING. After Jesus' strong statement against divorce, He blessed the little children, taking them up in His arms (vv. 13-16). Among the saddest D.P.'s of our day are the children of divorced parents. They often love both and want to live with both. But the sinful selfishness of the parents prohibits it.

Jesus was then confronted with the rich young ruler, who failed to pay the price of soul peace (vv. 17-22). For the third and last time He predicted His passion (vv. 32-34). The sordid sequel was the request of James and John that they might be first in His kingdom.

II. EXPOSITORY MEANING. The "cup" (v. 38) was a symbol of experiencing sorrow (cf. Ps. 75:8). "Baptism" was a figure for overwhelming floods of grief (cf. Isa. 43:2). It may be that the former suggests inner spiritual agony and the latter outer persecutions and afflictions. "Displeased" (v. 41) is "indignant." "Exercise lordship" (v. 42) is literally "lord it (over them)." "Minister" (v. 43) is *diakonos,* which simply means "servant." The verb (v. 45) may well be translated "not to be served, but to serve."

III. DOCTRINAL VALUE. The Greek word for "ransom" (v. 45) was used at that time for the redemption money paid for the freeing of a slave. "For" is *anti,* which in the papyri of that period most frequently means "instead of." Here it definitely supports the idea of Christ's substitutionary atonement. He not only died "for" us but in our place. He secured our release from sin by the payment of His own life's blood.

83

IV. PRACTICAL AIM. To see what true greatness is and also to appreciate Christ's atoning work for us.

V. HOMILETICAL FORM

Theme: "True Greatness."

Introduction: What a sorry spectacle of self-ambition! Jesus had for the third time predicted His coming suffering and death at Jerusalem. Right on the heels of that, James and John came to Him, requesting the seats of honor on either side of Him in glory. They were ready for a throne, but not for thorns. They wanted a coronation, not a crucifixion; self-indulgence, not sacrifice. How it must have hurt the heart of Jesus to see the selfishness and spiritual blindness of His disciples — yes, two who had been with Him on the Mount of Transfiguration. That vision seemed only to have whetted their anticipation of the coming kingdom. But they wanted to bypass the suffering that always must precede the glory.

A. *The Price of Greatness.* "Can ye drink of the cup that I drink of? and be baptized with the baptism that I am baptized with?"

Many people desire greatness, but few find it. The simple reason is that they are not willing to pay the price. True greatness never comes without a costly period of preparation. Only those who have experienced the discipline of suffering can develop the highest character.

When asked, "Can ye?" the disciples glibly replied, "We can." How little they understood the meaning of His words! What were they doing while He was agonizing in prayer in the Garden? Sleeping! What did they do when He was arrested? "They all forsook him and fled." Where were they when He was tried before Pilate and led away to be crucified? Missing!

But what of people today who thoughtlessly sing the song, "We are Able"? Do many, or any, really understand what they are singing. Too often it sounds like empty boasting.

B. *The Practice of Greatness.* "Whosoever will be great among you, shall be your minister [servant]."

When the other ten heard of James' and John's request they were indignant. Knowing the selfishness of their hearts we may wonder if they were jealous because they had not thought to ask first!

Jesus called them all to Him and gave them a lesson on true greatness. He reminded them of the world's way of looking at it: great men lord it over those under them. But the Master said that His men must be different. The one who would be great must be the servant of the rest, and the one who desired to be chief of all must be the slave (*doulos*) of all. This is the Christian way.

C. *The Paragon of Greatness.* "For even the Son of man came not to be ministered unto, but to minister, and to give his life a ransom for many."

The supreme example of true greatness is none other than Jesus Christ Himself. He practiced what He preached. But He went beyond anything that we can. Not only did He live a life of unselfish service, but He finally gave Himself as the supreme sacrifice for our sins.

The theological implications of this verse are tremendous. The price of our freedom from the slavery of sin was the death of Christ on the Cross. Gladly He paid the ransom, the redemption price of His own blood, that we might be released. He took our place as a condemned criminal and died in our stead. There could be no greater proof of infinite divine love.

Mark 11

THE TRIUMPHAL ENTRY

11:9. "Hosanna; Blessed is he that cometh in the name of the Lord."

I. HISTORICAL SETTING. The place was the Mount of Olives, across the Kidron Valley from Jerusalem. As the group of Galilean pilgrims came up the Jericho road and approached the village of Bethany on the east slope of the mount, Jesus sent two disciples ahead to Bethphage. He instructed them to bring a colt on which He could ride into Jerusalem. This was the first Palm Sunday at the beginning of Passion Week.

II. EXPOSITORY MEANING. The location of Bethphage is not certain. But references to it in the Talmud seem to place it on the western slope of the Mount of Olives, facing Jerusalem. Bethphage means "house of figs," Bethany "house of dates."

The Greek of verse 3 (latter part) reads thus: "Say: 'the Lord has need of it, and he is sending it immediately back here.' "

"Hosanna" (v. 9) literally means "Save now" or "Save, we pray." But here it seems to be more an exclamation of praise, like "God save the King!" Luke interprets it for his Greek readers as meaning "glory."

"Temple" (v. 11) is the Temple Area. His quick survey of conditions there was in preparation for His cleansing of the temple the next day.

III. DOCTRINAL VALUE. The striking fact is that when Jesus was acclaimed as the Messiah, He did not protest. If He was not the Christ, He was not even a good man, but a deceiver.

IV. PRACTICAL AIM. To encourage our hearts to welcome Christ as King of kings and Lord of lords in our individual lives.

V. HOMILETICAL FORM
Theme: "The Triumphal Entry."
Introduction: It was Jesus' last visit to Jerusalem. Frequently He had returned there for the annual festivals — Passover, Pentecost, Tabernacles — only to be criticized for His acts of mercy and to have His life threatened by the Jewish leaders. Now He would give them their last opportunity.

A. *The Preparation.* "He sendeth forth two of his disciples." Jesus never did anything haphazardly or without careful preparation. It was Sunday morning and He was approaching Jerusalem at the climax of His earthly mission. Before the final rejection of the Jewish nation as the special people of God, He must offer Himself publicly as the Messiah. They must be given every opportunity to accept Him as such.

So he sent for a colt. Zechariah had prophesied (9:9): "Behold thy King cometh unto thee: he is just, and having salvation; lowly, and riding upon an ass, and [even] upon a colt the foal of an ass." Deliberately Jesus acted out this prophecy as Himself the fulfilment of it. But even though the Jewish leaders were very familiar with this messianic passage, they refused to accept Jesus. In their minds and hearts they had already rejected Him and they stubbornly refused to change.

B. *The Procession.* "They that went before, and they that followed."
Though the leaders of the nation met the Master with final and full rejection, the Galilean pilgrims who had learned to love Him greeted Him with acclaim. For them it was truly a triumphal entry.

So stirred were they that many laid their outer garments in the road as a "red carpet" for Him to ride on. Others, with more caution, spread a litter of leaves on the path. All were mightily moved with the excitement of the moment. This was the hour toward which they had looked so long. The Messiah had come! A new age had dawned!

And so it was. But not in the way they anticipated.

C. *The Praise.* "Hosanna; Blessed is he that cometh in the name of the Lord: . . . Hosanna in the highest."

This was more than welcoming some new prophet. The language of verse 10 shows that the shouting pilgrims expected the immediate setting up of the messianic kingdom. Roman rule would be ended. The Golden Age had come. It was the fulfilment of the ages.

But sin triumphed that day. The reaction of the religious leaders (cf. Matt. 21:15; Luke 19:41-44) demonstrated conclusively that what the nation, and the world, needed was not a military conqueror but a Savior from sin. There were tears in the Triumphal Entry, and it left Jesus with a sob in His soul. Only He realized the tragic price the Jews must pay for their rejection of the Messiah.

It is still costly to reject the Savior — the most costly thing that one can do. What are we doing to Jesus today?

Mark 11

THE POWER OF FAITH

11:22. "have faith in God."

I. HISTORICAL SETTING. The Triumphal Entry was on Sunday. The next morning Jesus, on His way into Jerusalem from Bethany, saw a fig tree with leaves on it. He stopped to see if it might have fruit, but it had none. So He declared it should never again bear fruit. He did not curse it for not having fruit, but for giving the impression, by its leaves, that it did. Its destruction was a significant warning of what was to happen to the Jewish nation for claiming religion but having no fruit of genuine righteousness.

That same day, Monday, Jesus cleansed the temple. A corner of the Court of the Gentiles had been turned into a cattle and sheep market, as well as a money exchange. Jesus put an end to that and forbade the use of the sacred area as a thoroughfare for those carrying burdens across the city. He accused the priests of making God's house of prayer a den of robbers.

Tuesday morning, as they once more returned to the city, Peter noted that the fig tree had already withered, and called Jesus' attention to it. From it, the Master proceeded to teach His disciples a lesson on faith.

II. EXPOSITORY MEANING. "The time of figs" (v. 13) is normally June. But this was about the first of April. "Temple" (v. 15) does not mean a building (the Sanctuary), but the Temple Area and specifically the outer, open Court of the Gentiles. The "money-changers" were there because the annual temple tax had to be paid with the Phoenician silver half shekel, worth about thirty-five cents. The money in common use was Roman. "Thieves" (v. 17) should be "robbers." Robbery is theft with force. "Doctrine" (v. 18) is simply "teach-

89

ing." The imperfect tense of verse 19 probably indicates customary action: "and every evening he went forth out of the city" (ASV).

III. DOCTRINAL VALUE. Jesus' divine power was once more displayed in causing the fig tree to wither quickly. But He intimated that any one with full faith in God could accomplish miraclous things.

IV. PRACTICAL AIM. To show the great possibilities of faith and also the necessity for faith and a spirit of forgiveness if our prayers are to be answered.

V. HOMILETICAL FORM
Theme: "The Power of Faith."
Introduction: Jesus cursed the braggart fig tree, and it withered away. This was a parable of the death of the Jewish nation because of its hypocrisy.

Between the cursing and the withering came the cleansing of the temple. Against "all the sweltering of a dirty cattle-market and the haggling of a dirtier exchange of money" Jesus revolted with all His soul. The dishonesty and greed caused Him to call the temple a den of robbers. People had to have animals for sacrifice that were approved by the priests. It was safer to buy these cattle and sheep at the temple than to run the risk of having one's own animals rejected. Also the temple tax had to be paid with Phoenician money, and the priests' representatives charged about fifteen percent for exchanging Roman money. No wonder Jesus called the place a den of robbers!

Every evening Jesus went outside the city, where He would be safer from secret assassination. The city of the Great King was no safe place for the King when He came.

A. *The Command of Faith.* "Have faith in God."
God is both the source and object of our faith. The Greek of this text says literally, "Have faith of God." This could be the possessive genitive: "Have God's faith"; that is, the faith which God gives. In Ephesians 2:8 we read that faith is the gift of God. But here more likely it is objective genitive: "Have faith in God."

Faith in anything or anyone less than God spells inevitable disappointment. All else will let us down. But He never!

B. *The Character of Faith.* "shall not doubt in his heart." Faith is a firm conviction that what God has promised He will do. Ultimately it is trust in a Person — the all-wise, all-powerful, all-loving Heavenly Father.

Jesus said that if one commanded a mountain to be cast into the sea, and did not doubt in his heart, it would be done. Of course He was not talking about the Mount of Olives, as some have said. God does not busy Himself doing silly, unnecessary things. "Removing mountains" was a Jewish figure of speech for getting rid of a great difficulty. The disciples would understand what the Master meant. Christians are still seeing impossible barriers moved out of the way in answer to believing prayer.

But faith must be constant. "Believe" (v. 24) is literally "keep on believing." That is one of the main requirements for answered prayer. Too often we get discouraged and quit believing before the fulfilment of our petition.

C. *The Condition of Faith.* "Forgive."

Faith without forgiveness is impossible. The reason some people cannot believe is their wrong attitude. If we have an unforgiving spirit toward anyone it effectually blocks our prayers and destroys our faith. Faith will not operate in the atmosphere of unforgiveness.

The first requirement for successful praying is utter sincerity of soul. We must bare our hearts before God if we expect Him to hear and answer our prayers.

Mark 11

SHOULD WE PAY TAXES?

12:17. "Render to Caesar the things that are Caesar's, and to God the things that are God's."

I. HISTORICAL SETTING. After Jesus gave the lesson of faith, based on the barren fig tree, He once more entered Jerusalem. Here He was confronted by members of the Sanhedrin, who demanded to know on whose authority He had cleansed the temple. In turn Jesus asked them a question: Was John the Baptist's authority divine or human? The disgraceful ethical attitude of these religious leaders is laid bare in verses 31 and 32. They were governed by expediency rather than moral righteousness. Christ was altogether justified in asking what He did, for the correct answer to His question would be the answer to theirs.

Then Jesus told the parable of the wicked husbandman. The leaders recognized that they were the villains of the parable and wanted to kill Jesus. But they were afraid of the people. So they bided their time.

II. EXPOSITORY MEANING. The Herodians are not mentioned by Josephus. But their name indicates that they were supporters of the Roman rule of the Herods. The Greek word for "catch" (v. 13) means to "catch" or "take" by hunting or fishing. "In his words" is "by a word" or "in a statement." The "tribute" (v. 14) was the poll tax. The "penny" was a denarius, worth about twenty cents.

III. DOCTRINAL VALUE. Jesus' teaching included man's civic and social, as well as spiritual, responsibilities. On the subject of paying taxes compare Romans 13:7; I Peter 2:13f.

IV. PRACTICAL AIM. To show that one should fulfill his lawful obligations to the government and also to God.

V. HOMILETICAL FORM

Theme: "Should We Pay Taxes?"

Introduction: The Pharisees and the Herodians were sworn enemies. The former were the nationalists, who hated foreign rule. The latter were politicians who supported it. But they got together in their common enmity for Christ. Men still do that today.

A. *The Question.* "Is it lawful to give tribute to Caesar, or not?"

Note the "softening" process. They tried to flatter Jesus by saying they knew He did not care what anybody thought about His teaching; He told the truth always, fearless of the consequences. They thus hoped to put Him off His guard, so that He might carelessly make a statement that would get Him into trouble. Then they popped their question: "Is it lawful to pay a poll tax to Caesar or not?

They thought they had Him caught on either horn of the dilemma, so that He could not escape. If He said "Yes" the Pharisees would tell the people that He was unpatriotic, a traitor to the nation. But if He said "No" the Herodians would promptly report Him to the authorities as a dangerous revolutionary who was teaching the people not to pay their poll tax as an acknowledgment of Roman rule. It would be impossible for this upstart prophet to escape now!

B. *The Request.* "Bring me a penny."

The Jewish leaders had not reckoned with Jesus' insight into their character. He saw right through their hypocrisy. Instead of answering their question He asked for a denarius. Looking at it He asked whose picture was on it. It was a bust of Tiberius Caesar, the reigning emperor at Rome. On the other side of the coin was his inscription.

C. *The Command.* "Render to Caesar the things that are Caesar's and to God the things that are God's."

Jesus' logic was incisive, inescapable: "Well, if this coin carries Caesar's image and superscription, it looks to me as if it belongs to him; so you had better give it back to him." He might have implied: "Why are you carrying Caesar's picture around in your pocket if you hate him so?"

Jesus made himself perfectly clear on the subject of paying taxes. He taught that taxes are a debt we owe the government for services rendered. The verb "render" is literally "give back." We do not *give* taxes or tithe; we *pay* them. They are an obligation which it is our responsibility to meet.

Jesus did not stop with answering their question. As often, He went the second mile and gave more than was asked. Here He added: "and to God the things that are God's."

What are the things that are God's? Primarily the soul. For it bears on it, though marred, the image and superscription of its Creator. But the statement is all-inclusive. Everything we have comes ultimately from God and should be held at His disposal. It is really His. We are just the stewards of His property. Christian stewardship demands a complete consecration to God of all our time and talent, our strength and energy.

Mark 12

THE PRIMACY OF LOVE

12:30. "Thou shalt love the Lord thy God with all thy heart, and with all thy soul, and with all thy mind, and with all thy strength."

12:31. "Thou shalt love thy neighbor as thyself."

I. HISTORICAL SETTING. After the Pharisees and Herodians asked their question about paying taxes, the Sadducees had their try. Since they did not believe in any resurrection, they presented the hypothetical case of a woman who had seven husbands. Which one would claim her at the resurrection? They hoped to show how absurd this doctrine of the Pharisees (and Jesus) was. But Christ charged them with error due to not knowing the Scriptures or the power of God and proceeded to prove that the resurrection is implied in the Pentateuch, the only Scripture accepted by the Sadducees.

II. EXPOSITORY MEANING. The "scribes" (v. 28) were mostly Pharisees, who believed in the resurrection. One of them, pleased that Jesus had so effectually answered the Sadducees, asked a point of information. Literally the question reads: "Of what kind is the principal commandment of all?" That is, the scribe wished to know what was of highest importance in religion. The Rabbis had divided the 613 precepts of the Law (248 commands and 365 prohibitions) into "weighty" and "light." The scribe wanted to know which was most weighty.

In reply Jesus referred him to the Shema (Deut. 6:4, 5), which every pious Pharisee repeated twice a day. This was the most significant single Scripture passage in the eyes of the Pharisees, and the scribe expressed his approval of Jesus' answer (vv. 32, 33).

III. DOCTRINAL VALUE. Three doctrines are here set forth. The first is the unity of God. The second is the supreme love for God which is the duty of every man made in the image of God. The third is love for one's fellowmen, which is both the result of divine love in our hearts and the demonstration of it.

IV. PRACTICAL AIM. To show the supremacy of love. Also the importance of love for others as a proof of our love for God. This love for one's fellowmen should be shown in the daily life.

V. HOMILETICAL FORM
   Theme: "The Primacy of Love."
   Introduction: What is the most important thing in religion? That was the question with which a scribe one day confronted Jesus. The Master's answer can be summed up in one word: *love*. That is the heart of religion.
   A. *The Basis of the Divine Commandment.* "The Lord our God is one Lord."
   The ground of God's authority over man is here stated briefly but clearly. If there are many gods, why should Jehovah alone be obeyed? The answer is that there is only one true God, the Jehovah of Israel. Literally the statement reads: "The Lord (Jehovah) our God, the Lord is one." Explicitly this asserts the unity of God. Implicitly it affirms His aloneness, as well as His oneness. Israel's great contribution to a world plagued with polytheism was its central emphasis on monotheism. By this is meant not only that Jehovah is the *one* God for Israel (henotheism) but that He is the *only* God who exists (monotheism). Christianity carries on this testimony to the uniqueness of the one true God.
   Since Jehovah is the Creator and Lord of the universe He has a right to command our love and obedience. This is the basis of all divine law.
   B. *The First Commandment.* "Thou shalt love the Lord thy God with all thy heart, and with all thy soul, and with all thy mind, and with all thy strength." The Hebrew text of the Old Testament says: heart, soul, and might. But the Septua-

gint (Greek translation of O.T.) has: mind, soul, and might. Jesus combined these in naming the four terms.

It is almost impossible to distinguish "heart" and "soul." Furthermore, the Hebrew word for "heart" sometimes means "understanding." The distinction between these is not the most important point here. Rather, it is recognizing that the meaning is: You are to love God with your whole being, with all your faculties. Emotion, intellect and will are all to be centered in Him. Religion must be a matter of the whole man. What God desires is the complete response of our total being.

C. *The Second Commandment.* "Thou shalt love thy neighbor as thyself."

So far as is known Jesus was the first to combine these two commandments of love to God and love to one's neighbor (Deut. 6:5 and Lev. 19:18). Mystics often emphasize only the first, and too many evangelicals have fallen into this same trap. Social gospelers tend to talk only of the second. But true religion recognizes the supreme importance of both.

There is no use for one to profess love to God if he shows no love to his neighbor (I John 4:20). The only proof one can give that he really loves God is by showing it in love to others. Furthermore, His love is "perfected" (completed) in us only as we let it flow through us in love to those about us (I John 4:12). Love unexpressed is no love at all. Love cannot exist in a vacuum. It is not something abstract. Only love concretely manifested in kindness to our fellowmen is actual love. Too many Christians have missed this truth.

Mark 13

THE WHOLE GOSPEL
FOR THE WHOLE WORLD

13:10. "And the gospel must first be published among all nations."

I. HISTORICAL BACKGROUND. After the three questions that Jesus had been asked — by the Pharisees and Herodians, by the Sadducees, and by a scribe — He posed one of His own: How can the Messiah be both David's Lord and David's son? No reply was offered. But the incarnation gives the answer: Jesus Christ was both God and man, both David's Lord and his descendant.

The incident of the widow's mite followed. Jesus declared that giving is not measured by the amount given but by the amount left over. The widow gave most because she gave all.

As Jesus left the temple, where He had been teaching, His disciples called attention to its massive stones and magnificent buildings. In reply He made the startling prediction that all of this would be destroyed. A little later, as He was sitting on the Mount of Olives opposite the temple the four fisherman disciples asked Him when all this was to happen. Christ's extended answer is called the Olivet Discourse, because it was given on the Mount of Olives.

II. EXPOSITORY MEANING. Mark gives the question of the disciples as twofold: "When shall these things be? and what shall be the sign when all these things shall be fulfilled?" (v. 4). Matthew makes it threefold: "When shall these things be? and what shall be the sign of thy coming, and of the end of the world?" (Matt. 24:3).

The exposition of the Olivet Discourse is not easy. Rather clearly some elements in it refer to the destruction of Jerusalem and of the temple, which took place 40 years later (A.D.

70). Just as clearly some things can be taken only as predicting events still future now, connected with the Second Coming and the close of this age. But how to separate these items is the problem.

Probably the best solution lies in the recognition of the telescopic principle of prophecy. There is a nearer, partial fulfilment in the time of the prophet. But there is also a distant complete fulfilment in Christ, in connection with either His first or His second coming. To fail to recognize this is to become entangled in hopeless confusion. Incidentally this is the solution to the much debated problem of Isaiah 7:14.

III. DOCTRINAL VALUE. The doctrine of the Second Coming bulks large in the New Testament. Hence we have no right to ignore it today. Although eschatology has been an open field for all kinds of wild speculation, it is an important part of Biblical theology. What is needed is sane and sensible handling of the subject.

IV. PRACTICAL AIM. To show how we may hasten the coming of Christ, and show what our responsibility is in the matter.

V. HOMILETICAL FORM

Theme: "The Whole Gospel for the Whole World."

Introduction: The Olivet Discourse is the only lengthy message of Jesus which is recorded in all three Synoptic Gospels. Hence its importance should not be overlooked. It is significant that the longest common discourse should be on the Second Coming.

Just because many people have gone "off the deep end" in foolish speculation on this subject — setting dates and trying to identify the Antichrist — is no excuse for our neglect of this important Biblical theme. Rather we should seek to discover our responsibility. Can we do anything to help bring an end to the rising tide of wickedness? Our text gives the answer.

A. *The Gospel.* Missions is more than a matter of medicine or education, important as these are. It is fundamentally the giving of the gospel.

What is the gospel? It is the good news that Jesus Christ came into the world to save sinners. It begins with the recognition of human sin, but goes on to the proclamation of a divine Savior. Only a whole gospel can save a lost sinner.

B. *The Giving.* A gospel that is not given benefits no one. A truth that is kept to ourselves saves no sinner. It is only the gospel *preached* which is the power of God unto salvation to everyone that believeth. How shall they call upon Him of whom they have not heard? How shall they hear without a preacher? Those are still crucial questions.

To be responsible for souls being forever lost? To enjoy the gospel but fail to share it? Are we guilty?

C. *The Going.* Giving the gospel to the whole world means that someone must go. In fact it means that all Christians must go, at least by money and prayers.

Jesus declared that the gospel must first be published to all nations. Matthew (24:14) adds: "and then shall the end come." The end of what? The end of this age. The end of the horrible reign of wickedness. Only the coming of Christ in power and glory (v. 26) will bring an end to sin and the beginning of His reign of righteousness.

For this all Christians devoutly pray. But can we do anything about it? A familiar Scripture speaks of "Looking for and hasting unto the coming of the day of God" (II Peter 3:12). But a more accurate rendering is "expecting and speeding" the day of God. That is, by our work we are to hasten the coming of Christ!

This supplements what Jesus said. When will He return? When the gospel has been preached to all nations. Has that happened? Nearly so. Not every individual, not every tribe has heard the Word of God. But is there any "nation" that has not been reached at all?

Our responsibility is to see that this task of world evangelization is completed. With the modern means of communication and transportation the job can be done. It must be done! We should not pray for Christ to come unless we are willing to help answer our prayers.

Mark 13

THE MASTER'S RETURN

13:33. "Take ye heed, watch and pray: for ye know not when the time is."

I. HISTORICAL SETTING. This is the same as for the last text. Jesus probably uttered these words in A.D. 30, a few days before His death. Forty years later, in A.D. 70, they found a partial fulfilment in the destruction of Jerusalem. In the final war (A.D. 66-70) the Christians in Jerusalem remembered the warning of Jesus and fled from the city, finding a safe refuge at Pella, east of the Jordan River. Thus they escaped the awful horrors of the last months of the siege, as well as the death or slavery that followed. This was the worst "affliction" that had ever overtaken the Jews (v. 19) because they unjustifiably expected supernatural deliverance which did not come. The mental and spiritual anguish aggravated the physical torture of those days.

II. EXPOSITORY MEANING. It would seem that the Olivet Discourse may be divided into three sections. The first (vv. 5-13) is perhaps a general introduction, dealing with both A.D. 70 and the end of the age. The second (vv. 14-23) deals primarily with the former event, while the third (vv. 24-37) relates to the latter. This division will give some guidance in the interpretation.

"Sorrows" (v. 8) is literally "birth-pangs." The troubles at the end of this era will be the birth pains of the Messianic Age. In a more limited way the troubles of the first century could be described in the same way.

Whether the language of verses 24 and 25 should be taken literally or figuratively has been much debated. In favor of the latter interpretation is the general nature of apocalyptic language as highly symbolical. But in our atomic space age we

are faced with the evidence that these signs might be more
literally fulfilled in physical creation than had ever been
deemed possible.

The statement of verse 30 is admittedly difficult. If taken as
referring to A.D. 70 there is no problem, of course. But we
have suggested a reference to the Second Coming in this last
section (vv. 24-37). Some would translate "generation" as
"race." Others suggest that the generation which saw the beginning of sorrows would also see their end; that is, the events
predicted for the close of this age will all take place within
the period of a generation. No final solution of this question
has been reached.

III. DOCTRINAL VALUE. Again, the Second Coming. Also
verse 32 relates to the doctrine of the Kenosis. What self-
limitations of knowledge or power did the Son of God impose
upon himself in the Incarnation? That is an important question, but one not easy to answer.

IV. PRACTICAL AIM. In the last text we noted the responsibility of the church to hasten the return of Christ by evangelizing the world. In this text we see the challenge to personal preparedness by watching and praying.

V. HOMILETICAL FORM
Theme: "The Master's Return.

Introduction: The subject of the Second Coming is one
from which the majority of Christendom has shied away. This
is understandably due to the fanatical extremes of foolish
exposition often associated with it. But there is far too much
on this theme in the New Testament — Gospels, Epistles, and
Revelation alike — for us to pass it by. The careful reader of
God's Word will realize that there are few things more important for us as individual Christians than to be ready for
our Lord's return.

A. *When?* "Of that day and that hour knoweth no man."
Seldom has more breath and ink been wasted on any subject
than on the time of Christ's coming again. This is all the
more amazing in the light of Jesus' careful, repeated warning
that no one knows the day or the hour. Some have gone so far

as to affirm: "Yes, but He did not say we could not know the year." That kind of exegesis leads only into the quagmire of senseless confusion.

Jesus said that even He himself did not know. Only the Father had the schedule. How silly, then, for men to claim more knowledge than Christ by setting dates. But this plague has afflicted the church from early days.

B. *Watch.* "Take ye heed, watch and pray."

Not "when?" but "watch!" That is the emphasis in Jesus' teaching about the Second Coming. It is also Paul's and Peter's and John's. It should be ours.

It is a sad thing that some who have speculated about the date of Christ's return have failed to be prepared for it. Their contentious, dogmatic spirit shows an un-Christlike character that has no place in the kingdom of God.

Our most important concern personally should be to keep our hearts in tune with heaven. This can come about only as we fellowship with our tarrying Lord, as we "pray" with a sense of His presence with us. If there is unbroken, unhindered communion with Christ, we have the assurance that we are ready for His return.

The word "watch" in verse 33 means "do not be sleeping"; that is, "keep awake." A different verb for "watch" is used in verses 35 and 37, but with essentially the same emphasis; namely, "be watchful." Taken together the threefold warning means: "Keep awake; be always on the alert." That is Christ's closing word in this great discourse.

C. *Why?* "For ye know not when the time is."

If the watchman knew when the thief was coming, he would be prepared at that time. Not knowing, he must be prepared all the time.

Thus it is with us. We need to maintain a continuous watch, be on the alert constantly. Only thus shall we be ready when the Master returns at that unexpected hour.

Mark 14

GETHSEMANE

14:36. "Abba, Father, all things are possible unto thee; take away this cup from me: nevertheless not what I will, but what thou wilt."

I. HISTORICAL SETTING. Apparently the Olivet Discourse was given on Tuesday afternoon. Thursday evening Jesus with His disciples celebrated the last passover (vv. 12-21) and instituted the Lord's Supper (vv. 22-25). This took place in an upper room in Jerusalem (v. 15).

After the supper they sang a hymn (v. 26). This was probably the last part of the Great Hallel ("praise"), which consisted of Psalms 115-118. Then they left for the Mount of Olives. On the way Jesus predicted that Peter would deny Him (vv. 27-31).

II. EXPOSITORY MEANING. Gethsemane (v. 32) means "oil-press," a place where oil was squeezed out of olives. This was appropriate at the foot of the Mount of the Olive Trees. Evidently Jesus entered an olive grove. "Place" in the Greek suggests a small enclosure.

"Sore amazed" (v. 33) is a rare, strong compound verb in the Greek, suggesting "terrified surprise." The same can be said for "very heavy," which means "be in anguish" or "distressed." These, with verse 34, give us just a little glimpse into the agony of "the hour" (v. 35). "Fell" is literally "was falling" (imperfect tense). It suggests the picture of Jesus staggering and stumbling until He finally fell on His face on the ground, crushed by the burden of His heart. "Abba" (v. 36) is the Aramaic word for "father." "One hour" (v. 37) may suggest the length of Jesus' first prayer. "Flesh" (v. 38) probably means the physical body. "Words" (v. 39) is singular in the Greek. The meaning is: "uttering the same petition."

The apparent conflict between verses 41 and 42 may be resolved in either of two ways. Some would make Jesus' words ironical: "Sleep then, since it is your will to do so; rest if you can." But the atmosphere of agony seems to preclude irony. The best solution is to take the words as a question: "Are you still sleeping and taking your rest?" The Greek can with equal accuracy be translated that way, and this fits the situation perfectly.

III. DOCTRINAL VALUE. The subordination of the Son to the Father is central here. Also the meaning of Christ's passion.

IV. PRACTICAL AIM. To note Christ's complete submission to the Father, as an example for us. Also to face the question: are we failing to share His sufferings?

V. HOMILETICAL FORM
    Theme: "Gethsemane."
    Introduction: Christ had His Gethsemane. If we would follow Him we must also pass through the Garden — the place of full submission to the will of God.

A. *The Sorrowing Christ.* "Take away this cup from me."
    The picture of Jesus' sorrow is described with startling vividness. Leaving eight disciples at the gate of the garden, He took Peter, James, and John with Him into the olive grove. Terrified surprise and extreme anguish of soul seized Him, as the black shadow of the Cross came over His consciousness. In deep distress He said to the three: "My soul is exceeding sorrowful unto death." In other words, My sorrow is killing me, is crushing the life out of me! Asking them to watch and pray, He moved a little farther into the depths of the grove. There He "was falling" on the ground, crushed to the earth by the unbearable burden of a world's sin.

What was the "cup" from which He begged to be delivered? Scoffers have called Jesus a coward. They have accused Him of cringing before the cross, of shrinking from death. But His was no martyr's fate. It was not the physical pain He dreaded. It was that moment of separation from His Father's face, when

He who knew no sin would be made sin for us. This was the deepest sorrow of Jesus' soul.

B. *The Submitting Christ.* "Nevertheless not what I will, but what thou wilt."

This was the time when Jesus deliberately took up His cross, in order to pay redemption's price. The battle was fought now, not the next day. Then He simply carried through what He had already accepted as the Father's will.

The highest prayer that any Christian can pray is: "Not my will, but thine, be done." This involves a crucial self-surrender and also a continuous self-submission. God demands of all of us nothing more and nothing less than a complete consecration to His will. That is the cost of being a Christian.

C. *The Sleeping Disciples.* "He found them asleep."

Imagine the pain and disappointment of finding the three sentries sleeping soundly at their post. But the General did not court-martial them. Reproachfully He said to Peter: "Simon, are you asleep?" This was the first time he had been addressed by that name since he was chosen as an apostle (3:16). He was not now Peter, the stone. Then to all three He said: "Watch ye and pray, lest ye enter into temptation." That is still a salutary word of warning.

Three times Jesus agonized alone in prayer. Three times He returned to the supposed prayer-partners, only to find them sound asleep. How that must have added to the sorrow of His soul.

But do we do any better than they? How often have we failed Christ in the hours of His grief over men's sins today? "If we suffer, we shall also reign with him" (II Tim. 2:12).

Mark 14

THE BIG FISHERMAN'S WORST HOUR

14:72. "When he thought thereon, he wept."

I. HISTORICAL BACKGROUND. At the close of Jesus' prayer in Gethsemane He was arrested and forsaken by all His disciples (vv. 43-52). His captors took Him to the house of the high priest, where an informal meeting of the Sanhedrin condemned Him to death (vv. 53-65). In connection with that came Peter's denial of his Lord.

II. EXPOSITORY MEANING. "The chief priests and the elders and the scribes" (v. 53) comprised the Sanhedrin, or "council" (*synedrion*, v. 55). "The Blessed" (v. 61) was a euphemism the Jews employed for God, as also "power" (v. 62). The language of verse 62 is a combination of Daniel 7:13 and Psalm 110:1.

"Palace" (v. 66) should be "courtyard." The homes of the wealthy were built around a central, open court. In the middle of this the soldiers had lighted a fire, since the spring nights are cold in the mountainous height where Jerusalem is located. The "porch" (v. 68) was the "vestibule" between the inner court and the outer door opening on the street. Peter tried to get away from the light of the fire. But his Galilean accent had given him away (v. 70).

"To curse and to swear" (v. 71) does not mean that Peter used profanity, although he may have lapsed into the rough language of a fisherman. The first verb (*anathematizo*) is used elsewhere in the New Testament only in Acts 23:12, 14, 21, where it is correctly translated "bound under a curse," and "bound with an oath." The second verb means to swear an oath, as one does in court. So what Peter was saying was this: "Let me be subject to a curse if I am not telling you the truth.

107

I solemnly swear under oath that I do not know this man."
This, of course, was perjury.

III. DOCTRINAL VALUE. Here, certainly, was a demonstration of the depravity of the human heart. Peter had spent three years with Jesus. He loved his Lord. Yet disgracefully he denied that he had ever known Him.

IV. PRACTICAL AIM. To show the danger of over-confidence, of a misplaced trust in ourselves. In themselves, strong men are weak. Also to show the forgiving grace of God for one who fails miserably.

V. HOMILETICAL FORM

Theme: "The Big Fisherman's Worst Hour."

Introduction: Everyone has played the part of Peter in the great drama of life. Sometime, somewhere, each of us has denied his Lord.

But the crucial question is: Have we followed Peter's role to the finish? Have we repented with bitter tears? Have we been forgiven and restored? Have we been called and commissioned? Have we been empowered by the Spirit? Have we, who failed in the past, found a fruitful ministry of blessing to humanity?

A. *Peter's Mistakes.* "Warming himself."

Peter made three serious mistakes which paved the path to failure.

1. *He disregarded warning.* Jesus said: "Verily I say unto thee . . . thou shalt deny me thrice" (v. 30). Peter thought he knew better than his Lord. He replied vehemently: "If I should die with thee, I will not deny thee in any wise" (v. 31). And he meant it. When the mob (v. 43) seized Jesus, Peter quickly unsheathed his sword and swung at one of the servants. He would probably have gone down fighting with his last breath had not the Master commanded him to put away his sword.

2. *He followed afar off* (v. 54). He wanted to play it safe. But he got into trouble. Marginal living is actually dangerous living.

3. *He sat down with the wrong crowd.* It was when the high priest's maid saw Peter "warming himself" (v. 67) with

the soldiers that she challenged him. The person who goes with wrong companions makes it easy for him to deny his Lord.

B. *Peter's Denials.* "I know not this man."

All four Gospels say that Peter was first questioned by a maid. In the garden he was a brave warrior. He was ready to defend his Master against unnumbered foes. But he wilted before the accusing finger of a maid. It is sometimes harder to meet the small things in life than the large ones.

There followed a confusion of several people confronting Peter with the charge that he was "one of them" (v. 69). This confusion is reflected in the differing accounts in the four Gospels.

Finally those standing by joined in a general accusation, based on Peter's Galilean accent. This time he declared under oath, invoking a curse on himself if he were not telling the truth, that he did not know the man they were talking about.

C. *Peter's Repentance.* "When he thought thereon, he wept."

The cock crew. Jesus turned and looked at Peter (Luke 22:61). The apostle flung himself out of the company and burst into bitter tears of repentance. Under pressure he had done what he never dreamed he would do: denied His Lord. But immediately he felt a godly sorrow which issued in genuine repentance. Peter was restored to fellowship with his Lord on the day of the Resurrection, later commissioned to feed Christ's flock, empowered by the Holy Spirit at Pentecost, and then became the foremost leader in the earliest days of the church.

Are we guilty of denying our Lord? Some do it directly, as did Peter. Others do it negatively, by failing to take their stand for Christ. Many more professing Christians deny their Christ by the way they live. Worldly, selfish, or un-Christlike living denies one's Lord. But still there is forgiveness for the repentant soul.

Mark 15

BARABBAS OR JESUS?

15:15. "And so Pilate, willing to content the people, released Barabbas unto them, and delivered Jesus, when he had scourged him, to be crucified."

I. HISTORICAL SETTING. The Jewish Sanhedrin was supposed to act with utmost justice. Its regulations required that while a verdict of acquittal could be given on the same day, a verdict of guilty must be postponed until the next day; that no criminal trial should be held at night; and that the judges who condemned a man to death must fast all day. Apparently all these rules were broken in the case of Jesus, making His trial illegal. But the Sanhedrin did hold a brief session at daybreak (v. 1), to make its sentence of condemnation official.

Then Christ was taken to Pilate. Here He maintained a poised silence, which made the governor marvel (v. 5). As Luke and John report more definitely, Pilate was convinced of Christ's innocence. Here it is noted that the governor recognized the real reason for Jesus' condemnation by the Jewish leaders (v. 10). So he sought to gain His release by way of a custom at the feast (v. 6). It did not work.

II. EXPOSITORY MEANING. Barabbas is an Aramaic name composed of *bar*, "son," and *abba*, "father"; so it means "son of the (a) father." The "insurrection" (v. 7) would be a revolt against the Roman government. This was the most serious crime in the eyes of the ruling officials. Rome was tolerant toward many things, but not when there was any threat to its authority.

It is noticeable that the chief priests took the lead in demanding Jesus' death (v. 11). Earlier, in Galilee, it had been the Pharisees who opposed Christ. But when Jesus cleansed the temple He touched both the authority and the income of

the priestly Sadducees. Now they were determined to get rid
of Him.

III. DOCTRINAL VALUE. The nature of sin shows up
sharply here. The thin veneer of outward righteousness covered an inner rottenness. The depravity of the human heart is
revealed in the way the people joined in the cry for the
execution of an innocent man.

IV. PRACTICAL AIM. To understore the choice every man
must make for or against Christ.

V. HOMILETICAL FORM
   Theme: "Barabbas or Jesus?"
   Introduction: Everyone has to make the supreme choice of
his life — for or against Jesus Christ. About a thousand and
one other things we can remain neutral or indifferent. But
Christ confronts every man at the crossroads of life and demands a decision. Either we follow Him along the path that
leads to eternal blessing or we turn our backs on Him and
walk away from the Light of the world into a darkness made
deeper by our own disobedience.

   A. *False Son of the Father.* "released Barabbas unto them."
   By a strange coincidence the name Barabbas means "son of
the father." As leader of a revolt against the Roman government he posed as the savior of Israel. If the people would
follow him, he would free them from foreign domination. He
promised them political liberty.
   This was what the people wanted. "And so Pilate, willing
to content the people, released Barabbas unto them." They
preferred to have a murderer loose in their midst than the
Savior of mankind.

   B. *True Son of the Father.* "and delivered Jesus, when he
had scourged him, to be crucified."
   Here was the true Son of the true Father, who had come to
show the way to heaven. Far from being a murderer, He was
the Giver of life. He never hurt or harmed anyone. Instead He
healed and helped all those in need. What a contrast! Yet
they clamored for His death.

C. *False and True Salvation.* The salvation the Jews wanted was deliverance from foreign domination. What they failed to realize was that the dominion of sin was a far worse calamity. They wanted material prosperity, but ignored their deep spiritual need.

When we view the Jewish choice of Barabbas rather than Jesus we say, "How could they be so foolish?" Yet millions of men still make that same choice. They prefer to hold on to the murderer, Sin, rather than accept the Savior, Jesus. They will follow a political or social savior who offers them economic security and political freedom, but reject the gospel of spiritual salvation.

Never were the lines more sharply drawn than right now. On the international level it is Communism versus Christ. On the national scene it is materialism versus righteousness. In each individual heart it is sin or the Savior. Barabbas or Jesus? That is the ultimate choice every man must make.

Mark 15

SAVING ONESELF OR SAVING OTHERS

15:31 "He saved others; himself he cannot save."

I. HISTORICAL SETTING. Instead of taking Christ immediately to the place of execution the cruel Roman soldiers first staged a mock coronation. Calling the whole cohort together, they put a purple robe on Jesus. On His head they placed a crown of thorns. Then they bowed on their knees before Him in mock worship and saluted Him: "Hail, King of the Jews!" Not content with that, they smote His head with a reed and spat in His face. Quite a different coronation from what the disciples anticipated in Jerusalem!

Finally they brought Him outside the city, impressing an African, Simon, into service to carry His cross. Apparently Jesus was now too weak to carry it. At Golgotha, the place of a skull, they nailed Him to a wooden cross. The crucifixion took place at nine o'clock, and Jesus was hanging there for six hours before He died at three in the afternoon. During that period the passersby mocked Him.

II. EXPOSITORY MEANING. "Golgotha" (v. 22) is the Aramaic word for skull. The Greek word is *kranion,* from which comes the English "cranium." The familiar term "Calvary" is from the Latin *calvarium,* meaning "skull." This may have been a skull-shaped hill north of Jerusalem. We cannot be sure of the location.

They "tried to give wine mingled with myrrh" (v. 23) — this is what the imperfect tense means. But he refused to take this drug that the women of Jerusalem kindly provided for crucified criminals. It was intended to deaden the pain, but He wanted to be fully conscious.

The "third hour" was 9:00 A.M. "Thieves" (v. 27) should be "robbers." The "sixth hour" (v. 33) was noon. The "ninth

113

hour" (v. 34) was 3:00 P.M. The cry of dereliction (v. 34) was in Aramaic. "Vinegar" (v. 36) is "sour wine." The "veil" (v. 38) was the inner veil before the Holy of Holies.

III. DOCTRINAL VALUE. The whole doctrine of the Atonement is wrapped up in this incident. It cost Jesus His life to act as Mediator between a holy God and sinful men. The combination (or better, union) of the divine and the human bulks large here.

IV. PRACTICAL AIM. To note why Jesus could not save himself and at the same time save others, and its application to us.

V. HOMILETICAL FORM
Theme: "Saving Oneself or Saving Others."
Introduction: It was bad enough to have the soldiers mock Jesus in Pilate's Praetorium. It was worse to have the Jews who passed by rail on Him, taunting Him with His declaration that He would rebuild the temple in three days, and shouting: "Save thyself, and come down from the cross."

But what are we to say of the chief priests, the supposedly holy attendants in the sacred sanctuary? Surely they would treat Him with respect, if not with reverence. But no, they mockingly remarked to eath other: "He saved others; himself he cannot save."

A. *The Jews Who Saved Themselves.* "Save thyself."
This was their philosophy of life. Look out for yourself, for nobody else will. They were always thinking of their own selfish interests. Over and over again in the Gospels we see evidence of this. Self was number one in their eyes.

B. *The Jesus Who Saved Others.* "He saved others."
Never had the Jewish leaders spoken truer words. They may have meant them sarcastically. But they were literally and abundantly true of His whole life. He spent the days of His public ministry healing the sick, making the lame walk, strengthening the paralytics, giving sight to the blind, hearing to the deaf, and feeding the hungry. Yes, He even raised the dead. Always He was saving others.

If we would follow Jesus we must live to save others as He did. That calls for a love that manifests itself all the way from little deeds of kindness — giving a cup of cold water in His name — to intercessory prayer for lost souls. For the minister it means preaching, praying, pleading, personal work — anything to save those lost in sin. If we are not saving others, we are not following the Christ whose name we bear.

C. *The Cost of Saving Others.* "Himself he cannot save."

Saving others is expensive business. For Jesus it meant not only a life of healing ministry, involving arduous toil, but also a cruel death on a cross. There was no other way.

When the Jewish leaders mockingly said, "He saved others; himself he cannot save," they spoke better than they knew. The exact truth was that he could *not* save himself and save others. Only by losing His own life could He save others' lives.

What was true of the Master must be true of His servants. If our first concern is to save ourselves, we cannot save those around us. Selfish service will save no one. Only a sacrificial ministry can be a saving ministry. By losing ourselves in loving service for our fellowmen we shall both find a larger life and lead others to Christ.

Mark 16

THE MESSAGE OF THE EMPTY TOMB

16:6. "ye seek Jesus of Nazareth, which was crucified: he is risen; he is not here: behold the place where they laid him."

I. HISTORICAL SETTING. Friday evening before sunset, when the Sabbath Day would begin, Joseph of Arimathaea went to Pilate and boldly asked for the body of Jesus. The governor was surprised that Christ was already dead, for criminals often hung for days on the cross before finally expiring.

Joseph buried Jesus' body in a new tomb hewn out of solid rock. Two Marys watched carefully where He was laid away. On Saturday evening, when the Sabbath had ended, they brought aromatic spices for anointing the corpse. Since it became dark too soon to carry out this project then, they waited until early Sunday morning.

II. EXPOSITORY MEANING. Mary Magdalene is well known as the woman from Magdala (on the sea of Galilee) out of whom Jesus cast seven demons. Mary the mother of James is often identified as the wife of Cleophas, or Alphaeus (variant forms of the same Aramaic original). Salome was the wife of Zebedee and mother of James and John.

"Spices" (v. 1) is *aroma* in the Greek. The "stone" (v. 4) was "very great," probably four or five feet in diameter and round like a millstone. "And Peter" (v. 7) is a beautiful touch, suggesting that the apostle was forgiven, or at least not forgotten, by his Lord whom he had denied. "As he said unto you" (v. 7) refers back to 14:28.

The first reaction of the women was quite naturally one of fear and fright. They fled from the tomb, scared by the angelic presence they had seen there. At first they said nothing to anyone (v. 8). But we know from the other Gospel ac-

116

counts that soon they recovered their equilibrium and told some of the disciples — specifically Peter and John. Naturally they would not tell outsiders what had happened.

III. DOCTRINAL VALUE. The doctrine of the resurrection bulks much larger in the New Testament than it does in modern preaching. Have we somehow missed its importance today?

IV. PRACTICAL AIM. To see what is the meaning for us of the empty tomb.

V. HOMILETICAL FORM
Theme: "The Message of the Empty Tomb."
Introduction: In the famous Home Moravian Church in Winston-Salem, North Carolina, there is an unusual group of four stained glass windows in the rear of the sanctuary. Looking at them from the inside, one sees on the left of the entrance the scenes of Gethsemane and Calvary. On the right are portrayed the Resurrection and Ascension. By a strange coincidence, which seems a divine Providence, an adjacent building is so located that Gethsemane and Calvary are always dark. On the other side, however, the bright afternoon sun shines through the Resurrection and Ascension. This seems a beautiful parable of the fact that while the lights went out at Calvary they came on again at the empty tomb on Easter morning.

A. *The Mystery of the Empty Tomb.* "He is not here."
It is difficult for us today to put ourselves in the position of these women on that momentous Sunday morning. We have nineteen centuries of Christian history to explain the meaning of Easter. All they had, at first, was an empty sepulcher. There was no Christ there. Not yet had they met Him alive. We have been brought up on the tradition of the risen, living Lord. But to them it was all strange and mysterious.

B. *The Miracle of the Empty Tomb.* "He is risen."
This is the greatest miracle of all history. The Resurrection has been under attack many times in the past. There are still radical liberals who seek to explain it away as a purely subjective experience of the disciples (e.g., Bultmann). But it is gratifying to see how many leading theologians and Biblical

scholars of our day are underscoring the fact of the Resurrection as the indispensable foundation of the Christian faith.

C. *The Meaning of the Empty Tomb.* "Go . . . tell."

The New Testament indicates at least three things that the Resurrection means to us today.

1. *An accepted sacrifice.* Paul writes of Christ in Romans 4:25 — "Who was delivered for our offenses, and was raised again for our justification." If Jesus had died but not risen again we would still be left without hope. It was His resurrection which attested the fact that His sacrifice for our sins had been accepted, that His atoning death is valid for us. The Resurrection is the absolutely essential complement to the Crucifixion, without which the latter would not be complete.

2. *An abiding presence.* Because Jesus rose from the dead we may have the living presence of our risen Lord with us all the time. The empty tomb testifies to the absence of a dead corpse. It thereby implies a spiritual Presence.

3. *An appointed judgment.* Before the Areopagus at Athens Paul declared that God has commanded all men to repent, "Because he hath appointed a day, in the which he will judge the world in righteousness by that man whom he hath ordained; whereof he hath given assurance unto all men, in that he hath raised him from the dead." (Acts 17:31). The Resurrection is both a guarantee of our salvation and a warning of the certainty of the judgment.

BIBLIOGRAPHY

Alexander, J. A., *Commentary on the Gospel of Mark,* Grand Rapids: Zondervan Publishing House, 1955 (reprint)

Barclay, William, *The Gospel of Mark,* Philadelphia: Westminster Press

Branscomb, Harvie, *The Gospel of Mark* (The Moffatt New Testament Commentary), New York: Harper & Brothers, 1937

Earle, Ralph, *The Gospel According to Mark* (The Evangelical Commentary on the Bible), Grand Rapids: Zondervan Publishing House, 1957.

Erdman, Charles R., *The Gospel of Mark,* Philadelphia: Westminster Press, 1917

Grant, F. C. and Luccock, H. E., *The Interpreter's Bible,* Vol. 7., New York: Abingdon Press, 1951

Hunter, A. M., *Gospel According to St. Mark* (Torch Bible Commentaries), London: S. C. M. Press, 1948

Lange, J. P., "Mark" in *Commentary on the Holy Scriptures,* Grand Rapids: Zondervan Publishing House

Lenski, R. C. H., *The Interpretation of St. Mark's Gospel,* Columbus: Wartburg Press, 1946

Maclaren, Alex., *Expositions of Holy Scripture: St. Mark,* London: Grand Rapids: Wm. B. Eerdmans Publishing Co., 1944 (reprint)

Morison, James, *A Practical Commentary on the Gospel According to St. Mark,* 6th ed. London: Hodder & Stoughton, 1889

Rawlinson, A. E. J., *Westminster Commentaries,* London: Metheun & Co., 1925

Ryle, J. C., *Expository Thoughts on the Gospels,* 4 vols., Grand Rapids: Zondervan Publishing House (reprint)

Taylor, Vincent, *The Gospel According to St. Mark* (Greek text), London: Macmillan & Co., 1952

PREACHER'S HOMILETIC LIBRARY

PROCLAIMING THE NEW TESTAMENT

The Gospel of Luke

The Gospel
of Luke

by
Ralph Earle

BAKER BOOK HOUSE
Grand Rapids, Michigan

Reprinted, January, 1972

Library of Congress Catalog Card
Number: 68-14986

ISBN: 0-8010-6912-2

Preacher's Homiletic Library
ISBN: 0-8010-6916-5

Photolithoprinted by Cushing-Malloy, Inc.
Ann Arbor, Michigan, United States of America

Author's Introduction

"The most beautiful book ever written." That was how Renan described the Gospel of Luke.

It has special human interest appeal. The personality of Luke shows through very clearly. He was an unusually gracious Christian gentleman. Probably he was the most widely read and most widely traveled man in the first century church. It is generally held that he was the single Gentile writer of Scripture. He wrote two of the twenty-seven books of the New Testament — the third Gospel and Acts. But they are the two longest and together they comprise more than one fourth of the total contents.

Luke was the friend of the underdog. He was the champion of the rights of the Gentiles, of the Samaritans, of women, of children, of the poor, of sinners, of outcasts. In a day when social justice is being strongly advocated, Luke has something to say to us.

Most of the best known parables, the all-time favorites, are found only in Luke. One only need enumerate a few: the Good Samaritan, the Prodigal Son, the Unjust Steward, the Rich Fool.

Luke was evidently a great man of prayer. This is shown by the fact that he gives more attention to prayer than do any of the other Gospel writers. He does this in two ways. First, he mentions Jesus as praying on six different occasions (e.g., at His baptism and transfiguration) where the other Gospels omit this feature. Secondly, he gives more of Jesus' teachings on prayers. He alone preserves for us the three great parables on prayer: the Importunate Friend at Midnight, the Importunate Widow (or Unjust Judge), and the Pharisee and the Publican. These are found in the eleventh and eighteenth chapters.

Luke presents Jesus as the Son of Man. He gives such beautiful domestic touches as the unforgettable picture of

Martha and Mary (10:38-42), of Jesus and the two disciples from Emmaus (24:13-35). Luke was an artist with words. There is an ancient tradition that he was a painter of pictures. He loved poetry. Paul calls him "the beloved physician" (Col. 4:14). He was a great soul. His Gospel can be rich resource for preaching.

Contents

Luke 1

SERVICE THAT IS SACRED

1:74-75. "That he would grant unto us, that we being delivered out of the hand of our enemies might serve him without fear, in holiness and righteousness before him, all the days of our life."

I. HISTORICAL SETTING. Luke was a great historian. After a brief Preface of four verses — a gem of classical Greek — he begins his Gospel proper at 1:5. Typically, his opening words are: "There was in the days of Herod, the king of Judaea." This was Herod the Great, who ruled Palestine 37-4 B.C. He was an Idumaean (Edomite) with some Jewish blood in his veins. The incident recorded here probably took place in 6 B.C., something over a year before Jesus was born in 5 B.C.

II. EXPOSITORY MEANING. The word for "delivered" basically means "rescued." Christ was to come to rescue people from the clutches of sin and Satan. Thus delivered, they are to serve their Deliverer.

Four different Greek verbs are translated "serve" in the King James Version of the New Testament. The one here is *latreuo.* It may also be translated "worship." Actually true worship is the primary element in acceptable service to God.

The Greek word for "holiness" is a rare one, found only here and in Ephesians 4:24. In both places it is associated with "righteousness." The essential meaning of *hosiotes* is "piety," or a devout attitude toward God. Cremer says that "it denotes the spirit and conduct of one who is joined in fellowship with God."

"Righteousness" is a very common word in the New Testament, occurring 100 times (41 times in Romans). The Greek word used here is *dikaiosyne.* Thayer gives this definition:

11

"integrity, virtue, purity of life, uprightness, correctness in thinking, feeling, and acting." Of *dikaiosyne* and *hosiotes* he says that "the former denotes right conduct toward men, the latter piety towards God."

III. DOCTRINAL VALUE. Redemption is the keynote here (cf. 1:68). God has bought back his people, ransomed them from the slavery of sin. This involves remission of sins, which brings to one salvation (1:77). The "dayspring" (dawn) had appeared, "to give light to them that sit in darkness" and to "guide . . . into the way of peace" (1:78-79). This is what salvation does for the one who responds to the light of God's love.

The material here is naturally couched in Old Testament language, for Zechariah properly belongs to the old dispensation. But he spoke better than he knew. He was prophesying under the inspiration of the Spirit (1:67) and so predicted the salvation which would be provided in the great Deliverer, Jesus Christ. The Old Testament prophecies were being fulfilled in the coming of the Messiah.

IV. PRACTICAL AIM. The purpose of this passage is to show that salvation does not come through our own efforts but by a divine deliverance. No man can save himself. All men must look to God and trust only in Him if they would be saved.

V. HOMILETICAL FORM

Theme: "Service That Is Sacred."

Introduction: What the Jews wanted was political salvation, deliverance from domination by Rome. What they needed was personal salvation, deliverance from the dominion of sin.

So it is today. Modern society is crying out for reformation — racial, social, economic, political. What it desperately needs is regeneration, a spiritual renewal.

The central theme of Zechariah's Benedictus (1:68-79) is salvation. This means the forgiveness of sins and the living of a holy life. We are to be saved, not *in* sin but *from* sin. Purity must precede peace. Christ brings both.

The service that is sacred is:

A. *Service without Fear*

We are saved by faith. But faith banishes fear. The trusting soul is not afraid.

Paul wrote to Timothy: "For God hath not given us the spirit of fear; but of power, and of love, and of a sound mind" (II Tim. 1:7). The fearful saint cannot serve God either acceptably or effectively.

The secret of forever banishing fear is to realize that we are "in Christ." In Him we are delivered from our great enemy, sin. In Him we are protected against the onslaughts of Satan. In Him we have peace and purity and power. Apart from Him we have none of these.

Fear is a denial of faith. God does not want His children to live in fear. Peter walking on the water was all right as long as he looked at Jesus. But when he let his eyes drop to his surrounding circumstances he was terrified and began to sink. And so shall we. But Jesus is right there to rescue us, as He did Peter.

B. *Service in Holiness*

Holiness has to do primarily with our relationship to God. This is primary. What we are is more important than what we do. Inner piety must precede and produce outward performance. We cannot live a righteous life before our fellow men unless we maintain a holy fellowship in our hearts with God.

The trouble with most modern religion is that it starts with the outside of man, rather than the inside. In fact, one prominent writer in the field of psychology of religion has defined religion as "the sum total of human relationships."

When humanism gets rid of God it has to deny the reality of sin. There is no sin and no Savior. But this is a far cry from the religion of the Bible. It begins with God, shows man guilty and enslaved to sin, and then presents the Savior.

Only with holy hearts can we serve God acceptably. But He must make us holy.

C. Service in Righteousness

While the vertical relationships of life are all-important, the horizontal ones are also important. We cannot retain our right relationship to God unless we continually maintain a right relationship to our fellow men. That is the main thrust of Hebrews 12:14, which literally reads: "Keep on pursuing peace with all men and the sanctification apart from which no one shall see the Lord."

That is why we need to meet God in the morning before we meet men all day. We need the inner touch of Christ if we are going to live the Christian life.

We cannot be right with our fellow men unless we are first right with God. Inward holiness of heart must precede outward righteousness of life. We need to be sure that we are "in Christ" — not only positionally but powerfully — when we meet men. They must be confronted with Christ in us.

Luke 2

GOD'S GLORY AND MAN'S GOOD

2:14. "Glory to God in the highest, and on earth peace, good will toward men."

I. HISTORICAL SETTING. We do not know with certainty the exact day, month, or year in which Jesus was born. Because it is said that the shepherds were "abiding in the field, keeping watch over their flock by night" (v. 8), some have claimed this could not have been in late December. So October has been suggested as a substitute. But Samuel Andrews (*Life of Our Lord*, p. 16) writes that there is "no good ground to affirm that shepherds could not have been pasturing their flocks in the field during the month of December."

What about the year? In the sixth century a man named Dionysius figured the time of Christ's birth, and his system of dating events A.D. became common during the reign of Charlemagne (ninth century). But we know now that Dionysius was at least four years off in his calculation. For Herod the Great died in 4 B.C., and he was ruling when Jesus was born (Matt. 2:1). It is generally agreed today that Christ was born at least as early as 5 B.C., and possible in 6 B.C. Palestine was under Roman rule.

II. EXPOSITORY MEANING. The word for "glory" (*doxa*) may be translated "praise" or "honor." It is stated that the angelic host was "praising God" (v. 13).

The Greek begins: "Glory in the highest to God." The literal Latin of this, *Gloria in Excelsis Deo*, has furnished the title to one of the great songs of the Christmas season. Appropriately it is called the "Angelic Hymn."

"Peace" is *eirene*, from which comes the name Irene. This was originally the name of the goddess of Peace. Thayer

15

points out the various usages of this term in the New Testament. It first meant "a state of national tranquillity; exemption from the rage and havoc of war." Then it was used for "peace between individuals, i.e., harmony, discord." Next it meant "security, safety, prosperity." Fourthly, there was a special sense (used here), "the Messiah's peace." Fifthly, there is the distinct Christian conception: "the tranquil state of a soul assured of its salvation through Christ, and so fearing nothing from God and content with its earthly lot, of whatsoever sort that is."

III. DOCTRINAL VALUE. Peace is one of God's best gifts to man. It should always be recognized as a divine gift, not a human attainment. Christ's presence *is* peace.

IV. PRACTICAL AIM. To show the only way that peace can be found by individuals or by society.

V. HOMILETICAL FORM
   Theme: "God's Glory and Man's Good."
   Introduction: When the divine pronouncement of peace was made it did not come in a king's palace or at a conference table. The announcement was given to a group of humble shepherds in the open field. But the splendor of that historical moment far exceeded anything that man could have provided. For, "the angel of the Lord came upon them, and the glory of the Lord shone round about them" (v. 9). The Shekinah of God's presence overshadowed the shepherds as they heard the long awaited news that the Messiah had now come. Born that day in the city of David, He was to be a Savior, Christ the Lord.

   A. *Glory to God*
   In the familiar words of the Westminster Catechism, man's true aim is "to glorify God and enjoy Him forever." Some have found fault with this, maintaining that social responsibility should be given the priority over spiritual devotion. But what we must recognize is that it is only God's glory that brings man's highest good.

There are three ways that we may give glory to God. The first is by praising Him with our lips. This can be done by joining with others in congregational singing or by giving personal testimony to God's goodness and love to us. The second way is by lifting up Christ in our lives, displaying the implanted divine nature in true Christian living. The third way is by winning souls to the Kingdom. All of these bring glory to God as well as blessing to man.

B. *Peace on Earth*

One of the things that men desire most is peace. But they seek it the wrong way. The Bible throughout teaches clearly that righteousness must precede peace. We cannot have "peace with God" until we have been made right with God.

1. Political peace is what most men pray for. They cry out for the cessation of war. If we could only live in peace, everyone would be happy!

The only trouble with this is that it is not so. Times of national and international peace are not marked by moral progress, by love and joy in men's hearts. Often there is strife and hatred. Outward peace and prosperity have not satisfied man's deepest needs.

2. Social peace is desired by all good men. We deplore racial discrimination and the hate it engenders. We are opposed to any clash of classes. There must be freedom, with justice for all. But social problems are not settled by legislation alone. There must be the will to do right.

3. Spiritual peace is what man needs most. This can come only through the presence of the Prince of Peace. When He rules in our hearts, there is peace within. And that is where all true peace begins.

C. *Good Will toward Men*

The best Greek text reads: "among men of good will." And yet this is not quite an adequate translation. *Eudokia* can also mean "favor, good pleasure." Most scholars feel that this is the correct meaning here — "among men with whom he is pleased." That is, peace comes to those who are recipients of God's grace.

Actually, the two ideas are closely related. Men of good will are those who have submitted to God's will. The two words "good" and "God" are closely related. In fact, the former is derived from the latter. In the ultimate sense only the godly are good.

God can give His gracious bequest of peace only to those who accept His favor and so become men of His good pleasure. Jesus said not to the world but to His disciples: "Peace I leave with you, my peace I give unto you" (John 14:27). When we receive Christ into our hearts, His presence becomes our peace.

What our nation needs to do today is to cease its human search for peace and turn in repentance to the Prince of Peace. And it is the same path that individuals must take. Peace is to be found not in psychology or sociology but in Jesus Christ.

Luke 3

GOD'S FOURFOLD FORMULA

3:4. "Prepare ye the way of the Lord. . . ."
3:5. "Every valley shall be filled, And every mountain and hill shall be brought low, And the crooked shall be made straight, And the rough ways shall be made smooth;"
3:6. "And all flesh shall see the salvation of God."

I. HISTORICAL SETTING. Luke was the leading historian in the early church. His historical bent of mind shows up sharply in this chapter. The beginning of John the Baptist's ministry is dated as coming "in the fifteenth year of the reign of Tiberius Caesar" (v. 1). Tiberius was the second emperor of the Roman Empire. The dates of his reign are usually given as A.D. 14-37. But he became associated with Augustus in the ruling of the empire in A.D. 11 or 12. This would make the fifteenth year to be A.D. 26, which fits in well with the death of Jesus in A.D. 30 (perhaps six months for John's preaching and three and a half years for Jesus' public ministry).

Altogether Luke names five rulers and two priests in giving the historical setting for John's ministry. Pontius Pilate was governor of Judea (A.D. 26-36). Herod Antipas, son of Herod the Great, was "tetrarch of Galilee" (and Perea). His brother Philip ruled over some areas to the northeast of Galilee, and Lysanias over territory farther north near Damascus.

Annas and Caiaphas are mentioned as "being the high priests" (v. 2). The official high priest at this time was Caiaphas (A.D. 18-36). But his father-in-law Annas still exercised the authority. He had held the office A.D. 6-15, and then was succeeded by five of his sons, as well as his son-in-law. All were wicked men, more politicians than

19

priests. The nation of Israel was in desperate need of a spiritual revival. This was the burden of John the Baptist's ministry.

II. EXPOSITORY MEANING. John preached a "baptism of repentance for the remission of sins" (v. 3). That is, it was a repentance-baptism. He would not baptize anyone in water without requiring first a confession of sins (Mark 1: 4-5).

The Greek word for "repentance" means "a change of mind." Thayer represents well the thrust of this when he writes: "Especially the change of mind of those who have begun to abhor their errors and misdeeds, and have determined to enter upon a better course of life, so that it embraces both a recognition of sin and sorrow for it and hearty deeds."

III. DOCTRINAL VALUE. Repentance is often superficially thought of as being sorry. More adequate is the suggestion that it means "being sorry enough to quit." But the real sense is a radical change of attitude — toward God, sin, the world, and ourselves.

IV. PRACTICAL AIM. To show the need for repentance, and the results of repentance in bringing God's blessing.

V. HOMILETICAL FORM
    Theme: "God's Fourfold Formula."
    Introduction: "Prepare ye the way of the Lord." The picture is that of an Oriental prince making an official visit to one of his provinces. The people in those outlying districts busy themselves filling in valleys, cutting down hills, straightening out curves, and smoothing out rough places. They are eager for their sovereign to have a good road on which to travel.
    So God was saying to Israel, and says to us today: "Prepare ye the way of the Lord." And then He spells out that preparation in four specific points, promising that if they

obey, "all flesh shall see the salvation of God" (v. 6). This is God's fourfold formula for a revival.

A. *Fill In the Valleys*

The first thing an engineer does in building a highway is to fill in the low spots. In our Christian experience these may be of two kinds.

1. Sags in Our Souls. These are due mainly to two things. The first is neglect of Bible reading. If a person were to go without eating at all for a week or two he would feel very weak. So it is spiritually. A person can no more keep strong spiritually without eating spiritual food than he can keep strong physically without eating physical food. We must feed our souls on the Word of God every day to maintain our spiritual health. The second thing that causes sags in our souls is neglect of prayer. We need to realize that prayer is the breath of our spiritual life. Paul says, "Pray without ceasing." Don't stop breathing!

2. Low Spots in Our Living. It is deadly to live on low levels. Too many people live in the malaria-infested swamps of unbelief and worldliness. This can prove fatal.

B. *Cut Down the Hills*

These may be hills of hindrance, such as pride, self-will, self-assertion and the like. They must be attacked with determination and resolutely leveled if we are going to prepare the way for the Lord to come. It is working on just such matters that often precipitates a revival.

Or they may be hills of difficulty. We think of restitution that seems hard to make. More frequently there are difficult adjustments in our daily lives — at home, at work, at school, at church. Adjusting to both unfavorable circumstances and unpleasant personalities can sometimes be difficult indeed. But adjust we must, if we are going to have the divine blessing.

C. *Straighten Out the Curves*

The most obvious application is to crooked conduct. This can be devastating to our own spiritual life and destructive of the church. People will not overlook any dishonest business dealings, or even what looks shady.

But there is a more penetrating application to the little deceptions that are easy to practice. There is nothing so deceiving as the temptation to deceive. We rationalize and then find ourselves in trouble.

D. *Smooth Out the Bumps*

These may be thought of first as bumps and humps in our personalities. We all have some. They hinder those around us and hurt both our fellowship with other Christians and our influence on outsiders.

A second way of looking at it would be that these represent holes in the road that come through the wear and tear of daily living. A lot of traffic goes over lives in these busy days. Soon we have "chuck holes" of impatience and irritability. These need to be taken care of promptly.

Luke 4

AN ANOINTED MINISTRY

4:18. "The Spirit of the Lord is upon me, Because he hath anointed me to preach the gospel to the poor; He hath sent me to heal the brokenhearted, To preach deliverance to the captives, And recovering of sight to the blind, To set at liberty them that are bruised."

I. HISTORICAL SETTING. Matthew (13:53-58) and Mark (6:1-6) both record a visit of Jesus to His home town of Nazareth. But they place it at a later point in his ministry. There has been considerable dispute as to whether the two visits are the same. If they are, Luke probably placed it first as "a dramatic frontispiece to Jesus' public ministry."

"As his custom was" (v. 16), Christ went into the synagogue on the Sabbath Day — thus setting us an example for regular church attendance. He "stood up" as an evidence that He would like to read the Scripture lesson. Since He was handed the scroll of the prophet Isaiah, it is obvious that the regularly prescribed portion from the Law (Pentateuch) had already been read. The synagogue services began with the repeating of the Shema (Deut. 6:4-9; 11:13-21; Num. 15:37-41), followed by a prayer, the reading of the lesson from the Law, and then a portion from the prophets. It is claimed that in Palestine the Pentateuch was read through in prescribed sections over a period of three years, whereas the reader of the prophets could choose his own selection. Jesus chose Isaiah 61:1 (with the first clause of v. 2).

II. EXPOSITORY MEANING. "Anointed" is the verb *chrio* from which comes *Christos*, the "Anointed One." Thus there is a significant connection in the Greek which is lost in English. "To preach the gospel to the poor" is only two words in

Greek — *evangelisasthai ptochois* (literally, "to evangelize poor people"). "Gospel" means "good news."

"To heal the brokenhearted" is not found here in the best Greek text (cf. recent translations). But it is in Isaiah 61:1, which is quoted here. So we have included it in the sermon outline. In the Septuagint of Isaiah 61:1 "the broken-hearted" is literally "those who have been crushed in their heart."

The second "preach" is a different word in the Greek from the first. This one is *keryxai*, from *keryx*, "herald." So it means to "herald" or "proclaim." "Captive" is basically a military term, "one taken in war." "Liberty" and "deliverance" are the same in Greek, *aphesis*, which means a "release," as from bondage or imprisonment. "Them that are bruised" is one word, *tethrausmenous* — literally, those who have been broken in pieces, shattered, broken down, and are still in that state.

III. DOCTRINAL VALUE. Salvation is pictured here as healing from the brokenhearted, deliverance from captivity, recovering of sight, and freedom from oppression. The point is that salvation is more than the forgiveness of sins, wonderful as that is. It is health and liberty.

IV. PRACTICAL AIM. To show what the real nature of salvation is and what it does for the one who receives it.

V. HOMILETICAL FORM

Theme: "An Anointed Ministry."

Introduction: Jesus was anointed with the Holy Spirit at His baptism (3:22). "Being full of the Holy Ghost," He was "led by the Spirit into the wilderness" (4:1). There for forty days He was tempted by the devil. Having overcome, "Jesus returned in the power of the Spirit into Galilee" (4:14). Now in His "home church" He makes the Messianic announcement: "The Spirit of the Lord is upon me, because he hath anointed me."

This anointing of the Spirit was for a fivefold ministry: evangelizing the poor, healing the crushed in heart, releasing the captives, giving sight to the blind, and freeing the oppressed.

A. *Good News for the Poor*

Too often the church has neglected the poor, while it has cultivated the cultured and ministered to those with means. But one of the glories of Christ's ministry was that He evangelized the poor. When John the Baptist sent emissaries to inquire whether Jesus was really the Messiah, the Master gave as the climactic, final proof: "the poor have the gospel preached to them" (Matt. 11:5) — literally, "poor people are being evangelized." If we would follow in Christ's footsteps, we too must minister to the poor. They are often more responsive than are the self-sufficient.

The gospel is surely good news for the poor. It tells them that they can have an inheritance in Christ equally with the cultured, the educated, and the wealthy. God pays no attention to these outward circumstances.

B. *Healing for the Brokenhearted*

Today many people are crushed in their hearts — and for many reasons. With some it is an unreasonable husband or an untrue wife. For others it is ungrateful children or ungodly parents. It sometimes seems as if almost everybody has a bit of heartache, if not heartbreak.

But Christ came to heal the hearts that have been hurt. His very presence brings peace and comfort to those who accept Him. He is the Great Physician, and the only one who knows how to heal broken hearts.

Never was this healing ministry more needed than now. An ounce of balm for people's emotional disturbances can often do more than a pound of cure for their mental illnesses. This is a day when the Christian ministry is confronted with its greatest challenge — but also its greatest opportunity.

C. *Release for the Imprisoned*

The sinner is in captivity to Satan. He has been captured

in the warfare of life. He is a prisoner of the enemy, not free to live as he knows he ought to live.

But Christ came to deliver the captive, to set him free. This again is good news.

D. *Recovery for the Blind*

In the Bible the sinner is portrayed as being dead, sick, diseased, imprisoned, living in darkness. Salvation is deliverance from all of these.

Out of compassion for their sad lot Jesus healed many blind men. But this was also a symbol of the fact that He gives sight to the spiritual eyes blinded by sin.

E. *Freedom for the Oppressed*

Many lives today are broken to pieces, shattered by sin, broken down under the burdens of life. To such the Christian can come with a message of hope. The compassionate Christ was also broken by sin — not His but ours. But His seeming tragedy on the cross has become a triumph for all who will accept Him. All who are in Christ Jesus are set at liberty. The oppressed are free.

Luke 5

THE SECRET OF SUCCESSFUL FISHING

5:4. "Launch out into the deep, and let down your nets for a draught."
5:5. "Nevertheless at thy word I will let down the net."
5:10. "From henceforth thou shalt catch men."

I. HISTORICAL SETTING. Whether this incident is the same as the call of the four fishermen in Matthew 4:18-22 and Mark 1:16-21 is still a matter of open debate. The best of scholars are divided on the question. Matthew and Mark place the call at the very beginning of Jesus' Galilean ministry. In Luke, on the other hand, the incident recorded here has been preceded by several miracles (4:33-41), as well as by a tour of Galilee (4:44).

II. EXPOSITORY MEANING. Jesus stood one day on the shore of "the lake of Gennesaret." This is the only place where this name is used in the New Testament. Matthew and Mark regularly refer to it as "the sea of Galilee," or simply "the sea." To the men who lived on its shores — Mark reflects Peter's point of view — it seemed like a sea. But Luke accurately calls it a lake, for it was only about thirteen miles long and seven miles wide. The name Gennesaret was derived from a small plain (about three miles long by a mile and a half wide) on the northwestern shore of the lake.

"Ship" is more properly translated "boat." Actually it was a small fishing craft, perhaps twenty to forty feet in length, such as can still be seen on the Lake of Galilee. "Nets" refers to seines, dragged through the water to enclose a large number of fish. One can see them today being washed and hung up in the sun to dry. "Standing by the lake" (v. 2) is better translated "lying at the water's edge" (NEB).

27

III. DOCTRINAL VALUE. Obedience to God's will always brings blessing. When Peter obeyed he reaped a rich reward.

IV. PRACTICAL AIM. To show how we may become successful fishers of men. By following the example of Peter we may hope for similar results.

V. HOMILETICAL FORM

Theme: "The Secret of Successful Fishing."

Introduction: It all happened on the shore of the Lake of Galilee, near Capernaum. The vast crowd of people pressed forward on Jesus until He was in danger of being pushed into the water.

Pulled up at the water's edge, or possibly on the beach, were two fishing boats. Climbing into one of them, Jesus asked its owner, Peter, to push out a little way from the shore. Then He sat down, as was the custom for Jewish rabbis, and taught the people who were thronging the beach.

Having asked for the use of the boat as an improvised "pulpit," Christ paid Simon a handsome rental fee by presenting him with an immense catch of fish. Jesus will not be in debt to any man.

A. *Pushing Out.* "Launch out into the deep."

Superficiality is one of the main secrets of failure. Shallow water cannot contain big fish. For success in any area of life one must heed the admonition: "Launch out into the deep."

"Nothing ventured, nothing won" is a principle that has wide application. Even in the business world it is the man who "launches out" into the deep water who makes the big haul. While others are content to catch a few little minnows in their tiny pond, this man pushes far out into the lake — and comes back with a boatload of fish.

Such a man was Bernard Gimbel. His poor father owned a little corner grocery. Bernard kept pushing out into bigger territory. Finally he envisioned something far beyond. Against the strong protest of his father and brother, he decided to enter the deep and dangerous financial waters of

New York City. It looked like sheer folly. But it made him a multimillionaire.

The same principle holds in Christian work. A succession of pastors — and the church is still the same size after a dozen or twenty years. Suddenly something happens. The "hopeless" situation springs to life, spurts down to the road to phenomenal success in a matter of months. What made the difference? The new pastor pushed out into the deep water of an aggressive campaign for reaching the lost in his community. He soon had a great catch of fish. The same thing is happening in large evangelistic crusades.

Courageous action is one of the great secrets of success. Timid souls never win great victories. Nor do lazy, inactive "saints."

B. *Putting Down.* "Let down your nets for a draught."

It was not enough for Peter to push out into deep water. There were fish there, lots of them. But he had to let down his net in order to catch them.

Occasionally a pastor, Sunday School superintendent, or church board plans a big project. Enthusiasm is gendered, excitement runs rife. Something great is going to happen!

But big talk does not guarantee big results. The "follow through" is what really counts. Planned projects can end up as pitiful problems. If the fish out there in the community are going to be caught, the church is going to have to let down the net in an earnest, persistent crusade of visitation evangelism. Seldom can the sophisticated "fish" of modern suburbia be lured by tempting bait, no matter how dazzling. If they are going to be caught, one must go where they are.

C. *Pulling In.* "They inclosed a great multitude of fishes."

When the Master issued His command to launch out into the deep and let down the net, Peter protested: "We have worked hard all night and caught nothing." It was foolish to waste any more time trying to do the impossible.

But fortunately Peter did not stop there. He went on to say: "Nevertheless at thy word I will let down the net."

When we are willing to realize that Christ knows better than we do, and follow His orders though they may seem foolish to us, we can hope to have success. Obedience is the most important secret of successful fishing for men.

When Peter obeyed, results came — surprising, spectacular. The net let down was filled with a large school of fish, so that it was beginning to break. Peter and Andrew waved frantically to their partners, James and John. Together the four men managed to haul in the net. The immense catch filled both boats until they were almost overweighted. Peter's obedience made it possible for his partners to share in the blessings he received.

Then Jesus said to Peter: "From henceforth thou shalt catch men." This was to be his supreme calling in life. And it is ours today.

Luke 6

MAKING MOUNTAINS OUT OF MOLEHILLS

6:2. "Why do ye that which is not lawful to do on the sabbath days?"
6:5. "The Son of man is Lord also of the sabbath."
6:9. "Is it lawful on the sabbath days to do good, or to do evil? to save life, or to destroy it?"

I. HISTORICAL SETTING. The two incidents from which our triple text is taken came at the end of a series of five conflicts between the Pharisees and Jesus. The first was over His authority to forgive sins (5:21). The second was a criticism of His associating with publicans and sinners (5:30). The third had to do with the question of fasting (5:33).

The first objection was due to a failure to recognize His deity. Only God has a right to forgive sins! Granted. But Jesus was God. So He had authority to pronounce men's sins forgiven.

The second was due to a failure to understand His humanity. Christ came to be one of us. He not only took upon himself a physical body but He entered into human living in a meaningful way. He became involved! The Pharisees were "separatists" — that is what the name means. Jesus got next to sinners in order to save them.

The third criticism reflected the overemphasis on asceticism on the part of the Pharisees of that day. The Mosaic law prescribed one annual day of fasting. But now the pious Pharisees were fasting twice a week (18:12). Jesus believed in living a normal, happy life that radiated joy instead of producing gloom. This was one great difference between Pharisaism and Christianity.

II. EXPOSITORY MEANING. The first incident in the Scripture lesson took place on "the second sabbath after the

31

first" (v. 1) literally, "a second-first (*deuteroproto*) sabbath."
The term is found nowhere else and its exact meaning is
unknown. It should be noted that the oldest Greek manuscripts have simply "on a sabbath."

"Corn fields" should be "grainfields" and "ears of corn"
should be "heads of grain." Actually the grain was either
barley or wheat, probably the latter. But in the British Isles
wheat is still spoken of as corn (cf. NEB). What is called
"corn" in the United States was unknown in the Old World.
Indian maize was given that name by the early colonists
from England simply because they were in the habit of
referring to all grain as "corn."

"Showbread" (v. 4) is literally "loaves of the presentation";
that is, "bread of the Presence." It was a beautiful type of
Christ as the Bread of Life on which we are to feed our souls.

"Watched" (v. 7) is a strong compound in the Greek, meaning "watched closely" or "observed narrowly." The Pharisees
were eyeing Jesus narrowly, hoping He would do something
they could criticize. This picayunish attitude caused them
to make mountains out of molehills.

III. DOCTRINAL VALUE. Sabbath observance is a part
of Christianity, as it was of Judaism. What we need to do is
to find out what Jesus had to say on this important subject.

IV. PRACTICAL AIM. To discover how our Lord would
have us to observe His day — what is in Revelation 1:10 called
"the Lord's day."

V. HOMILETICAL FORM

Theme: "Making Mountains out of Molehills."

Introduction: Little people major on minors. Big people
are busily engaged in things that really matter. This difference reveals the measure of our character. Are we majoring
on the truly important things of life?

The Pharisees were overly concerned about the minutiae
of Sabbath observance. In the Talmud no less than twenty-
four chapters are devoted to the subject. They found two

opportunities at this time to criticize Jesus and His disciples for failing to keep the man-made regulations of rabbinical Judaism.

A. *What Is Lawful?* "Why do ye that which is not lawful to do on the sabbath days?"

Jesus and His twelve apostles were walking through some fields of ripened grain. Hungry, the disciples began to pluck heads of wheat. They rubbed them in their hands, blew the husks away, and ate the raw kernels — one of nature's most nutritious foods.

All this was perfectly proper. The Mosaic law expressly said: "When thou comest into the standing corn of thy neighbor, then thou mayest pluck the ears with thine hand" (Deut. 23:25).

But the trouble was that this was on the sabbath day. The disciples were working. When they plucked the heads of wheat they were *harvesting*. When they rubbed off the husks in their hands they were *threshing*. When they blew the chaff away from the kernels they were *winnowing*. They really were breaking the Law!

These Pharisaic critics were typical legalists, making mountains out of molehills. As far as they were concerned the few innocent gestures of the disciples were just as bad as though they were working hard in the fields all day long on the Sabbath, harvesting, threshing, and winnowing their grain. The failure to make a proper assessment of moral values is the mark of a legalist.

B. *Who Is Lord?* "The Son of man is Lord also of the sabbath."

Over against all this rabbinical casuistry Jesus set His authority as Lord of the Sabbath. He had a right to declare what was allowable and what was forbidden. If He said it was all right for His disciples to eat some grain as they walked along, happily conversing with Him, then it was right.

Christianity is a religion of love, joy, and peace. These three virtues should characterize the life of every follower of Christ. These are the real mountains of religious experience. But the legalist turns these mountains into molehills with his harsh, unloving, joyless attitude. Everything is grim duty. Enjoyment of what one is doing is a sign that it must be sinful. Not so with Jesus. He lived life to the full and gave it new meaning and sacredness.

C. *Why Is Life?* "Is it lawful on the sabbath days to do good, or to do evil? to save life, or to destroy it?"

Why was the Sabbath instituted? Not just to make another regulation. Not to save religion, but to save life.

With Jesus life was all-important. He declared: "The sabbath was made for man, and not man for the sabbath" (Mark 2:27). The reason God ordained one day of rest and worship was that He knew man needed it — rest for his body, worship for his spirit.

What is proper to do on the Sabbath Day? This question has caused a lot of discussion. But Jesus had a very simple answer. Here it is put in the form of a rhetorical question: "Is it lawful . . . to do good, or to do evil?" The answer is obvious. Jesus himself put it in a categorical statement: "Wherefore it is lawful to do well on the sabbath days" (Matt. 12:12). Whatever is good for us and others — in the highest sense of "good" — is proper on the Lord's day.

Luke 7

THE COMPASSIONATE CHRIST

7:13. "And when the Lord saw her, he had compassion on her, and said unto her, Weep not."

I. HISTORICAL SETTING. The previous incident in this chapter is that of the healing of the centurion's servant at Capernaum. This officer sent elders of the Jews to ask Jesus to come and heal the servant who was at the point of death. The emissaries informed Christ that the centurion had built them a synagogue. He had helped others; now he needed help.

As Jesus approached the home, the centurion sent a further message. He was not worthy of having the Master come into his home. In fact, he had not felt worthy to speak to Christ directly. But all the Master had to do was speak the word, even at a distance, and his servant would be healed. The man thus exhibited a faith that made Jesus marvel. And his faith was rewarded.

From Capernaum Christ and his disciples walked down the western side of the Lake of Galilee to the village of Nain —a good day's walk of about twenty-five miles. Nain was situated on the slope of "Little Hermon," between Mount Gilboa and Mount Tabor in the Plain of Esdraelon (which separates Galilee from Samaria).

II. EXPOSITORY MEANING. For "bier" (v. 14) the margin of the King James Version has "coffin." But it seems evident that "bier" is the more correct translation, and it is followed in recent versions. At least it was not a closed coffin, for the young man "sat up" (v. 15). Probably it was just a flat platform of wooden boards on which the body was placed, as in Muslim funerals today. Burials in those days were crude and simple.

The young man had been dead for only a few hours. Because of the hot climate of Palestine and the lack of modern embalming techniques, it was required that the body should be buried the same day a person died.

III. DOCTRINAL VALUE. Luke portrays Jesus as the Son of Man. This incident is one of the many where he paints an unforgettable picture of the compassionate Christ. The Master has a tender love for sorrowing, suffering humanity.

IV. PRACTICAL AIM. To show how Christ comes to us in the emergencies of life to meet our needs fully. No situation is too hard for Him. No circumstances are impossible. No case is hopeless. "Jesus Christ is the same yesterday, and today, and forever." He can minister to us in our deepest sorrows and keenest sufferings, even as He did to this widow.

V. HOMILETICAL FORM

Theme: "The Compassionate Christ."

Introduction: Of Jesus in His earthly ministry it was said, "He went about doing good." He is still going about doing good. He is present at funerals as well as weddings. He shares our tears as well as our sunshine. Always He is there to meet our need.

A. *Compassing the Circumstances.* "A dead man . . . the only son of his mother, and she was a widow."

Nain was located on a hillside, right near the modern Arab village of Nein in Israel. Followed by a crowd, Jesus was walking toward the town. As He came past the cemetery and neared the gate of the city, He saw a scene that gripped Him with compassion. Men were carrying a bier, on which was lying the corpse of a young man. Behind the bier walked a lonely figure, a woman bent low with grief. No husband at her side, no son was there to attend to her needs. It was obvious that she was a widow and that the dead body was that of her only son.

All this Jesus took in at a glance. And He knew what that meant. Not only was the woman utterly bereft of loved ones;

she was completely uncared for economically. For when the husband in a home died, the oldest son became the head of the house — not the mother. He was fully obligated to provide for her. In this case, since there was no younger son, he was her sole support, socially and economically.

In those days a woman could not take a job as now — in office, store, or factory. This widow had lost her only source of income. To the sorrow of having lost both husband and only son was added fear of financial destitution. Her plight was indeed a sad one. The people of the city tried to show their concern. But her heart was utterly lonely.

B. *Comforting the Comfortless.* "Weep not."

When Jesus' understanding compassed the whole circumstance of the woman's tragedy, He was moved with compassion. He stepped to her side and said gently, "Don't weep any more."

She must have looked startled. If anybody had a right to weep, she did. Possibly she resented this intrusion. What business did He have interfering in her sorrow? To tell her to stop weeping seemed utterly heartless. This was the only release she had for her pent up grief.

But Jesus is never heartless, never unkind. He knew what He was going to do. Soon her weeping would be turned to rejoicing.

It takes confidence in Christ to obey His commands. But that is where faith comes in. If we believe that He knows best and that He is both able and willing to do that best, then faith becomes obedience.

C. *Commanding the Corpse.* "I say unto thee, Arise."

If telling the woman to stop weeping seemed unreasonable, ordering her dead son to arise sounded utterly ridiculous. But no sooner had Jesus said the word than the young man sat up. To prove that he was fully alive he began to talk. We do not know what he said. But presumably he spoke to his mother with tender love and thanked Jesus for restoring him to life.

The Master did not ask this man to follow Him in full time

service. Instead "he delivered him to his mother." The young man's first responsibility was in the home. His mother desperately needed him. Christ is concerned for all of life. He is interested in our social and economic, as well as spiritual, needs. And He is able to supply every need. He will do to trust.

Luke 8

LIFE'S THREE GREATEST THREATS

8:14. *"And that which fell among thorns are they, which, when they have heard, go forth, and are choked with cares and riches and pleasures of this life, and bring no fruit to perfection."*

I. HISTORICAL SETTING. Jesus was conducting a preaching tour of Galilee. We read that He "went throughout every city and village, preaching and showing the glad tidings of the kingdom of God" (v. 1). The two participles are literally "proclaiming and evangelizing."

Besides the twelve apostles, He was accompanied by "certain women" (v. 2). Three are named: Mary Magdalene, Joanna, and Susanna. Out of Mary Jesus had cast seven demons (not "devils"). Joanna was the wife of Chuza, a steward of Herod Antipas who ruled Galilee. Susanna is not further identified. These grateful women helped to provide food and clothing for the Lord; they "ministered unto him of their substance."

When a large crowd gathered on the shore of the Lake of Galilee, Jesus proceeded to give the people a parable. Recorded in all three Synoptic Gospels, the Parable of the Sower is one of the best known of Jesus' many parables. Fortunately, the Master himself gave a full explanation of its meaning.

II. EXPOSITORY MEANING. "Parable" comes from the Greek *parabole* — literally, "something thrown beside," and so a comparison. Unlike a fable, a parable is always true to life.

There were many footpaths leading through the fields. Hence in the process of scattering seed with wide sweeps of the hand as the sower strode across the ground, some seed would fall on the hard-packed path. Here the birds would devour it. Also the soil of Palestine is full of rocks, so that some seed would certainly fall on shallow earth above a ledge of rock. Having no depth of root, the plants would soon wither and die. In both these cases there was no grain.

III. DOCTRINAL VALUE. This parable shows clearly that the results of gospel preaching depend not only on the divine sowing but also on the human response. Jesus was talking first about the varying reactions to His teaching. All four kinds of soil described here were to be found in His audiences.

But the same is true today. No matter how clearly and forcefully the Word of God is presented, the results are largely governed by the attitudes of the hearers. And in almost any large congregation all four types of soil will be found. Jesus did not win all his hearers, and neither shall we.

IV. PRACTICAL AIM. To show the importance of responding "in depth" to the preaching of God's Word. Hearers need to be challenged to realize that they, not the preacher, are responsible for what they do with the messages they listen to. If they treat the gospel indifferently or superficially, they are the losers.

V. HOMILETICAL FORM

Theme: "Life's Three Greatest Threats."

Introduction: The Parable of the Sower may more properly be called the Parable of the Soils. For the emphasis is on four kinds of soil on which seed is sown. No fruit results from sowing on hard or shallow soil. But in this message we wish to concentrate our attention on only one of the four — the thorn-infested ground. Jesus interpreted the thorns as suggesting three things in life:

A. *Anxieties.* The Greek noun comes from a verb which means "to be drawn in different directions." It refers therefore to the distractions of the mind, or to "the worries of life."

This is one of the greatest threats to spiritual growth. And it is increasing rather than decreasing today. The time was when life was relatively simple. A person could spend a rather quiet day at home, with no distractions.

But this is forever in the past. The doorbell, the telephone, the radio, the television — all these clamor for our attention. Life has become complicated, and so more divisive. One feels drawn in many directions at once, pulled to pieces. Most people today do not know how to be quiet and give time for growth.

Then, too, it seems that our worries have multiplied. High pressure advertising helps to bring this about. We purchase more than we should — "It's so easy to charge it!" — and then worry about our monthly payments. The pressure of this keeps us from taking care of the more important things of life. We are ashamed to pray for help in our folly. So we keep on worrying.

Anxiety is high on the list of causes of emotional disturbance and mental illness. But long before it gets to the stage where we have trouble with our social relationships, it may be cutting off our fellowship with God. Anxiety chokes faith; it strangles trust; it separates us from the Lord.

B. *Riches.* There never was a time when income was so high as it is for most Americans today. Our wages and salaries are larger, but not our savings.

But the very fact that we handle more money than ever before makes the threat of riches increasingly serious. There are so many ways to make "big money" these days. Why be content with a hundred dollars a week when one can make two hundred? But we are not content to stop there. We go on to three hundred, perhaps four hundred.

If we do not watch out, about this time money will be getting a strangle hold on our hearts. All we can think about is making more money. It is our meat and drink. With the thought of it we go to bed at night and get up in the morning.

The Psalmist warned: "If riches increase, set not your heart upon them." For most people today riches are increasing.

If we would save our souls, we must not set our hearts on riches.

C. *Pleasures.* Was there ever a time when the entire population seemed so pleasure-bent as today? Entertainment is big business — not only in hundreds of kinds of amusement centers, but right in our homes. Constructive conversation has been replaced by wasted time watching television. With too many people helpful reading has suffered the same fate.

The price paid for pleasure annually in the United States would make a staggering total, if we could add it up. But this can never be done. Presumably data could be collected, and a financial report given. But this would not represent the tragic total. For we have paid the price of wasted time, jaded nerves, dissipated emotions, and weakened wills. Pleasure presents herself as a beautiful maidservant, ready to wait on our every whim. But she ends up a monstrous slave master. Bishop Ryle comments: "The money, the pleasures, the daily business of the world, are so many traps to catch souls."

Luke 9

TESTS OF DISCIPLESHIP

9:58. "The Son of man hath not where to lay his head."
9:60. "Let the dead bury their dead: but go thou and preach the kingdom of God."
9:62. "No man, having put his hand to the plough, and looking back, is fit for the kingdom of God."

I. HISTORICAL SETTING. The major part of Jesus' public ministry seems to have been spent in Galilee. But now He was leaving there for the last time. Luke records: "And it came to pass, when the time was come that he should be received up, he stedfastly set his face to go to Jerusalem" (v. 51).

For the next nearly ten chapters (9:51—19:28) we have what is usually referred to as the Perean Ministry of Jesus. For the next few months it would seem that the Master spent most of His time in this territory east of the Jordan River. Perea is from the Greek *peran*, "across," and was the ancient name of Transjordan. It was ruled, along with Galilee, by Herod Antipas.

It would seem that Jesus first planned to take the shortest route to Jerusalem, straight south through Samaria. He sent messengers ahead to arrange lodgings for the night. But the Samaritan village where they inquired refused accommodations because the party was headed for Jerusalem. James and John, the "sons of thunder," wanted to call down fire out of heaven to destroy these wretches. But the Master rebuked their wrong spirit and led the way to another village (9:55-56).

II. EXPOSITORY MEANING. The Greek word for "lay" (v. 58) is from the same root as that for "couch" or "bed." So it means "to rest." Jesus had no place of His own where

43

He might rest His head. He who created all things never possessed any property, as far as the record goes.

"Preach" (v. 60) is neither of the common words translated this way, but *diangello*, which means "publish abroad, proclaim." It was time to proclaim the Kingdom.

In Christ's day one would literally "put his hand to the plough" (v. 62). One can still see occasionally a crude plow consisting only of a crooked stick being pulled through stony ground by a calf and/or a donkey hitched together. The single end is held by one hand.

III. DOCTRINAL VALUE. The cost of discipleship was a favorite topic with Jesus. It shows up rather prominently in all three Synoptic Gospels. Here three men are tested as to whether they really mean business. It is not enough to say, "I will follow." One must be prepared to pay the price of putting Christ first.

IV. PRACTICAL AIM. To discover what it really means to be a disciple of Jesus. This Scripture shows that it requires more than good intentions or initial enthusiasm.

V. HOMILETICAL FORM

Theme: "Tests of Discipleship."

Introduction: It costs something to be a disciple of Christ. In fact, it costs everything. The Master warned: "If any man will come after me, let him deny himself, and take up his cross daily, and follow me" (v. 23). Now He spells out the implication of this a bit more specifically to three individuals. In doing so He indicates three tests of discipleship.

A. *Complete Consecration.* "The Son of man hath not where to lay his head."

As Jesus and His disciples were going on their way to Jerusalem an eager aspirant confronted Him. "Lord, I will follow thee whithersoever thou goest," he cried. But the Master perhaps sensed here a superficial enthusiasm. Quietly but firmly He replied: "Foxes have holes, and birds of the air have nests; but the Son of man hath not where to lay his head."

Large crowds were following Jesus. In some ways He may have been one of the most popular men in Palestine. It would be great to walk near His side and bask in the brightness of His presence.

But there was another side which this man needed to know. Jesus had nothing in the way of material compensations to offer His followers. If they went with Him all the way it would entail deprivation and hardship.

Was this man willing to pay the price? We are not told. Perhaps like the rich young ruler, this man decided that the cost was too great, and turned away. That is what many still do today.

B. *Prompt Obedience*. "Let the dead bury their dead: but go thou and preach the kingdom of God."

On the surface these words seem harsh and out of character for Christ. From our Occidental point of view we are apt to picture a man whose father is lying in the coffin and Jesus will not even let him attend the funeral!

The facts, of course, are far different. In Oriental countries the oldest son carries full responsibility for seeing that his father is given a decent burial. It is very likely that this man's father might be expected to live for several more years. In the meantime, what about the need for the proclamation of the kingdom of God?

Discipleship demands prompt obedience. Soldiers answering the call of their country have to make sacrifices. They have to respond at once. So must the soldiers of the Lord.

C. *Firm Determination*. "No man, having put his hand to the plough, and looking back, is fit for the kingdom of God."

Following Jesus is "for keeps." It demands a crucial decision, backed up by firm determination.

On the surface the man's request seemed reasonable enough: "Let me first go bid them farewell, which are at home at my house." What was wrong with that? The problem was that an Oriental "farewell" might take anywhere

from a few weeks to some months. Wedding feasts commonly
lasted two or three weeks. It might take this man a year to
settle all his family affairs and really leave to follow Jesus.
By then it would be too late.

The man said: "I will follow, but. . . ." There must be no
"buts" if we are going to follow Him. It must be: "I will
follow — now . . . forever."

Jesus used the figure of a man starting out to plow a field.
He becomes tired or distracted and quits before the job is
done.

That is what has happened to would-be followers of Christ.
Publicly they said, "I will follow Him." But the cost is so
great they falter and fail. Jesus said that such would not be
fit for the kingdom of God.

Luke 10

WHO IS MY NEIGHBOR?

10:29. "Who is my neighbor?"
10:37. "Go, and do thou likewise."

I. HISTORICAL SETTING. As Jesus came into the territory called Perea ("across" the Jordan) He realized that His
time was short. The passover season was only a few weeks
away, and He must be in Jerusalem at that time. What He
did, He must do quickly.

So He "appointed other seventy also, and sent them two
and two before his face into every city and place, whither
he himself would come" (v. 1). Their task was to heal the
sick and proclaim to their hearers the fact that the kingdom
of God was now being presented to them. By repentance
the people could enter that kingdom. They were also to prepare the way for their Master, so that His necessarily brief
visits would be more fruitful.

After an interval — we are not told how long — "the seventy
returned with joy, saying, Lord even the devils [demons]
are subject unto us through thy name" (v. 17). Jesus made
the significant reply: "In this rejoice not, that the spirits are
subject unto you; but rather rejoice, because your names
are written in heaven" (v. 20). Christ himself "rejoiced in
spirit" that the Father had revealed heavenly truths to such
simple folk as His disciples (vv. 21-24).

II. EXPOSITORY MEANING. The word for "tempted" is
probably better translated "tested." Only when there is evil
intent should it be rendered "tempt," and there is no direct
indication here that this lawyer was trying to trap Jesus.

The term "lawyer" does not properly carry the same connotation that it has for us today. We think of one who argues

cases in court. But in the New Testament it means an expert in the law of Moses, one who studied and taught the Law.

Among the Jews "neighbor" (v. 29) meant a fellow Jew. That is the point of the man's question. But Jesus rejected this concept emphatically. He showed that one's neighbor is anyone who is in need, regardless of race, color, or creed.

"Pence" (v. 35) is in the Greek *denaria*. The denarius was a Roman silver coin, worth approximately twenty cents. It was, however, the equivalent of a day's wages (Matt. 20: 2). Presumably the "two pence" would have taken care of the wounded man for several days.

Every "priest" (v. 31) was a Levite; that is, of the tribe of Levi. But not every "Levite" (v. 32) was a priest. The Levites who were not descendants of Aaron would act as assistants to the priests in the work of the Temple. A "Samaritan" (v. 33) was a half-breed, part Jew and part Gentile. The Samaritans lived in the central portion of Palestine, between Galilee and Judea, and were despised by Jews of both areas.

III. DOCTRINAL VALUE. There is an emphasis here on love as the basis of correct relationship both to God and to one's fellow man.

IV. PRACTICAL AIM. Jesus vividly underscored the truth that one should love everyone, without discrimination. Whoever needs your help is your neighbor.

V. HOMILETICAL FORM

Theme: "Who Is My Neighbor?"

Introduction: One day a lawyer challenged Jesus with the question: "What shall I do to inherit eternal life?" In reply Christ pointed the man to the Sacred Scriptures: what did the Law say? Correctly the lawyer quoted the very heart of Old Testament teaching, what the Master himself had declared to be the "first" and "second" commandments (Matt. 22:37-40). Putting together Deuteronomy 6:5 and Leviticus 19:18, the man said: "Thou shalt love the Lord thy God with all thy heart, and with all thy soul, and with all thy strength, and with all thy mind; and thy neighbor as thyself" (v. 27). Jesus told him to do this and he would have eternal life.

Eager to justify himself as having kept this dual commandment, the lawyer replied: "And who is my neighbor?" If Jesus said, "Pious Jews like yourself," the man would have considered himself secure. Even if the Master broadened it a bit to "your fellow Jew," the lawyer probably would have claimed that he met the demand.

But Christ had in mind a very different concept. To make the point vividly and unforgettably clear, He told what we commonly call the Parable of the Good Samaritan.

A. *The Robbed Traveler.* "Fell among thieves."

A certain man was going down the road from Jerusalem to Jericho. The Jericho Road was a winding mountain thoroughfare, descending steeply some three thousand feet in fifteen miles. As he walked around a sharp curve, suddenly some robbers sprang out from behind a rock. Disappointed to find no money on him — apparently he was walking, for no donkey is mentioned — they stripped off his clothes to take as loot and wreaked their vengeance on him by beating him half to death. Then they fled.

B. *The Religious Cleric.* "There came down a certain priest that way."

Thousands of priests lived at Jericho, where the climate was more balmy than at Jerusalem in the mountains. One of them was returning home after his tour of duty in the Temple. When he saw the bleeding body beside the road, "he passed by on the other side." He probably said to himself: "I offered this man's sacrifice the other day in the Temple. So I have discharged my responsibility to him." Perhaps the poor victim had put his last penny in the offering at Jerusalem!

C. *The Righteous Layman.* "Likewise a Levite."

As had the priest, the Levite kept as far away as he could from the robbed man. Perhaps a quick glance satisfied his conscience that the man was dead. If so he could not afford to risk becoming ceremonially unclean by touching a dead body. After all, there was no use in taking a chance! He wasn't to blame for the man's pathetic condition.

D. *The Renegade Samaritan.* "A certain Samaritan . . . came where he was."

This man was not an ordained minister, nor even a lay member of the congregation of Israel. He was a despised, rejected outcast. Apparently a man of some means, he may well have been a merchant on a business trip. Probably he had more reason to be in a hurry than either the priest or the Levite.

Yet when he saw the poor victim, he was immediately "gripped with compassion," as the aorist tense suggests. He did five things for the man: (1) "went to him"; (2) "bound up his wounds, pouring in oil and wine" — oil for balm, wine for antiseptic; (3) "set him on his own beast," walking beside the man and helping to hold him on; (4) "brought him to an inn," perhaps where the Good Samaritan Inn is situated today; (5) "took care of him," not only paying for the man's board and room, but promising to provide any more funds that might be needed.

Three basic philosophies of life are revealed in this story. That of the robbers was: "What's yours is mine, and I'll take it." That of the priest and the Levite was: "What's mine is mine, and I'll keep it." That of the Samaritan was "What's mine is yours, and I'll share it." Put a little more briefly and bluntly, these three philosophies might be summed up this way: (1) "Beat 'em up"; (2) "Pass 'em up"; (3) "Pick 'em up." Many in the world practice the first. Too often the church has been guilty of practicing the second. How many of us actually practice the third?

Having finished this fascinating story, Jesus asked who was neighbor to the robbed man. There was only one answer. Then the Master commanded: "Go, and do thou likewise." Those are His orders to us today.

Luke 11

PRAYER THAT PREVAILS

11:9. "Ask, and it shall be given you; Seek, and ye shall find; Knock, and it shall be opened unto you."

I. HISTORICAL SETTING. Luke's Gospel is the great Gospel of prayer. Six times Luke specifically mentions Jesus as praying where the other Synoptics omit it — at His baptism (3:21), after cleansing the leper (5:16), before calling the twelve apostles (6:12), before Peter's confession at Caesarea Philippi (9:18), at His transfiguration (9:29), and before giving the Lord's Prayer (11:1).

It was very fitting that when the disciples heard their Master praying, one of them should plead: "Lord, teach us to pray, as John also taught his disciples." Prayer is the very heart of the religious life.

In response to this request, Jesus taught His disciples the so-called Lord's Prayer (vv. 2-4). He followed this by the striking Parable of the Importunate Friend.

II. EXPOSITORY MEANING. Luke's form of the Lord's Prayer is somewhat shorter than that given in Matthew (6: 9-13). This is even more strikingly true in the earliest Greek manuscripts, which have simply:

Father, let thy name be sanctified; let thy kingdom come;

Our daily bread give to us each day;

And forgive us our sins, for we also ourselves forgive everyone who is indebted to us;

And do not lead us into temptation.

"Lend" (v. 5) means "grant the use of, as a friendly act." The "loaves" of Jesus' day were something quite different

51

from our modern, sliced, baker's loaves of bread. They were like flat breakfast biscuits or small pancakes. The man wanted three loaves so that he could offer one to his guest, eat one with him for fellowship, and have an added one to offer his host for "seconds."

"In his journey" may be translated "out of his way." But in the hot season in Palestine people commonly traveled at night. So it was not necessarily unusual that a traveler should arrive at midnight. But it was inconvenient for the host. In those days it was the custom for the women to grind the barley or wheat each morning with little handmills, and make fresh "loaves" of bread for the day. Normally these would be eaten before night.

The Greek word for "importunity" (v. 8) is found only here in the New Testament. It literally means "shameless-ness." When one knows his cause is just he has to be shameless in asking.

When "ask," "seek," and "knock" are listed one under the other, the initial letters form the acrostic ASK. However, this is true in English but not at all in the Greek. So probably the significance of this coincidence should not be stressed overmuch.

III. DOCTRINAL VALUE. The doctrine of prayer is of the highest practical value. Its importance in the life and teaching of Jesus is given a prominent place in Luke's Gospel. Here the emphasis is on prevailing prayer.

IV. PRACTICAL AIM. To discover the secret of an-swered prayer.

V. HOMILETICAL FORM
Theme: "Prayer That Prevails."
Introduction: One day the disciples heard Jesus praying — one of six such times recorded only by Luke. They were stimulated to ask Him to teach them to pray. They did not say, "Teach us how to pray," but "Teach us to pray." No matter what number of how-to-do-it books on prayer one

may read, the only way anyone can learn to pray is by praying.

In response to their request, Jesus gave them the Lord's Prayer. It is marked by brevity and simplicity. Not a single word is wasted. The few brief petitions are right to the point. The primary petitions are for God's glory and kingdom. The secondary petitions are for our personal needs.

To encourage the disciples to pray persistently, the Master gave them the Parable of the Importunate Friend at Midnight. It consists of three parts and is followed by the application in the words of our text.

A. *Applying for Help.* "Send me three loaves."

Jesus portrayed a true-to-life situation — the hallmark of a parable. A man suddenly finds himself confronted with an embarrassing crisis. A friend arrives unannounced at midnight. Oriental hospitality requires that he be taken in for the night, but also that he be offered something to eat before retiring. Unfortunately, there is not a bite of food left in the house. To grind the grain and bake the tiny biscuit-like loaves at that hour is utterly impractical. What can he do?

There is only one thing: borrow from a friendly neighbor. So the man hurries to a nearby home and knocks at the door.

B. *Answering with Annoyance.* "Trouble me not."

Without getting up to open the door, the neighbor calls out: "Stop bothering me. My children are with me in bed." This would be literally true. In those days a "bed" usually consisted of a padded quilt stretched out on the floor. The entire family would lie down on this and pull a blanket over the group. If this man got up he would disturb the whole household. So he says, "I cannot rise and give thee."

C. *Asking with Persistence.* "Because of his importunity."

The distraught host was desperate. He had to have the loaves. So he could not take "No" for an answer. Shamelessly he kept on knocking and pleading.

Finally the neighbor rose and handed him the requested loaves. He did not do it because he felt friendly: he probably felt quite the opposite at the moment. But he decided he would have to comply sooner or later, and he wanted to get back to sleep.

D. *Application by Jesus.* "Ask . . . seek . . . knock."

If a selfish neighbor would answer a request because of the persistence of the asker, how much more will a loving heavenly Father respond to the prayers of His children. The contrast makes the lesson all the more forceful.

It would seem that "ask . . . seek . . . knock" suggest three stages of intensity in prayer. If one asks for something he feels he needs and that he has reason to believe is pleasing to the Lord, he may expect to receive it. If, however, the answer does not seem to be forthcoming, he should ask more earnestly. If the answer is still delayed, and he continues to feel that it is in divine order, he should get desperate and "knock." Sometimes God tries our patience and persistence. But He will finally answer. Prevailing prayer works!

Luke 12

THE RICH FOOL

12:20. "Thou fool, this night thy soul shall be required of thee."

I. HISTORICAL SETTING. Jesus apparently was still in Perea. Though some of the teaching here overlaps that found in Matthew's account of His Galilean ministry, it is probable that He repeated His main emphases in the new areas.

To "an innumerable multitude of people" Jesus said: "Beware ye of the leaven of the Pharisees, which is hypocrisy" (v. 1). He also warned: "Be not afraid of them that kill the body, and after that have no more that they can do. But I will forewarn you whom ye shall fear: Fear him, which after he hath killed hath power to cast into hell" (vv. 4-5). Most commentators feel this means that one should fear God rather than man.

The immediate background of the Parable of the Rich Fool was the request of a certain man: "Master, speak to my brother, that he divide the inheritance with me" (v. 13). Jesus protested that He was not appointed as judge over such matters. Then He issued the significant warning: "Take heed, and beware of covetousness: for a man's life consisteth not in the abundance of the things which he possesseth (v. 15). In other words, life is more than "things." The truth of the Master's statement is illustrated vividly in the parable that follows.

II. EXPOSITORY MEANING. In Christ's day a man's wealth was apt to be measured by the amount of land which he possessed. Here was a rich man with a large farm.

The Parable of the Rich Fool was apparently provoked by the covetous request of one whose father had recently died.

It would appear that he was the younger son. If so, he would receive a third of the family estate and his older brother two-thirds, according to the custom of that day. It looks as though this younger son wanted an equal division of the property.

The parable is followed by teaching similar to that found in the sixth chapter of Matthew, a part of the Sermon on the Mount. Right in line with the main lesson of the parable is this statement: "The life is more than meat [food], and the body is more than raiment" (v. 23). The climax is: "But rather seek ye the kingdom of God; and all these things shall be added unto you" (v. 31). Then Luke alone subjoins this beautiful saying of Jesus: "Fear not, little flock; for it is your Father's good pleasure to give you the kingdom" (v. 32).

III. DOCTRINAL VALUE. This parable emphasizes two important truths: the immortality of the soul and the certainty of the final judgment. The man planned to live a long time and enjoy his wealth. But God told him his time was up. He must give account of his life on earth, as every man must do.

IV. PRACTICAL AIM. To warn against the folly of a gross materialism that neglects the spiritual values of life.

V. HOMILETICAL FORM

Theme: "The Rich Fool."

Introduction: "The fool hath said in his heart, there is no God" (Ps. 14:1; 53:1). The man in this parable may not have been a theoretical atheist. In fact, he may have been in good standing in the synagogue. But he was a practical atheist. He lived his life as if there was no God to whom he was accountable. The fool is the one who says in his heart: "There is no God as far as I am concerned. I can live without God."

The man Jesus described was a fool for three reasons: (1) He thought more of his body than of his soul; (2) He thought more of himself than of others; (3) He thought more of time than of eternity.

A. *He Forgot His Soul.* "What shall I do?"

On the surface it appears that he was thinking of his soul, for he addresses it in verse 19. But what does he say? "Soul, thou hast much goods laid up for many years; take thine ease, eat, drink, and be merry." He seemed to think he could feed his soul on wheat and meat. No wonder God called him a fool!

The tragedy is that too many people today have not yet learned that material things do not satisfy the soul. If only they could have a better car, a boat, a beautiful home, expensive clothes, plenty of money to purchase entertainment — then they would be happy! But many are gaining all these, only to feel more miserable than ever before. A few years ago one man acknowledged that he was the wealthiest man in his state, but went on to say that he was the most miserable man in the state. Soon after that he committed suicide.

Material things cannot meet the spiritual hunger of the heart. The sooner people recognize this, the better off the world will be.

B. *He Forgot Others.* "I will pull down my barns, and build greater."

As is true in almost every Oriental country, this rich man was surrounded by multitudes of the poor. When he found himself burdened with a bumper crop, there was just one logical, humanitarian thing to do: distribute his surplus to the needy nearby. Instead he decided to build bigger barns in which to store his grain. But what good would this do for him? A man can eat only so much in a lifetime. What would happen to the surplus?

Greediness is one of the greatest robbers of mankind. It drives men on in an insane, insatiable quest for more — and more — and more. There is no end to it. Never satisfied with what they have. Always reaching out for something else. Covetousness robs a man of love, joy, and peace. It steals life's highest values and leaves him with only the bare husks of materialism. It robs him of rest and urges him ever on. Contentment — this he never enjoys. To think of others is to find oneself.

C. *He Forgot Eternity.* "Then whose shall those things be, which thou hast provided?"

When man lives only for this life he is living like an animal. Man was made for a larger world than this.

Yet most people give little thought to the next life. If you remind some people of the inevitable, inescapable fact of death, and ask what they will do then, they shrug their shoulders and say they are not worrying, or they will take a chance.

This attitude God calls foolish. And why not? This life lasts only a few decades, and then comes an endless eternity. There is no real comparison of their relative importance.

Suppose a man should have his choice between having on the one hand a life of unrestrained pleasure for a year followed by seventy years of tormenting misery, and on the other hand a year of hardship followed by seventy years of glorious happiness. If he should choose the first, would not everyone call him a fool?

Luke 13

THE FRUITLESS FIG TREE

13:7. "Behold, these three years I come seeking fruit on this fig tree, and find none."

I. HISTORICAL SETTING. Certain people reported to Jesus that Pilate had murdered some Galileans and mingled their blood "with their sacrifices" (v. 1). That is, they had been slain in the Temple while they were offering sacrifices there.

We have no secular confirmation of this event. But Josephus indicates that Pilate's administration in Judea was marked by many massacres. As has been said, "The Galilean zealots were notoriously turbulent, and Pilate was ruthlessly cruel." Probably the incident took place during some religious festival when the fires of nationalism were often fanned into flame.

Jesus himself mentioned another calamity that had recently transpired. At the pool of Siloam, in the southern part of Jerusalem, a tower had collapsed and killed eighteen persons. Again, we have no external testimony to this. But in those days it was not uncommon for walls to fall. In this instance it could have been due to either earth tremors or poor building — or both. Siloam is on sloping ground where a wall might easily not be too firm.

II. EXPOSITORY MEANING. The Galileans were thought by the Jews of Judea to be less pure and pious than they. The fact that some had been killed by Pilate showed they were even worse than the common run of the Galileans. So it was thought; but Jesus said, "No."

"Dresser" is literally "vine-worker," and so "vinedresser." "Cumbereth" is a strong term in Greek. It means "to make idle or inactive." Here the best translation is, "Why does it use up the ground?"

III. DOCTRINAL VALUE. It is easy for people to think that natural catastrophes are divine judgments. That they sometimes are seems to be indicated clearly in the Old Testament. At the same time, that they are not always so is proved by the Book of Job.

In the opening verses of this chapter it is evident that people thought the murdered Galileans must have been more wicked than other Galileans. Their tragic fate proved it. So also with the eighteen killed by the falling tower of Siloam. The Master denied this false concept. The righteous suffer along with the wicked in auto, train and plane accidents, as well as in such natural calamities as wind, fire, and flood. It simply is not true that tragedies are always punishments.

Jesus took advantage of this opportunity to give a much needed lesson on repentance. Instead of complimenting themselves on being so good that they had escaped disaster, the informers should realize that unless they repent they would all "likewise perish." The important thing is not to try to analyze the divine connection with physical calamities but to make sure that we are right with God.

IV. PRACTICAL AIM. To sound the warning that unfruitfulness can be sufficient cause for perishing. Are we bearing fruit as Christians. If not we shall finally be "cut down."

V. HOMILETICAL FORM

Theme: "The Fruitless Fig Tree."

Introduction: A horrible massacre had just happened. It was the talk of the town. Pilate had slain a group of Galileans right in the Temple as they were offering their sacrifices. Everybody was enraged — and scared.

About the same time a tower near the pool of Siloam had suddenly fallen and killed eighteen people. Certainly the victims of these two calamities must have been awful sinners.

But Jesus said, "No," — twice, emphatically. He warned: "Nay: but except ye repent, ye shall all likewise perish"

(vv. 3, 5). To enforce the point He told the Parable of the Fruitless Fig Tree. It was a sort of final warning to the Jewish nation.

A. *The Condition of the Tree.* "He came and sought fruit thereon, and found none."

A fig tree has one function: to bear fruit. If it fails in this it is useless.

This tree had been carefully cultivated. It had received all due attention. Yet when the owner came he found no fruit.

It was a picture of the Jewish nation, God's people. It had been planted in the Promised Land. Priests and prophets had ministered to its religious life. There was no excuse for its failure to bear fruit.

But it did lack the fruit of true piety. Too many of the religious leaders were hypocrites. They had the leaves of outward observance. But they lacked the fruit of inward character.

B. *The Condemnation of the Tree.* "Cut it down; why cumbereth it the ground?"

The owner complained to the gardener that he had been looking for fruit on this tree for the past three years, but so far had found none. There was no point in having the tree use up valuable space any longer. So he gave the order: "Cut it down."

It is difficult not to see a connection between the "three years" of the parable and the three years of Jesus' public ministry. For this length of time Christ had been confronting the nation with the command: "Repent; for the kingdom of heaven is at hand" (Matt. 4:17). But it had not repented. Instead it had rejected Him and His message. Now the three years were almost ended. Could there be any more respite?

C. *The Consideration for the Tree.* "Lord, let it alone this year."

The plea was made: give it a little more time. The gardener pleaded for one more chance for his fig tree. He wanted to cultivate and fertilize it once again. Perhaps it might yet bear fruit.

But to be fair he had to add: "And if it bear fruit, well; and if not, then after that thou shalt cut it down" (v. 9). Continued failure must ultimately bring judgment.

Jesus knew that the Jews would still reject him, remain fruitless, and so have to be cut down. A little later He cried out: "O Jerusalem, Jerusalem, which killest the prophets, and stonest them that are sent unto thee; how often would I have gathered thy children together, as a hen doth gather her brood under her wings, and ye would not! Behold, your house is left unto you desolate: and verily I say unto you, ye shall not see me, until the time come when ye shall say, Blessed is he that cometh in the name of the Lord" (vv. 34-35).

The cutting down could refer to the church of Jesus Christ taking the place of the Jewish nation as God's people. Or it could be related to the destruction of Jerusalem in A.D. 70. Perhaps both.

Are we bearing fruit? The term "fruit" suggests two things: (1) the fruit of the Spirit in Christian character; (2) the fruit of witnessing, in bringing other souls to Christ.

Luke 14

NO EXCUSES, PLEASE!

14:24. "None of those which were bidden shall taste of my supper."

I. HISTORICAL SETTING. In spite of the frequent clashes between the Pharisees and Jesus, He sometimes dined in their homes. One such occasion is described here. It was on the Sabbath Day, apparently the meal eaten after they came home from the synagogue. As usual, the Pharisees "watched him" (v. 1) with narrow, critical eyes.

"Before him" Jesus saw a man "which had the dropsy" (v. 2). It seems altogether possible that the man had been "planted" there to see what Christ would do — whether He would break the Sabbath by healing the afflicted man.

If so, the schemers were not disappointed. When the lawyers and Pharisees refused to answer His question, "Is it lawful to heal on the sabbath?" Jesus healed the victim and sent him on his way. Strict observers of the Sabbath would pull a donkey or an ox out of the ditch on the Sabbath Day. Why shouldn't He rescue this man?

The dinner became an occasion for a bit of practical teaching. When Christ observed some guests eagerly choosing the best places, He warned them of the folly of this. They were apt to be ousted in favor of some more honorable guest. The divine principle that works in life is: "For whosoever exalteth himself shall be abased; and he that humbleth himself shall be exalted" (v. 11).

Jesus also gave some advice to His host. Instead of inviting his friends, relatives, and rich neighbors, he should bring in the poor. They would not be able to recompense him, but he would have his reward in heaven.

II. EXPOSITORY MEANING. It is claimed that in the time of Christ the Jews ordinarily ate only two meals on week days, but three on the Sabbath. Strack and Billerbeck note: "The chief meal took place after the close of morning service — that is, more or less in the neighborhood of noon. The participation of guests in the Sabbath meal was a general custom."

Instead of "ass" (v. 5), the best Greek text has "son." The phrase would then read: "the son of which of you, or even only his ox."

III. DOCTRINAL VALUE. This Parable of the Great Supper teaches several truths. One is that every man is free to decide whether he will accept or reject the call of God. Not everyone who is called elects to accept. Those who are lost are not damned forever because of the arbitrary dictum of deity. They are lost because they refuse Christ's invitation, "Come." There is also here a strong emphasis on aggressive evangelism: "Go out . . . and bring in" (v. 21), even "Go out . . . and compel them to come in" (v. 23).

IV. PRACTICAL AIM. To show the importance of accepting the divine invitation rather than rejecting it, and to emphasize the responsibility which each one bears in deciding his destiny.

V. HOMILETICAL FORM

Theme: "No Excuses, Please!"

Introduction: One day Jesus found himself eating dinner in the home of a wealthy Pharisee. After healing a dropsied man, He turned His attention to the guests. He reproved the pride and selfishness of those who picked out the best places at the feast.

Then He spoke to His host. "Don't entertain just your friends, relatives, and rich neighbors. Invite the poor, the maimed, the lame, the blind. They will not be able to recompense you in this life, but you will get your reward in heaven."

When one of the guests observed, "Blessed is he that shall eat bread in the kingdom of God," Jesus used that remark as the springboard for a story. He proceeded to tell the Parable of the Great Supper. In it He dealt with invitations, excuses, and substitutes.

A. *Invitations.* "A certain man made a great supper."

1. "and bade many." The Orientals were fond of having big feasts. Servants were plentiful and so a man would be limited only by the cost of the food. Banquets were common, as they are apt to be today.

2. "Come, for all things are now ready." It was the custom not only to issue invitations ahead of time, as we do now, but also to send special messengers to notify the guests when the banquet was ready. Geldenhuys suggests the application here to God's feast for those who will enter the kingdom of God: "The first invitation refers to the promises of the Old Testament and the messenger who takes round the final invitations is especially Jesus "Himself." There is a further application to evangelism today.

B. *Excuses.* "And they all with one consent began to make excuse."

1. "I have bought a piece of ground." This man was more interested in viewing his newly acquired field than he was in enjoying the fellowship at the feast. He put materialistic interests above social and spiritual values.

This man is a type of those with whom "Business is first!" Nothing must be permitted to interfere with it. Other things are unimportant.

2. "I have bought five yoke of oxen." Here was a man who couldn't wait. Impatient, impulsive, he had to check out his new oxen. There was no time to be bothered with a feast.

3. "I have married a wife." This excuse has always seemed especially unreasonable. What better place to take his new bride than to a bountiful banquet? There they could enjoy a happy time together and meet friends new and old.

Unfortunately, most excuses are alibis. They are not backed up by reason but by personal desire.

C. *Substitutes.* "Then the master of the house being angry said to his servant. . . ."

1. "Go out quickly into the streets and lanes of the city, and bring in hither the poor, and the maimed, and the halt, and the blind." There is no enterprise in the world that calls for more urgency than evangelism. "Go out quickly" should ring in the ears of every Christian worker. While we tarry, millions more are born to live and die without knowing Christ as their Savior. The early church felt a sense of urgency which is too rare today.

The servant was commanded to go "into the streets and lanes of the city." That is where the people were. We must go outside our church walls and walk or drive the streets and roads if we are going to find those who need Christ.

The servant was also instructed: "Bring in hither the poor, the maimed, and the halt and the blind." Do we bring into our Sunday Schools and church services these kinds of people? Or do we pass them by? They are among those for whom Christ died.

2. "Go out into the highways and hedges, and compel them to come in, that my house may be filled." God is "not willing that any should perish, but that all should come to repentance" (II Peter 3:9). Godly people should feel the same way about the salvation of every last, least lost soul.

Evangelism demands not only a sense of urgency but a sense of compulsion. We must feel as Paul did when he wrote: "The love of Christ constraineth us" (II Cor. 5:14). These words found an echo in the motto of David Livingstone, carved on a stained glass window in the home of his birth in Blantyre, Scotland: "The love of Christ compels me."

Love for Christ and for the lost — this is the twofold motivation for effective evangelism. We must be willing to go out into the highways and byways of life in search of those for whom Jesus was willing to die. They must feel compelled by love — Christ's and our's.

Luke 15

THE SON WHO CAME HOME AGAIN

15:18. "I will arise and go to my father."
15:20. "And he arose, and came to his father."
15:24. "For this my son was dead, and is alive again; he was lost, and is found."

I. HISTORICAL SETTING. Two of the outstanding emphases of Luke's Gospel are lostness and salvation. The fifteenth chapter contains three parables of lost things: the Lost Sheep (vv. 3-7), the Lost Coin (vv. 8-10), and the Lost Son (vv. 11-32). The latter is more popularly known as the Parable of the Prodigal Son. The Parable of the Lost Sheep is found also in Matthew (18:12-14). The other two parables are found only in Luke.

Also Luke is the only one to record the story of Zacchaeus, the chief tax collector whom Christ won to himself at Jericho (19:1-9). At the close of that incident is found the key verse of this Gospel: "For the Son of man is come to seek and to save that which was lost" (19:10).

The opening two verses of Chapter 15 present a startling contrast. The first reads: "Then drew near unto him all the publicans and sinners to hear him." These despised renegades (collecting money for the Roman government) and "unclean" sinners were eagerly hearing and accepting Jesus' message. But the second verse says: "And the Pharisees and scribes murmured, saying, This man receiveth sinners and eateth with them."

It was evidently this attitude which caused the Master to tell the three parables following. The link with the first two verses shows up strikingly in verse 7: "I say unto you, that likewise joy shall be in heaven over one sinner that repenteth, more than over ninety and nine just persons, which

67

need no repentance" — or perhaps "think they need no repentance." The first part of this verse is repeated in verse 10.

II. EXPOSITORY MEANING. "Publicans" (v. 1) is more correctly translated "tax collectors" or "tax-gatherers." The *publicani* were wealthy Romans who received the right of getting the taxes from certain large areas and turning in a specified amount to the imperial government. They let out the actual collection of taxes to local individuals, who were underlings. These local tax collectors are the ones who are mentioned in the Gospels. They were not publicans.

"Sinners" (vv. 1-2) does not necessarily mean wicked men. The Pharisees applied this label to any who were careless about observing all the meticulous and multitudinous regulations of "the tradition of the elders" concerning ceremonial cleanness. Actually it was almost impossible for the common working man to keep all these rules. So he was considered unclean, a "sinner."

"Receiveth" is a compound verb in the Greek meaning "welcomes to himself." This is exactly what Jesus did, but it cut squarely across the religious policy of the Pharisees. "Scribes" were teachers of the Law. Most, if not all, of them were Pharisees.

"With riotous living" (v. 13) is literally "living wastefully." It was used in the sense of "living dissolutely or loosely."

III. DOCTRINAL VALUE. The supreme emphasis here is on God's love for the lost, which leads Him to seek and recover lost souls. Saving the unsaved — this is the main theme of Luke's Gospel.

IV. PRACTICAL AIM. To see how salvation is intended to reach every sinner.

V. HOMILETICAL FORM

Theme: "The Son Who Came Home Again."

Introduction: A familiar story in school readers is that of the man who had the goose that laid the golden eggs. Greedy to get all the gold at once, he killed the goose. Result: no more golden eggs.

This was the way it was with the younger son in our story. Not content with the daily golden eggs of kind parents and a good home, he wanted everything all at once. He got it, and then promptly lost it.

A. *The Possessor.* "And he divided unto them his living."

The younger son asked his father to give him his share of the family estate. According to the custom of that day this would be one-third, for the oldest son received a double portion — perhaps because he was obligated to care for his widowed mother.

Having received his part of the family fortune, the proud possessor started off down the road with his head high in the air. If he had seen the pigpen waiting for him he would not have been so eager and enthusiastic!

B. *The Prodigal.* "Took his journey into a far country, and there wasted his substance with riotous living."

The proud possessor had become a profligate prodigal. He evidently had not been used to having lots of money, with freedom to spend it as he pleased. Now he went literally "hog-wild" — and soon landed in a hog pen! "A fool and his money are soon parted." The prodigal quickly demonstrated the truth of this old proverb.

C. *The Pauper.* "And when he had spent all, there arose a mighty famine in that land; and he began to be in want."

Getting rich is ordinarily hard work and takes time. But getting poor is as easy as riding a toboggan down a slope; and usually one picks up speed and gets to the bottom very soon.

Thus it was with profligate prodigal. Before long he became a penniless pauper. And to add to his difficulties, a severe famine set in. Those with money found it hard enough to obtain food. For the pauper it was impossible.

Driven to desperation, the young man hired out to a farmer in that foreign country, who sent him into his field to feed the pigs. For a Jew this was bottomless abyss of disgrace. The pig was an unclean animal. The Jews were to keep away from hogs. But this young Israelite had gone so low that he actually envied the hogs because they had something to eat! Nobody would give him any food.

D. *The Penitent.* "And when he came to himself, he said . . . I will arise and go to my father."

Too often it is true that a person has to come to "the end of his rope" before he will come to himself and face reality. Sin is insanity. Now this sinner "came to himself," came back to his senses.

In striking contrast to the filthy pigpen and his own desolate condition, the pauper remembered the plentiful abundance at home. His father's hired servants were much better off than he. So he decided, "I'm going home."

But good resolutions are not enough. There must be action. Too many resolve to return home but never do it. This young man arose and went.

E. *The Pardoned.* "But the father said . . . Bring forth the best robe and put it on him."

His father had been waiting for him. As soon as he saw the pitiful, emaciated figure in rags coming down the road, he rushed to meet him. There was first the kiss of forgiveness. The son's confession was cut short as the father commanded the servants to bring the best robe and put it on his son in place of the filthy rags. Next a ring was put on his hand. This was doubtless the family signet ring which authorized the son to transact business in his father's name. What amazing forgiveness! What full restoration!

This was not all. Shoes were put on his bare feet. The fatted calf was killed and a big celebration was soon in full swing. The prodigal had returned. The lost was found.

Luke 16

THE RICH MAN AND LAZARUS

16. "Son, remember."

I. HISTORICAL SETTING. Both this chapter and the next begin with the statement that Jesus "said unto his disciples." It is clear that in the closing days of His ministry the Master was spending most of His time instructing His disciples in preparation for leaving them.

The same phrase occurs in both 16:1 and 16:19 — "a certain rich man." But two different parables follow. In the first instance it is that of the unjust steward. In the second it is the story of the rich man and Lazarus.

The point of the Parable of the Unjust Steward (vv. 1-8) is that "the children of this world (literally, "the sons of this age") are in their generation wiser than the children of light." That is, worldly business men use better judgment in preparing for the future than do most Christians. Geldenhuys puts it well: "In contrast with the diplomatic, clever conduct of such people, those who are members of the kingdom of light too often act unwisely and undiplomatically towards others. Instead of behaving in such a manner that they bind others to themselves, they act so that people are unnecessarily repulsed."

Then follows the enigmatic command: "Make to yourselves friends of the mammon of unrighteousness; that, when ye fail, they may receive you into everlasting habitations" (v. 9). Money is so often acquired and spent in an unjust way that it is here called "the mammon of unrighteousness." But it can be invested in kingdom enterprises. Geldenhuys asks: "Do we use our worldly possessions in such a manner that there will be persons in Eternity who will be glad to receive us?"

71

II. EXPOSITORY MEANING. It should be obvious that the language of the story of the Rich Man and Lazarus was intended to be taken figuratively, not literally. For "Abraham's bosom" (v. 22) cannot mean the breast of that man's body, which had been laid in a grave. Strack and Billerbeck write: "Lying or sitting in Abraham's bosom is . . . a pictorial expression to indicate the loving fellowship which exists in the beyond between Abraham and his pious descendants, derived from the love of a mother, who cherishes and protects her child in her lap."

"Hell" (v. 23) is not the Greek word Gehenna, but Hades. This word was first used as the name of the god of the underworld. Then it came to be used for the underworld itself, the place of departed spirits. It is the Greek equivalent of the Hebrew Sheol, which is translated Hades in the Septuagint. It appears that now all believers who die are immediately with Christ (II Cor. 5:8; Phil. 1:23), whereas unbelievers go to Hades. That Hades is not the place of eternal punishment is shown clearly by the statement that "Death and Hades were cast into the lake of fire. This is the second death" (Rev. 20:14). That is, the lake of fire is the final hell.

III. DOCTRINAL VALUE. The story of the Rich Man and Lazarus is a vivid warning of the horror of being lost. It also suggests that the wrongs of this life will be made right in the next.

IV. PRACTICAL AIM. To show the seriousness of life in this world as a preparation for eternity.

V. HOMILETICAL FORM

Theme: "The Rich Man and Lazarus."

Introduction: Any serious-minded person cannot avoid wondering about the seeming injustice of life in this world. The wicked prosper and live in luxury. The righteous are often poor and suffer hardship. It doesn't seem fair! How can we believe in a God of love and justice?

Our trouble is twofold. In the first place we measure things by material rather than spiritual values. In the second place, we measure things by time rather than eternity. The fact is that suffering is one of the important factors in producing the noblest Christian character. And perfect bliss throughout an endless eternity will more than compensate for all the lacks of this life.

To illustrate these truths vividly Jesus told the story of the Rich Man and Lazarus. It is a study in contrasts. The two men were at the opposite poles in life, in death, and after death.

A. *Two Men in Life.* "There was a certain rich man. . . . There was a certain beggar."

A greater contrast could hardly be imagined. The rich man "was clothed in purple and fine linen, and fared sumptuously every day." The beggar Lazarus "was laid at his gate, full of sores, and desiring to be fed with the crumbs which fell from the rich man's table: moreover the dogs came and licked his sores."

There is no direct statement that the rich man lived in immorality. But he was guilty of selfishness, and this is the very heart of sin. His dress and food were luxurious. He "fared sumptuously every day," oblivious to the harrowing hunger of the poor beggar at his gate. The least he could have done would have been to have a servant take some food to the sick, wasted form.

Instead all that Lazarus could do was to long for even "the crumbs that fell from the rich man's table." These would have fed him well. But probably they were swept up and thrown into the garbage containers. Only the dogs had pity on the poor man; they "came and licked his sores." They were more "human" than the rich man!

B. *Two Men in Death.* "The beggar died . . . the rich man also died."

The first thing that this verse says to us is that all men alike must die — the wealthy as well as the poor, the educated as well as the ignorant, the cultured as well as the crude. Death knows no partiality.

The second thing we note is the difference that took place at death. Lazarus may well have starved to death; the rich man may have eaten and drunk himself to death. Lazarus doubtless had no undertaker to care for his body, but his spirit was "carried by the angels into Abraham's bosom." On the other hand, the rich man "was buried." This does not tell us much. But we are fully justified in assuming that the funeral was a very elaborate affair, with a long procession to the place of burial. As far as the bodies were concerned, one was probably placed in the potter's field and the other given a burial marked by pomp and ceremony. But the story was different with their spirits.

C. *Two Men after Death.* "In hell . . . being in torments." "Abraham afar off, and Lazarus in his bosom."

An instant after death situations were suddenly reversed. The rich man, who had lounged luxuriously on thick cushions with a servant to fan him in hot weather, found himself "in torments." So severe was his agony that he cried: "Father Abraham, have mercy upon me, and send Lazarus, that he may dip the tip of his finger in water, and cool my tongue; for I am tormented in this flame." But there was no relief to be had.

In sharp contrast was the former beggar, now resting in Abraham's bosom. For him there would be no more hunger, pain, or suffering; "now he is comforted."

After death every man's destiny is fixed and irrevocable. Between the wicked and the righteous there is "a great gulf" which no one can cross. It is either Paradise or Torment; there is no place between.

Too late to receive any help himself, the rich man begged Abraham to send Lazarus back to his brothers, to warn them not to come to the place of torment. If one rose from the dead, they would listen to him. But Abraham sadly replied: "If they hear not Moses and the prophets, neither will they be persuaded, though one rose from the dead." This strong assertion receives striking confirmation in the case of another Lazarus who did rise from the dead. Instead of listening to him, the Jewish leaders tried to put him to death (John 12: 10).

Luke 17

REMEMBER LOT'S WIFE

17:26. "So shall it be also in the days of the Son of man."

I. HISTORICAL SETTING. Jesus was still giving private instruction to His own disciples (cf. vv. 1, 5, 22). He warned them against causing any weaker Christians to stumble (vv. 1-2). They were to forgive an erring brother, even seven times a day if necessary (vv. 3-4). He talked about faith (vv. 5-6) and service (vv. 7-10).

Verse 11 marks the beginning of the third and last part of Jesus' "Journeys on the Road to Jerusalem." "Through the midst of Samaria and Galilee" should rather be translated "between Samaria and Galilee."

As He entered a village in this area ten lepers met Him. They were required by law to stand "afar off." When they called to Jesus for mercy for their pitiful condition, He healed them. Only one, a Samaritan, returned to give thanks. The others were guilty of the gross sin of ingratitude. Once more Luke puts the Samaritans in a good light (cf. 10:33-35).

II. EXPOSITORY MEANING. Jesus told the disciples that if they had "faith as a grain of mustard seed" they could say to a "sycamine tree, Be thou plucked up by the root," and it would obey (v. 6). The roots of a sycamine tree were considered to be unusually strong. The Jews had a saying that this tree could stand in the earth for six hundred years.

The fact that it is stated that the grateful leper was a Samaritan implies that the other nine, or at least some of them, were Jews. It may seem surprising that they mingled here, in view of the sharp animosity between the two races. But a common misery would tend to draw them together: they were all "unclean," outcasts from society. Furthermore

76

this was on the border between Samaria and Galilee (see above), where the two peoples were in close proximity.

III. DOCTRINAL VALUE. The doctrine of the Second Coming bulks large in the latter part of all three Synoptic Gospels. Luke's main teaching on it is in Chapter 21. But here he anticipates that with some foregleams of truth.

IV. PRACTICAL AIM. To emphasize the importance of being ready for the return of our Lord, not drawn away by the spirit of the world.

V. HOMILETICAL FORM

Theme: "Remember Lot's Wife."

Introduction: One day the Pharisees demanded of Jesus "when the kingdom of God should come" (v. 20). In reply He said: "The kingdom of God cometh not with observation"; that is, not by observing signs in the sky. Instead, "the kingdom of God is within you." In a sense it was already in their midst in the person of Christ, the King. It was also an inward, spiritual kingdom, not an outward, political one.

Then Jesus turned to His disciples. Said He: "The days will come when ye shall desire to see one of the days of the Son of man, and ye shall not see it." In other words, you will long for the coming of the Messiah; but you will have to wait. That is our situation right now, in the midst of hot wars and cold wars and strife between nations.

The Son of man would come suddenly, like lightning. But before that took place, He must suffer many things, even death, being rejected by that generation.

A. *The Days of Noah.* "And as it was in the days of Noe, so shall it also be in the days of the Son of man."

The days of Noah were times of extreme lawlessness. The record reads: "And God saw that the wickedness of man was great in the earth, and that every imagination of the thoughts of his heart was only evil continually" (Gen. 6:5). This condition is being too closely approximated in our day for anyone to feel easy about the outcome. When we pray for peace, for an end to the tragic waste of lives in war, we are reminded that our nation has wandered far from the paths of righteousness. Can we expect God to preserve and protect us when we flout His standards and desecrate His name?

The description of the people of that day seems innocent enough: "They did eat, they drank, they married wives, they were given in marriage." It sounds like "business as usual." There was nothing wrong with doing these things except that they left God out of their lives. But that made them god-less; and the godless shall perish, as these did in the Flood.

B. *The Days of Lot.* "Likewise also as it was in the days of Lot. . . ."

Here we are given a similar picture: they did eat, they drank, they bought, they sold, they planted, they builded." All of these things are innocent in themselves. But independence of God makes a man a sinner. And that is what these people were guilty of.

As in the case of Noah's contemporaries, we have evidence that the people of Lot's day were far from being morally blameless. For we read: "But the men of Sodom were wicked and sinners before the Lord exceedingly" (Gen. 13:13). Their particularly obnoxious vice has come down to us in the very term "sodomy." One of the most alarming things about society in the United States and Europe today is the shocking growth of this sex perversion. A recent essay in a leading news magazine revealed the fact that weddings are already being performed, uniting men with men and women with women. It was for sodomy that God "rained fire and brimstone from heaven, and destroyed them all." For the same sin, along with others, we face the danger of new fire and brimstone raining from the sky in the form of nuclear missiles. We can only pray for God's mercy on America.

C. *The Days of the Son of Man.* "Even thus shall it be in the day when the Son of man is revealed."

There are too many startling similarities between the days of Noah and of Lot on the one hand, and present days on the other, to leave us feeling very comfortable about the future. When we see the flood of filth pouring out of Hollywood, with its daring change of movie standards, together with the deluge of pornographic magazines cluttering our newstands, we pause and wonder. If ever there was a time when we needed a voice in our modern wilderness to call for repentance it is right now.

The closing warning is: "Remember Lot's wife." Her heart was still in Sodom, and she stood there looking longingly back at the city. She was left a pillar of salt, a monument of warning to those who are tempted to hold on to the world. One has to turn his back on the world in order to follow Christ.

Luke 18

THE MAN WHO PRAYED TO HIMSELF

18:11. "The Pharisee having taken his stand was praying these things to himself" (literal translation).

I. HISTORICAL SETTING. We have already noted that Jesus' main teachings on prayer are to be found in the eleventh and eighteenth chapters of Luke. In the earlier chapter we found the so-called Lord's Prayer and the Parable of the Importunate Friend. Here we have two parables together, that of the Importunate Widow (or unjust Judge) and that of the Pharisee and the Publican. In both cases the purpose of the parable was given. In connection with the first it is stated: "And he spoke a parable unto them to this end, that men ought always to pray, and not to faint" (v. 1). The second is introduced with these words: "And he spake this parable unto certain which trusted in themselves that they were righteous, and despised others" (v. 9). Discouragement and self-righteous conceit — these were the two things the Master warned against.

II. EXPOSITORY MEANING. "Faint" (v. 1) is better translated "lose heart." Two things are perhaps suggested. The one is that we should not become discouraged if we do not receive the answer to our prayers at once, but should keep on praying. The other is that the best way to avoid discouragement is to maintain an atmosphere of prayerful trust. This brings God consciously into focus against our daily problems and enables us to commit everything to Him continually.

"Feared" (v. 2) means to have reverence for. "Regarded" is better translated "respected." This judge had neither reverence for God nor respect for man. "Avenge me" means vindicate me" or "give me legal protection."

"Weary me" is a very weak rendering. The verb literally means "to strike under the eye" or "to give a black eye." This woman was getting desperate for help.

The Pharisees are mentioned some one hundred times in the New Testament. They were strict legalists who insisted on the meticulous observance of all religious regulations, not only those in the law of Moses but also those contained in the unwritten "tradition of the elders." They were the ones who taught in the local synagogues. "Pharisee" means "separatist." They were thus originally the Puritans of their day. By the time of Christ too many of them had become hypocritical in their religion. Jesus declared that some of them were clean on the outside but full of uncleanness in their hearts. They proved this in their jealous hatred of Him.

III. DOCTRINAL VALUE. Once more we have significant teaching on prayer. We are not only to pray persistently but humbly and sincerely.

IV. PRACTICAL AIM. To show the necessity of the right attitude in prayer. Above all, one must be utterly honest before God, for He reads our hearts as well as hears our words.

V. HOMILETICAL FORM.

Theme: "The Man Who Prayed to Himself."

Introduction: One of the most important lessons the disciples needed to learn was how to pray. They realized it and requested help. So Jesus taught them the Lord's Prayer — a perfect gem of brevity, simplicity, and straightforwardness. Its petitions are few but to the point.

To illustrate His teaching He told three parables. The principle of persistence was emphasized in the parables of the Importunate Friend at Midnight and the Importunate Widow. Humility and sincerity were the main points underscored in the Parable of the Pharisee and the Publican. It was told particularly for the benefit of "certain" (Pharisees) who "trusted in themselves that they were righteous, and despised others."

A. *Two Men.* "Two men went up into the temple to pray; the one a Pharisee, and the other a publican."

The Pharisees were the strict religionists of their day. They laid great stress on purity, but it was mainly a matter of maintaining ceremonial cleanness by avoiding contact with anything that would contaminate. They emphasized holiness, but it was of a formal, legalistic type. "Separation from sinners" — this was their motto. This tended to make them proud and haughty. The common people naturally resented this attitude. Self-righteousness is always offensive.

"Publican" is more accurately translated "tax collector." The men who belonged to this group were hated by almost all Jews. For one thing, they represented the foreign rule of the Roman Empire. Nationalism was strong among the Jews of Jesus' time. They eagerly awaited the day when they would be delivered from foreign oppression. For another thing, at least some of the tax collectors overcharged the people and this unpatriotic dishonesty naturally enraged the populace. Also the Pharisees considered that the tax collectors were rendered "unclean" by their contact with the Gentiles.

B. *Two Prayers.* "God, I thank thee, that I am not as other men." — "God be merciful to me a sinner."

The Pharisee "stood" — literally, "took his stand," probably in a prominent place where many could see and hear him. He was eager to put his piety on parade, to get praise of men.

He prayed "with himself." But the Greek says, "to himself." He was praying to himself, not to God.

One Sunday an exquisitely worded prayer was uttered in Trinity Church in Boston. The next morning an editorial in the newspaper observed that it was "the most beautiful prayer ever prayed to a Boston audience." The editor wrote better than he knew. It was prayed to the people rather than to God. Jesus taught His disciples to pray with simplicity and sincerity.

The Pharisee's prayer was a perfect example of how one should not pray. Instead of thanking God for gracious blessings from heaven, he thanked God for his own superior goodness. Actually all that he was doing was congratulating himself in public. To be thankful that we are better than everybody else shows the worst kind of spiritual pride.

But the Pharisee did not stop there. He proceeded to categorize "other men" as "extortioners, unjust, adulterers." Then flinging a contemptuous glance toward the nearby figure he added: "or even as this publican."

Then he proceeded to recite his virtues: "I fast twice in the week, I give tithes of all that I possess." This surely should give him high status in the eyes of God. What he forgot was that God was looking inside his heart rather than listening to his words. The attitude of pride and self-righteousness he had there, with contempt for his fellow men, was utterly godless. In the sight of heaven this man was a deep-dyed sinner.

In contrast the publican prayed a prayer that was a model of brevity, honesty, and humility: "God be merciful to me a sinner." That was all. But it was enough. He showed the genuine penitence of his heart by smiting his breast in consternation.

C. *Two Results.* "This man went down to his house justified rather than the other."

God can only justify those who repent and believe. The Pharisee did neither. The publican did both. His deep repentance demonstrated his true faith. For to obey is to believe.

The Pharisee justified himself, but Christ condemned him. On the other hand, the publican condemned himself, and Christ justified him. This is the way it works. Jesus concluded by saying: "For every one that exalteth himself shall be abased; and he that humbleth himself shall be exalted."

Luke 19

TEARS IN A TRIUMPHAL ENTRY

19:41. "And when he was come near, he beheld the city and wept over it."

I. HISTORICAL SETTING. Near Jericho Jesus had healed a blind beggar (18:35-43). While passing through the city, He saw Zacchaeus perched in a tree. This wealthy chief tax collector of the district was short of stature. Prevented by the crowd from seeing Christ, he had run ahead and gained his observation point.

The Master startled the little, big man by inviting himself to the tax collector's home. Overjoyed at this attitude — so different from what he usually received from the Jewish rabbis — Zacchaeus offered Jesus a hearty welcome.

But the people began to murmur and complain because Christ "was gone to be guest with a man that is a sinner" (v. 7). Zacchaeus acted quickly to squelch this criticism. Standing still, he said to Jesus: "Behold Lord, the half of my goods I give to the poor; and if I have taken anything from any man by false accusation, I restore him fourfold" (v. 8). The Master's reply settled it: "This day is salvation come to this house, forsomuch as he also is a son of Abraham" (v. 9). Zacchaeus was no longer "a sinner"! Then Jesus uttered the key verse of this Gospel: "For the Son of man is come to seek and to save that which was lost" (v. 10).

"Because he was nigh to Jerusalem, and because they thought that the kingdom of God should come immediately" (v. 11), Christ told the Parable of the Pounds (vv. 12-27). This suggested that the setting up of the kingdom would be delayed. Having spoken the parable, "he went before, ascending up to Jerusalem" (v. 28). It was His last journey to the Holy City.

II. EXPOSITORY MEANING. The exact location of Beth-phage is a matter of dispute. Both it and Bethany were doubtless situated on the slopes of the Mount of Olives. Bethany was evidently on the eastern side, where the "village of Lazarus" is today. But many scholars think that Bethphage may have been on the western slope of the mount, facing the city of Jerusalem across the narrow Kidron valley. If so, it was counted as being within the sacred area for purposes of eating the Passover. Putting all the Gospel accounts together, it seems evident that the colt on which Jesus rode came from Bethphage (cf. Matt. 21:1). "The descent of the mount of Olives" (v. 37) would be the west side of the hill, leading down into the Kidron valley.

Verses 43 and 44 seem clearly to refer to the destruction of Jerusalem by the Romans in A.D. 70, only forty years after Jesus uttered this prophecy. Josephus, the Jewish historian, agrees that there was not left "one stone upon another."

III. DOCTRINAL VALUE. Jesus was greeted as "the King that cometh in the name of the Lord." This was clearly a Messianic expression. In the minds of the people the man from Nazareth was more than just another prophet.

IV. PRACTICAL AIM. To show the need of real repentance, not just outward acceptance of Christ.

V. HOMILETICAL FORM

Theme: "Tears in a Triumphal Entry."

Introduction: It was the first Palm Sunday. As Jesus approached the Mount of Olives He sent two of His disciples to secure a colt. He was about to ride into Jerusalem in fulfilment of Zechariah 9:9. In doing so He was presenting himself to the nation as its Messiah. But it rejected Him.

A. *The Cry of the Crowd.* "Blessed be the King that cometh in the name of the Lord: peace in heaven, and glory in the highest."

Somewhere about the top of the Mount of Olives, apparently, some people put their outer garments on the colt which

had just been brought. Then they set Jesus on it. As the
procession started down the western slope toward the city,
many ran ahead and threw their loose outer garments on the
path. As we would say today, they were rolling out the red
carpet for Him.

It was a joyous occasion. We read that "the whole multitude of the disciples began to rejoice and praise God with a
loud voice for all the mighty works that they had seen."
These were the Galilean pilgrims to the feast of the Passover.
They had seen the feeding of the five thousand on the shores
of the Lake of Galilee. They had seen how Jesus made the
blind to see, the deaf to hear, the dumb to speak, the lame
to walk, the paralytic to carry his pallet. In their estimation
He had given adequate proof that He was the Messiah.

So they greeted Him with a Messianic title: "Blessed be
the King that cometh in the name of the Lord." These ardent
nationalists from Galilee no doubt expected Christ to ride
right into Jerusalem, overthrow the government of Rome, and
set up His Messianic throne instead. This was the hour they
had long waited for. No wonder they shouted for joy. As
far as they were concerned this was the Messiah's inaugural
parade.

B. *The Complaint of the Critics.* "Master, rebuke thy
disciples."

In the crowd were some Pharisees. They became increasingly disturbed at the emotionalism of the multitude. They
were also probably horrified that these pilgrims should
acclaim Jesus as the King, the Coming One, the Messiah.
To them this perhaps seemed blasphemous. In any case, for
a shouting crowd to welcome a man as "King" was an extremely dangerous thing. The Roman rulers were apt to
wreak revenge for this.

But Jesus answered: "I tell you that, if these should hold
their peace, the stones would immediately cry out." So
epochal was the occasion that if man did not respond all
nature would burst forth into praise.

There are always those who will criticize any "religious

excitement." They want everything nice and quiet — and dead. The Book of Acts shows clearly that the early church was marked by excitement and enthusiasm. The movement of the Spirit is always accompanied by some movement of people's emotions. Every great revival has witnessed to this fact. The only alternative to life, expressed by some emotion, is death.

C. *The Cry of the Christ.* "He beheld the city, and wept over it."

The criticism of the Pharisees was but a foretaste of the condemnation of Jesus which would take place before the week was ended. No wonder He wept! He saw the doom that must inevitably result from rejecting the Messiah.

And so there broke forth from His heart almost a wail of woe. If only the people of Jerusalem had realized the significance of the hour. He was presenting himself as the fulfilment of Old Testament prophecy, as the Messiah of promise. This was Israel's greatest opportunity. But she turned it down.

What would be the consequence? The destruction of Jerusalem forty years later; the scattering of the Jews all over the world — a people without a country; persecution such as no other people have suffered, culminating in the horrible massacre of some five or six million Jews by Hitler. It was all "because thou knewest not the time of thy visitation."

Luke 20

RIGHTEOUS RETRIBUTION

20:16. "He shall come and destroy these husbandmen, and shall give the vineyard to others."

I. HISTORICAL SETTING. On Monday of Passion Week, as Mark 11 clearly indicates, Jesus cleansed the Temple (19:45-48). This appears to have precipitated violent opposition to Him on the part of the Sadducees. He had not only hurt their pocketbooks — for the priests operated the cattle market in the Court of the Gentiles — but had also challenged their authority. They could never forgive Him for this.

So they came to Him, along with the scribes and elders, and demanded of Him: "Tell us, by what authority doest thou these things? or who is he that gave thee this authority?" (v. 2). In return Jesus asked them a question: "The baptism of John, was it from heaven, or of men?" (v. 4). In other words, what was the source of John the Baptist's authority? This was a fair question, for the answer to it would be the same as the answer to their query. That is, Jesus was going to make His opponents answer their own question. This is always a wise thing to do.

The reasoning of the Jewish religious leaders described in verses 5 and 6 shows an utter lack of moral conscience. They were moved by considerations of expediency, not ethics. When they answered that they "could not tell whence it was" (v. 7), they were guilty of deliberate lying. It was not a case of "could not" but of "would not."

As a further answer to their question Jesus told the Parable of the Wicked Husbandmen (vv. 9-18). In it He clearly identified himself as the son sent by the owner of the vineyard, who symbolized God. Thus He clearly indicated His deity and the divine source of His authority.

88

II. EXPOSITORY MEANING. "Preached the gospel" (v. 1) is all one word in the Greek — *evangelizomenou*, "evangelized." "The chief priests . . . scribes . . . elders" were the three component parts of the Sanhedrin, the Supreme Court of the Jewish nation. They, not Jesus, were the ones who had authority to say what could be done in the Temple.

The "vineyard" (v. 9) represented the Jewish nation (cf. Isa. 5:1-7). The "husbandmen," or tenants, were the rulers of that nation (which in this case was the same as religious leaders). These leaders were given "a long time" to care for their responsibility.

"At the season" would be the time for ripe grapes, in August or September. The tenants were to pay their rent in kind, giving the owner his share of the grape harvest.

The three servants (vv. 10-12) represent the prophets of the Old Testament. "My beloved son" symbolized Christ. "Reverence" means "regard" or "respect."

The reasoning of the tenants has often been pointed out as utterly ridiculous. How could they hope to get legal possession of a property by killing the heir? But Geldenhuys has a good answer for this criticism. He says that "it is precisely Jesus' intention to call attention to the folly of the Jewish leaders' attitude towards Him by using as an example the foolish reasonings of the husbandmen."

Christ pointed out the consequences of the tenants' criminal action: "He shall come and destroy these husbandmen, and shall give the vineyard to others" (v. 16). That is, God will destroy the leaders of the Jews — and the people that identified themselves with them — and will give the vineyard (the true Israel, or people of God) to "others" (the leaders of the Christian church).

"The stone which the builders rejected" (v. 17) was, of course, Christ. Rejected by the leaders of the Jewish religion, He would become "the head of the corner" in the new church. The language of verse 18 was fulfilled partially in the destruction of Jerusalem (A.D. 70). Its complete fulfilment awaits the Second Coming.

III. DOCTRINAL VALUE. The doctrine of the Gentile church as the new people of God is highlighted here. Israel lost her special status.

IV. PRACTICAL AIM. To show the tragic results of rejecting Jesus Christ.

V. HOMILETICAL FORM

Theme: "Righteous Retribution."

Introduction: Every man must ultimately decide whether the authority of Christ is human or divine. If we realize that it is divine, we must submit to it. To fail to do so means that we perish forever. For He is the only one who can save us. To reject Jesus Christ is to sign our own death warrant.

A. *The Servants.* "He sent a servant. . . . another servant. . . . a third."

To show the seriousness of their rejection of Him as the Messiah, Jesus told the Jewish leaders the Parable of the Wicked Husbandmen. A man planted a vineyard and let it out to tenants, who were to pay him in kind. At the time of the grape harvest he sent a servant to procure the owner's share of the crop. But the tenants beat him and sent him away empty-handed. They did the same with a second servant, in addition to insulting him. The third one they wounded and cast out of the vineyard.

These three servants represent the prophets of the Old Testament. Many of them were treated shamefully, and some of them were even put to death.

B. *The Son.* "I will send my beloved son: it may be they will reverence him."

"Beloved son" in the Bible often means "only son." This was the owner's last resort. When the tenants saw him, they realized that he was the only heir. If they killed him, the family inheritance would be theirs.

This, of course, was foolish reasoning. But the point Jesus was making was that this was the way the Jewish leaders were treating Him. They thought that if they could get rid of

Him they could remain in control of the religious life of the nation and do as they pleased. They could cash in on their place of leadership to get wealthy while they left the people starved spiritually. Foolishly, they failed to realize that they were accountable to God, who knew their motives as well as their actions.

So the tenants cast the owner's son outside the vineyard and killed him. Likewise Jesus would soon be led outside the city of Jerusalem and put to death.

C. *The Substitution.* "He shall come and destroy these husbandmen, and shall give the vineyard to others."

The tenants had a good opportunity to enjoy peace and prosperity. They could have continued to care for the vineyard and would have been amply rewarded with their share of its fruit. But instead they were greedy. They wanted to keep everything for themselves. And in doing so they lost it all, plus their own lives.

This is the way it is for those who reject Jesus Christ and wish to hold on to themselves. They seek to save themselves and are lost forever. To find the best and highest in life one has to accept God's way and do His will.

Luke 21

SIGNS OF THE SECOND COMING

21:25. "And there shall be signs. . . ."
21:26. "Men's hearts failing them for fear."
21:27. "And then shall they see the Son of man coming in a cloud with power and great glory."

I. HISTORICAL SETTING. The Olivet Discourse — so called because it was given on the Mount of Olives — is the only long discourse of Jesus given in all three Synoptic Gospels. It is also known as the Prophetic Discourse because of its contents. It is found in Matthew 24 (and 25), Mark 13, and Luke 21:8-36.

The occasion of the discourse is clearly indicated in verses 5-7. Some of the disciples called their Master's attention to the beautiful stones and gifts that adorned the Temple. With its marble walls nearly 150 feet high and its gold dome it was one of the wonders of that day.

Then Christ made the startling prediction that the day would come when there would not be left one stone upon another. Distressed, the disciples asked: "But when shall these things be? and what sign will there be when these things shall come to pass?" The discourse is a response to these two questions.

II. EXPOSITORY MEANING. It seems clear that Christ's reply is divided into two main parts. Verses 8-24 deal with the destruction of Jerusalem in A.D. 70. Verses 25-36 look forward to the time of the end and the second coming of Christ.

The signs that are given in the first section were all fulfilled in the first century. The frequent wars (vv. 9-10), earthquakes and famines (v. 11), persecution by Jews and Gentiles (vv. 12-19) — all these are documented in the excellent commentary by Geldenhuys (Eerdmans, 1951).

The actual destruction of Jerusalem is dealt with in verses 20-24. "Compassed with armies" (v. 20) is literally "being compassed with armies." That is, when the siege began the Christians in Jerusalem were to "flee to the mountains." Eusebius records how they did this, making their escape to Pella, a town on the east side of the Jordan River and south of the Lake of Galilee. It was here that the Jewish Christian church was preserved after the horrible massacre that took place at Jerusalem in A.D. 70, when the siege ended in the fall of the city.

Jesus predicted this awful judgment: "And they shall fall by the edge of the sword, and shall be led away captive into all nations: and Jerusalem shall be trodden down of the Gentiles, until the times of the Gentiles be fulfilled" (v. 24). It is claimed that about 100,000 Jews perished when the city was taken, and another 100,000 were led away into captivity. Jerusalem has continued ever since to be "trodden down of the Gentiles." Though the Jews regained possession of a considerable part of Palestine, including the newer city of Jerusalem to the west of the walls, yet the Old City within the walls remained in Arab hands until 1967. The new state of Israel was set up in 1948. Just when "the times of the Gentiles" will end no one on earth can tell.

III. DOCTRINAL VALUE. The doctrine of the Second Coming, though often neglected today, bulks large in the New Testament. It is dominant in the only long discourse found in all three Synoptic Gospels. It is the main theme of what may well have been Paul's first two epistles (I and II Thessalonians). It also shows up prominently in II Peter, Jude, and Revelation.

IV. PRACTICAL AIM. To call attention to the signs of the Second Coming and urge all people to be prepared for it.

V. HOMILETICAL FORM

Theme: Signs of the Second Coming."

Introduction: It is popular today to scoff at those who believe in a second coming of Christ. What we need to remember is that His first coming was predicted for many centuries before it took place. But in spite of doubt and disbelief, He did finally come nearly two thousand years ago. Just as all the promises concerning His first advent were fulfilled at that time, so shall all concerning His second advent be fulfilled.

A. *Fearful Signs.* "There shall be signs . . . men's hearts failing them for fear."

We are not told what these signs will be. But in this age of space exploration we realize that a whole new dimension has been opened up to us. What relation this may have to the signs in the heavens we cannot tell.

Verse 26 certainly describes our times in a graphic way. Until recent years wars were confined to a small section of the earth. Then came two World Wars which forever changed the picture. But though fierce fighting took place on the continents of Africa, Asia, and Europe, it never touched the shores of North and South America.

We all know that this will not be true in a third World War. Intercontinental ballistic missiles suddenly raining death on our cities could well herald the beginning of that war. And every continent would probably soon be involved, especially with the wide spread of Communism.

But when things get their worst, "then shall they see the Son of man coming in a cloud with power and great glory." So "when these things begin to come to pass, then look up, and lift up your heads: for your redemption draweth nigh." This is the blessed hope of the Christian.

B. *Fig Tree Lesson.* "Behold the fig tree."

When the trees begin to put forth their leaves, we know that summer is near. "So likewise ye, when ye see these things come to pass, know ye that the kingdom of God is nigh at hand." That many of the things mentioned here are coming to pass in our day in a new and larger way, no well-informed person can deny.

What did Jesus mean when He said, "This generation shall not pass away, till all be fulfilled"? Some apply this to the destruction of Jerusalem in A.D. 70, only forty years later. Others take the Greek word for "generation" in another proper sense it has — "race." That is, the Jewish race will not perish before the return of Christ. It must be said that the preservation of the Jews through all their many persecutions, culminating with the massacre of 5,000,000 — 6,000,000 under Hitler, is nothing short of a miracle. But there is a third possible interpretation: the generation that sees the beginning of these signs will live to see the end. In view of the amazing speeding up of affairs in our day, we realize that ours could very well be that generation.

C. *Faithful Watching.* "Watch ye therefore, and pray always, that ye may be accounted worthy to escape all these things that shall come to pass, and to stand before the Son of man." This was the main concern of Christ. This was regularly His closing note of emphasis (cf. Matt. 24:42, 44; 25:13).

We cannot always interpret the signs of the times. We certainly are warned against setting dates. But we all must watch and be ready at any time for the coming of Christ.

Luke 22

THE LAST PASSOVER

22:15. "With desire I have desired to eat this passover with you before I suffer."

I. HISTORICAL SETTING. Passion Week began with the Triumphal Entry on Sunday. On Monday Jesus cursed the barren fig tree and cleansed the Temple. Tuesday morning He taught the disciples a lesson of faith as they looked at the withered fig tree. Perhaps on the same day we have the questions and answers given in Chapter 20. Either Tuesday or Wednesday was marked by the Olivet Discourse. Now on Thursday comes the Passover.

The chief priests and scribes were trying to kill Jesus, but they were afraid the people would mob them if they did (v. 2). Then, from their point of view, they had an unexpected stroke of fortune. One of Jesus' own twelve apostles, inspired by Satan, offered to betray his Master into the hands of the Jewish hierarchy. Overjoyed, they agreed with him on the amount they would pay. Did ever the love of money provoke a more heinous crime? Judas now sought an opportunity to betray Jesus "in the absence of the multitude" (v. 6). This dastardly deed must be done quietly and secretly.

II. EXPOSITORY MEANING. The chapter begins with the statement: "Now the feast of unleavened bread drew nigh, which is called the Passover." According to the Old Testament account (Lev. 23:5-6; Num. 28:16-17) the Passover was to be celebrated each year on the 14th Nisan, followed by seven days of the Feast of Unleavened Bread. But by now both names were applied to the whole period of eight days. The language of Luke here is almost exactly paralleled by the words of Josephus, a contemporary Jewish historian.

He writes: "This happened at the time when the feast of unleavened bread was celebrated, which we call the passover"
(Ant. xiv. 2.1).

The Jews used a lunar calendar: every month began with
the new moon. The Passover always came in the middle of
the month. That is why the date of Easter varies from
roughly the middle of March to the middle of April.

The Jewish leaders were afraid to arrest Jesus in public,
lest a riot ensue. The pilgrims from Galilee and Perea who
had acclaimed Him so ardently on Sunday could not be expected to stand by and watch their hero taken. So the rulers
sought to take Him "in the absence of the multitude" (v. 6).

"With desire I have desired" (v. 15) is a typical Hebraistic
construction, found frequently in the Bible. It means, "I
have earnestly desired." The Master was eager to have this
last fellowship meal, with its rich religious meaning, before
His death.

The "bread" (v. 19) was unleavened bread. The Jews
were very strict about searching their homes on the 14th
Nisan to make sure that there was no leaven (yeast) in the
house. "This is my body" obviously means "This represents
my body," for the physical body of Jesus was intact before
their eyes.

"Testament" should be "covenant." The Greek word is
diatheke, an agreement or contract made between two par-
ties. Our word "testament" (Latin, *testamentum*) means a
"will." But the Jews did not make wills, as the Greeks and
Romans did. Semitic peoples were strong on making cove-
nants. What we call the "New Testament" is really the New
Covenant which God had made with men through Christ.
All those who accept Christ as Savior and Lord enter into
that covenant.

III. DOCTRINAL VALUE. The Passover looked forward to
the sacrifice of the great Paschal Lamb for the sins of humanity. The Lord's Supper looks back to that central point
of all human history and memorializes it. Thus Holy Communion is the Christian substitute for the Jewish Passover.

IV. PRACTICAL AIM. To show the significance of Jesus'
inauguration of the Lord's Supper and what that sacramental
meal should mean to us.

V. HOMILETICAL FORM

Theme: "The Last Passover."

Introduction: It was the last Passover which Jesus ever
ate. True, it was not the last Passover of history, for both
Jews and Samaritans still celebrate the Passover every spring.
But it was the last Passover in a very significant sense. After
Christ had died as the Paschal Lamb, the meaning of the old
Passover had been fulfilled, and so the ceremony lost its
value. This was the last Passover under the old covenant
between God and Israel.

A. *The Passover Prepared.* "Go and prepare us the passover, that we may eat."

Finally came "the day," on which the Passover lamb was to
be killed and cooked for eating that night. Jesus sent Peter
and John into the city to prepare the meal. They were given
cryptic directions. On entering the city they would see a man
with a pitcher of water. This would be such an unusual
sight — since women alone carried water jars on their heads
— that they would have no difficulty picking him out. They
were to follow him home. There they would find a large
upper room furnished with rugs, cushions, couches, and tables. They would then prepare the Passover meal.

The rabbinical rule was that each lamb must be eaten
between sunset and midnight by a group of not less than ten
nor more than twenty. So Jesus and His twelve apostles
fitted in very well with the requirements. Presumably the
two disciples would purchase a lamb, have it slain by a priest
in the Temple, and roast it for the evening meal. With it
they would eat bitter herbs and unleavened bread, and drink
"wine" — grape juice, whether fermented or unfermented.

B. *The Passover Repeated.* "And he took the cup, and
gave thanks, and said, Take this, and divide it among yourselves."

Acting as head of the household, Jesus distributed the bread and wine for the meal. It is generally considered that this was the third cup of the Passover, handed round after the lamb was eaten. The fourth cup would then be the one used for the so-called Lord's Supper (v. 20). Christ was simply repeating the ceremony which had been observed by the Jews for over a thousand years.

C. *The Passover Replaced.* "This is my body. . . . This cup is the new testament in my blood."

The Last Supper became the Lord's Supper. For in these words we find Jesus giving new meaning to the bread and the wine. The bread symbolized His body "which is given for you." He added: "This do in remembrance of me."

So the Lord's Supper is a memorial meal, commemorating the death of Christ on the cross. But it also is a time of anticipation, for it looks forward to the return of our Lord (I Cor. 11:26). This gives it double significance.

Then Jesus distributed a common cup, that each one might drink from it in a closely knit fellowship. The fruit of the vine was red, symbolical of the blood of Christ "which is shed for you." Thus each time we partake of the sacrament we are reminded of the shed blood which atones for our sins and cleanses our hearts. Apart from the blood of Christ there is no salvation from sin.

Luke 23

THE INNOCENT MAN WHO WAS EXECUTED

23:4. "I find no fault in this man."
23:24. "And Pilate gave sentence that it should be as they required."

I. HISTORICAL SETTING. When Jesus was arrested in the garden He was taken to the house of the high priest (22:54). Here the Sanhedrin held an informal meeting, for it was illegal to hold a trial at night.

So in the morning it met in an official session (22:66-71). Two questions were asked of Jesus. The first was: "Art thou the Christ?" — that is, the Messiah. Instead of giving a direct answer, He said: "Hereafter ye shall see the Son of man sit on the right hand of the power of God." Obviously by "the Son of man" He meant himself. He would sit at God's right hand.

This caused the members of the Sanhedrin to ask the second question: "Art thou then the Son of God." He replied: "Ye say that I am." The Greek could equally well be translated: "Ye say, because I am." But probably Jesus purposely gave an ambiguous answer because of their wrong conceptions of the Messiah (Christ, Son of man, Son of God).

At any rate, the members of the Sanhedrin took it that He had answered in the affirmative. They condemned Him as worthy of death (cf. Mark 14:61-64). But the Roman government reserved to itself the power of capital punishment. So the Sanhedrin had to turn His case over to Pilate (23:1).

The charge on which the Jews condemned Jesus to death was blasphemy (Matt. 26:63-66). But they were smart enough to know that this religious accusation would carry no weight in a Roman court. So they trumped up a threefold political charge: "We found this fellow perverting the na-

100

tion, and forbidding to give tribute to Caesar, saying that he himself is Christ a king" (23:2).

This, of course, was barefaced lying. Jesus had not been perverting the people. Instead He had affirmed positively that He did not come to destroy the Law but to fulfill it (Matt. 5:17). In the second place, all three Synoptics record that far from forbidding to pay taxes to Caesar He had emphatically said: "Render to Caesar the things that are Caesars" (Matt. 22:21; Mark 12:17; Luke 20:25). In the third place, He had carefully avoided claiming to be king — although the people had acclaimed Him as such in the so-called Triumphal Entry on the previous Sunday.

II. EXPOSITORY MEANING. The elders, chief priests, and scribes (22:66) were the three component parts of the Sanhedrin. They led Him into the "council" (Greek, *synedrion*); that is, they brought Him before an official meeting of the Sanhedrin. The Christ (22:67), Son of man (22:69), and "Son of God" (22:70) were all of them designations of the Messiah.

"This fellow" (v. 2) is a slurring expression of contempt. "Perverting the nation" was intended to convey the idea of causing sedition, which was the worst crime in Roman eyes.

"Thou sayest it" (v. 3) is probably purposely ambiguous (cf. 22:70). Jesus was a king, but not in the political sense that Pilate had in mind (cf. John 18:33-38).

"Fault" (v. 4) is hardly an adequate translation. The Greek word means "cause for punishment" or "crime." It was not the responsibility of a Roman court to decide whether a man was faultless. It was concerned with whether a man had broken the law and so deserved punishment for his crime.

III. DOCTRINAL VALUE. If Jesus had died as an actual criminal, obviously His death would have no value for us. But He was thrice declared to be innocent by a Roman governor.

IV. PRACTICAL AIM. To appreciate the fact that the innocent Christ died as a criminal in our place, for our sins.

V. HOMILETICAL FORM

Theme: "The Innocent Man Who Was Executed."

Introduction: Many innocent men have been put to death unjustly. But none compares with Christ. Not only did a Roman court three times declare Him guiltless, but His own conscience enabled Him to say what no other man could: "The Father hath not left me alone; for I do always those things that please him" (John 8:29).

A. *The First Declaration of Innocence.* "I find no fault in this man" (23:4).

The Jewish leaders had brought a threefold political charge against Jesus. They said that He was: (1) "perverting the nation"; (2) "forbidding to give tribute to Caesar"; (3) "saying that he himself is Christ a King." All of these were very serious accusations. In fact, any one of them alone would have been sufficient cause for executing Jesus as an enemy of the Roman Empire. Of course, the religious leaders were well aware of this.

Pilate talked with Christ. He evidently became satisfied that the charges were all false. For he came back to the chief priests and the people with the verdict: "I find no fault in this man." That is, "He is not guilty."

B. *The Second Declaration.* "I, having examined him before you, have found no fault in this man touching those things whereof ye accuse him" (23:14).

Not at all happy with Pilate's attitude, the religious leaders "were the more fierce, saying, He stirreth up the people" (v. 5). They were bound to prove Him a trouble-maker.

When they inadvertently mentioned Galilee, Pilate tried to get rid of the responsibility of deciding Jesus' case by sending Him to Herod Antipas, ruler of Galilee, who had come for the Passover. But this proved to be no escape. Herod mocked Christ and sent Him right back to Pilate.

Pilate then called together the Jewish rulers. He had examined Jesus in open court and had not found Him guilty of any charges laid against Him. Even Herod had found nothing wrong with Him. Pilate suggested that he have Jesus beaten and then release Him.

By this time the religious leaders were getting desperate. It looked as though they were going to lose their case. So they began yelling in unison: "Away with this man. . . . Crucify him, crucify him" (vv. 18, 21).

C. *The Third Declaration.* "I have found no cause of death in him" (23:22).

This should have settled it. If Pilate had been a man of honesty and moral courage he would have climaxed his three declarations of innocence with the verdict, "Not Guilty."

But the governor was weak and wobbly. As the pressures increased, he "caved in." In one of the greatest miscarriages of justice in all history, "Pilate gave sentence that it should be as they required" (v. 24). In doing so he abdicated all right to be a ruler and judge. He was a political puppet.

So he released to the people one who was a murderer and insurrectionist, and ordered the Prince of Life to be put to death. And that is virtually what people have been doing ever since.

Our hearts ought to be stirred with fresh gratitude that Jesus, the sinless One, was willing to die in our place. We should pledge Him our full love and loyalty.

Luke 24

THE UNCONSCIOUS PRESENCE

24:15. "Jesus himself drew near, and went with them."

I. HISTORICAL SETTING. The last chapter in the life of Christ is the story of the Resurrection. This is shown in each of the Gospels.

In common with Matthew, Luke tells of the visit of certain women to the sepulcher on Sunday morning. But he adds a note as to their purpose. They were "bringing the spices which they had prepared" (v. 1), in order to anoint the corpse of Christ.

Instead of finding the body they were confronted by two angels, who declared: "He is not here, but is risen" (v. 6). The women promptly reported the matter to "the eleven" — Judas was gone. The disciples reacted in typical masculine fashion: "And their words seemed to them as idle tales, and they believed them not" (v. 11). But Peter — with John (cf. John 20:2-10) — did go to the tomb to investigate. Sure enough, the body was gone. But, strangely, the grave clothes were lying there empty. It was all beyond Peter's comprehension.

II. EXPOSITORY MEANING. The location of Emmaus (v. 13) is still uncertain. "Threescore furlongs" (Greek, *stadious*) was about seven miles and a half. "Cleopas" (v. 18) is mentioned only here, and nothing further is known about him.

The Messianic concepts and expectations of the Jews are revealed strikingly in the words of these two disciples: "But we trusted that it had been he which should have redeemed Israel" (v. 21). That is, they believed that Jesus was the Messiah. So they expected Him to expel the Romans and "redeem" the nation of Israel from foreign domination. Doubt-

104

less they were among the ones who acclaimed him King in the Triumphal Entry just a week before this. But instead of His driving out the Romans, He had allowed them to put Him to death. When this happened, all Messianic hopes disappeared. What these disciples did not realize, of course, was that the very death of Jesus was to bring a larger redemption in spiritual salvation.

"Christ" (v. 26) should be translated "the Messiah." What Jesus proceeded to show these Jewish believers was that their "scriptures" (our Old Testament) taught that the Messiah was to suffer before He entered His glory. Christ started with Moses and went through the Old Testament, proving this point. He doubtless called attention especially to Psalm 22 and Isaiah 53. In verse 44 we have the threefold division of the Hebrew canon: "the law of Moses . . . the prophets . . . the psalms" (or Writings). Our thirty-nine books were classified under these three headings.

III. DOCTRINAL VALUE. The spiritual presence of Jesus with each of His own is a precious truth. If we believe that God is Spirit, we know that He can be with all of us all the time.

IV. PRACTICAL AIM. To emphasize the fact that Jesus walks life's road with us and that we ought to be more conscious of His presence.

V. HOMILETICAL FORM

Theme: "The Unconscious Presence."

Introduction: Jesus is "The Christ of Every Road." The pitiful thing is that too often we are unconscious of His presence. We need to have our spiritual eyes opened so that we can see Him. For He is there.

A. *Sad Hearts.* "What matter of communications are these that ye have one to another, as ye walk, and are sad?" (24:17).

Two disciples of Christ were walking home one Sunday afternoon from Jerusalem to Emmaus. Their hearts were

heavy, their faces sad. They had believed that Jesus of Nazareth was the Messiah. They had joined in the triumphal
procession the Sunday before, as the Passover pilgrims shouted
"Blessed be the King that cometh in the name of the Lord"
(19:38). They had expected Him to ride into Jerusalem,
drive out the Romans, and set up His Messianic kingdom.

But a week from that day everything was different. In
almost stupefied unbelief they had heard Pilate give in to the
pressure of the crowd and order Jesus crucified. They had
followed Him outside the gate to the place of execution.
There with agonized hearts they had heard His cries and
seen Him expire. And with that all their Messianic hopes
expired, too. No wonder they were sad.

All this they related to the stranger who had joined them
on the road and now walked by their side. So clouded by
sorrow was their vision that they did not recognize who He
was.

B. *Slow Hearts.* "O fools, and slow of heart to believe all
that the prophets have spoken" (24:25).

When they had finished their recital, Jesus chided them for
their failure to understand their Scriptures. "And beginning
at Moses and all the prophets, he expounded unto them in
all the scriptures the things concerning himself" (v. 27).

Probably everyone who has read that statement carefully
has thought: "How I would like to have been there and to
have heard the Great Teacher expound the Christology of
the Old Testament!" It would be a rare treat indeed. But
Jesus promised to give us the Holy Spirit who would teach us
all things (John 14:26). With His help we can understand
the Scriptures.

C. *Seeing Hearts.* "And their eyes were opened, and they
knew him" (24:31).

How long Jesus had been with them we are not told. But
it was probably an hour or two. All that time they had not
recognized Him.

As they approached their home, the Stranger naturally

acted as though He was going on His way. But since it was getting toward night, they constrained Him to stay with them.

It was at the supper table that it happened. In the old familiar way "he took bread, and blessed it, and brake, and gave to them" (v. 30). Suddenly they recognized who it was. But even as they really saw Him for the first time that day, He vanished out of their sight.

Then the meaning of that afternoon's conversation dawned upon them. With awed tones they exclaimed: "Did not our heart burn within us, while he talked with us by the way, and while he opened to us the scriptures?" Always our hearts burn when His voice speaks in our souls. What the world sorely needs is more burning hearts and less careless, cold, cruel hearts.

D. *Sharing Hearts.* "And they rose up the same hour, and returned to Jerusalem" (24:33).

They were weary. They had walked the seven miles from Jerusalem. It was late and would probably be dark before they reached the city.

But this news was too wonderful to keep to themselves. They must share it with the sorrowing disciples back in Jerusalem.

So, tired though they were, they headed right back to town. A bit footsore they finally arrived. When they reached the Upper Room they found the eleven gathered, with a few others.

Before the Emmaus disciples could get in a word, some of the Jerusalem folk excitedly said: "The Lord is risen indeed, and hath appeared to Simon" (v. 34). Poor Peter; he had been in misery since denying his Lord. Compassionately Christ met him that day and forgave him. Now there was a general rejoicing together.

What we need to do is to recognize the presence of Christ with us on every mile, even at every step, of life's way. He need not be for us "the Unconscious Presence."

BIBLIOGRAPHY

Arndt, William F., *The Gospel According to St. Luke.* "Bible Commentary." St Louis: Concordia Publishing House, 1956.

Barclay, William, *The Gospel of Luke.* "The Daily Study Bible." 2nd ed. Philadelphia: Westminster Press, 1956.

Bruce, A. B., *The Synoptic Gospels.* "The Expositor's Greek Testament." Edited by W. Robertson Nicoll. Grand Rapids: Wm. B. Eerdmans Publishing Co., n.d.

Burton, Henry, *The Gospel According to St. Luke.* "The Expositor's Bible." Edited by W. R. Nicoll. New York: A. C. Armstrong and Son, 1896.

Creed, J. M., *The Gospel According to St. Luke.* London: Macmillan and Co., 1930.

Erdman, Charles R., *The Gospel of Luke.* Philadelphia: Westminster Press, 1931.

Farrar, F. W., *The Gospel According to St. Luke.* "Cambridge Greek Testament." Cambridge: University Press, 1884.

Geldenhuys, Norval, *Commentary on the Gospel of Luke.* "New International Commentary on the New Testament." Grand Rapids: Wm. B. Eerdmans Publishing Co., 1951.

Godet, F. L., *Commentary on the Gospel of Luke.* Grand Rapids: Zondervan Publishing House, n.d.

Leany, A. R. C., *A Commentary on the Gospel According to St. Luke.* "Harper's New Testament Commentaries." New York: Harper & Brothers, 1958.

Lenski, R. C. H., *The Interpretation of St. Luke's Gospel.* Columbus, O.: Wartburg Press, 1946.

Maclaren, Alexander, *Expositions of Holy Scripture.* Vol. IX. Grand Rapids: Wm. B. Eerdmans Publishing Co., 1944 (reprint).

Manson, William, *The Gospel of Luke.* "The Moffatt New Testament Commentary." New York: Harper and Brothers, 1930.

Miller, Donald G., *The Gospel According to Luke.* "The Layman's Bible Commentary." Edited by Balmer H. Kelly. Richmond, Va.: John Knox Press, 1959.

Morgan, G. Campbell, *The Gospel According to Luke.* New York: Fleming H. Revell Co., 1931.

Plummer, Alfred, *A Critical and Exegetical Commentary on the Gospel According to St. Luke.* "The International Critical Commentary." New York: Charles Scribner's Sons, 1896.

Plumptre, E. H., *The Gospel According to St. Luke.* "Commentary on the Whole Bible." Edited by C. J. Ellicott. Grand Rapids: Zondervan Publishing House, 1954 (reprint).

Ragg, Lonsdale, *St. Luke.* "Westminster Commentaries." London: Methuen & Co., 1922.